SHOW OF HANDS

Published February 2009, by 826 Valencia
Copyright © 2009 by 826 Valencia
All rights reserved by 826 Valencia and the authors.

ISBN: 978-1-934750-10-0

VOLUNTEER EDITORIAL STAFF:

Adrianna Ely, Ana Soriano, Andrea Drugan, Andrea Torres, Angel Chaparro, Angie Colon-Chin, April De Costa, Ashley Arabian, Cynthia Patricia, Cynthia Shannon, Dorrian Lewis, Dustin Platt, Eamon Doyle, Eduwiges Rivas, Elissa Bassist, Erin Archuleta, Eryn-Rose Manzano, Heather Rasley, Henry Arguedas, Idalia Beltran, Ingrid Reis, Jessica Hansen, Jorge Pinto, Josué Henriquez, Karen Schaser, Karen Siercke, Karla Poot-Polanco, Kate Bueler, Kate Viernes, Kehinde Whyte, Kenya Lewis, Leonard Cetrangolo, Linsey Sandrew, Loretta Stevens, Lucy Kirchner, Mena Adlam, Mercedes Logan, Michele Lobatz, Nancy Spector, Nancy Ware, Ranon Ross, Ravon Anderson, Rebecca Kaden, Renee Ashbaugh, Ryan Lewis, Ryan Noll, Sarah Buishas, Sarah Million, Tracey Cooper, Whitney Phaneuf, Vicky Wu, Victor Greene & Zoe Brock

COPYEDITORS:
Juliet Litman, Michelle Orange, Eric Wilinski & Maggie Wooll

PROJECT MANAGER:
Marisa Gedney

MANAGING EDITOR & BOOK DESIGNER:
Alvaro Villanueva

Printed in Canada by Westcan Printing Group
Distributed by PGW

SHOW OF HANDS

Young Authors Reflect on the Golden Rule

WRITTEN BY STUDENTS OF MISSION HIGH SCHOOL
IN CONJUNCTION WITH 826 VALENCIA

A NOTE ABOUT THIS BOOK

The seeds for this book were planted a year ago at the 2008 TED Conference. TED, which stands for Technology, Entertainment, and Design, annually brings together inspiring thinkers and doers from around the world. At the conference, three individuals are awarded with the opportunity to unveil their "One Wish to Change the World."

Dave Eggers, co-founder of 826 Valencia, gave a talk in which he wished for people to engage directly with their public schools. Another honoree of last year's TED prize was noted scholar and religion writer Karen Armstrong, whose wish was to assemble a Council of Compassion—a forum through which religious leaders could work together for peace. Armstrong's wish focused on the power of the Golden Rule, the moral code which states, "Do unto others as you would have them do unto you."

One of last year's TED Conference attendees, Mark Dwight (founder of Rickshaw Bags), was inspired by both Armstrong and Eggers. To fulfill both of their wishes, he came to 826 Valencia, an organization devoted to working with public schools, with an idea to infuse one of our student projects with the Golden Rule. We would like to thank Mark Dwight for his help in shaping the idea for this, our seventh annual Young Authors' Book Project, for his help with the funding of the project, and for ensuring this book's inclusion in the welcome bag of all 2009 TED Conference attendees.

FOREWORD

by Joe Loya

The Golden Rule: Do to others what you would have done to you.

You will find the Golden Rule, or slight variations of it, in many cultures. The sturdy principle evolved, no doubt, as each infant society formed, and neighbors needed to figure out rules to guide their behavior as they dwelled next to each other.

Don't throw your garbage on your neighbor's clean laundry if you don't want garbage thrown on yours.

Don't steal your neighbor's goat to cook for dinner if you don't want your goat stolen for someone else's meal.

And so on.

As a child I was taught to live in accordance with the Golden Rule. As the son of a strict preacher, the Golden Rule was sort of beaten into me with my father's school ruler. If not his belt. Or his fists. He abused my brother and me. X-rays once revealed that a beating he gave me resulted in a fractured elbow and rib. He practiced a perversion of the Golden Rule. He was doing bad to others the same way bad had been done to him.

So I too grew up and explored the reverse of the Golden Rule. I became a criminal caring not how my actions affected others. First as a petty crook. Then as a car thief. Finally I became a bank robber.

My crooked life was dedicated to subverting the Golden Rule. I hated society. Their rules. Their limitations on my vices. Their command that I behave fairly with others. So I lived out of bounds. I lured people to trust me, then I intentionally defrauded them. I terrorized bank tellers. I wanted to make them victims so they would become more suspicious of their neighbors. I wanted them to turn fearful and cynical, like me and my father. I wanted nothing less than to make people lose their trust in their fellow citizens.

I eventually tired of the criminal life. I'll never forget the day I threw the towel in. I was serving an eight-year term for bank robbery. My moral shift came during a two-year stint in solitary confinement. It occurred to me in isolation that the culmination of my adult antagonism with regulations had effectively exiled me from the society I despised. But I was not happy with this arrangement. I felt despair, actually, for being alone. The loss of nearness to good family. Friends. Neighbors. The absence of community. So I dedicated myself to returning to the society which I had been cast from. I wanted to prove to be good and worthy, if a community would have me.

But I had created so many convoluted reasons to hate society, cultivated so many skills for hurting people, that I suspected I might have disqualified myself from going straight.

And yet I dreamed of reconciliation with honest people.

Fortunately, one day I stumbled across the idea that my reconnection with society didn't have to be some daunting ordeal, but could, in fact, be as simple as applying the Golden Rule in all facets of my life. The Golden Rule is essentially an admonition to do the fair and decent thing in every decision you make regarding another human being.

I lay on my bunk in my cell and created many scenarios in my head to test my new theory of living right.

How would I handle someone bumping into me and not apologizing?

How would I handle being called a violent racist name?

How would I handle being injured by someone I love?

All these issues had once provoked me to behave violently. Now I could see how I didn't have to take these affronts personally. And this comprehension freed me from thinking only about me. This was a start. Because this is the fundamental premise of the Golden Rule: You must be able to step outside of yourself in order to think about someone else's well-being.

As my release date approached, I told myself that at every opportunity I would ask myself what option I had to show society that I could be entrusted to look out for the well-being of my new community. In essence, I promised myself that I would always do what was fairest and most decent for my neighbors.

I got an opportunity to demonstrate this new ethic one rainy afternoon in Pasadena.

I was seated in a bank lobby, waiting for the bank manager to finish with a customer. I wanted to open a checking account. I saw a man enter the bank and immediately I thought, *That guy looks like a bank robber.* He wore sunglasses in the rain. Baseball cap. Heavy jacket, scruffy beard, military boots, and more importantly, he didn't hold a checkbook or deposit slip in his hands. Plus, he looked around as if he were casing the joint.

I sat there and asked myself, "Okay, if this guy robs a teller, what is my responsibility to all the citizens in this bank?" And it was instantly clear. If I was being robbed and somebody could help me, I would certainly like their help. At that moment I felt an obligation to protect my fellow citizens. And I knew I had the precise and necessary skill to make it happen. I was a man who could act in a split second to violently disable a person.

As the suspicious man got to the front of the line I rose from my comfortable chair and meandered toward the exit, clocking him, aware that I would be almost exactly behind him when he reached the teller station. If he robbed her, I would recognize the terror on her face.

He walked to his teller, pulled out a check from his pocket and slid it to her with his ID. It was a smooth exchange. A legitimate interaction.

I returned to my seat.

The naked eye would not have noticed that anything happened to me. But my interior world was thrilled. You see, that man was a possible bandit in my imagination, and if he had proven to be real then it was clear to me that I no longer felt like criminals were my community. I was willing to protect those I once resented. My desire to defend the local citizenry even overrode my desire to protect myself. Because I would want them to now protect me as one of their neighbors.

Today, when my actual neighbors leave for vacation, they knock on my door and ask me to look after their place while they are away. I ask them to do the same when I travel.

The Golden Rule guided me back from the brink. It was no longer merely a pretty, poetic phrase. The Golden Rule has become the ethos of my daily redemption.

And this is why this book of essays by brilliant students from San Francisco's Mission High School is relevant. They speak to those who have an antagonism with the Golden Rule. They address the forces that would subvert the safety of community. The folks who would throw garbage on clean laundry, or steal your goat. Or, of course, do much worse, like not help a young lady who's been stabbed in the back by a stranger for no apparent reason—an anti-Good Samaritan act. Or the people who would disparage a young gay man out of unadulterated hate for the gay lifestyle.

These essays smartly identify the many spaces between human interactions where unfairness and indecency reside. The students rail against the "worthless violence" of gang retaliation that leaves young bodies in its wake. They chastise bullies, and in some cases, they scold themselves for selfishly promoting their own leisure and comfort over others.

I met with these students and spoke to them not only about writing to an audience, but also about how writing can inspire the reader, as well as themselves. These high schoolers were very alert, and asked questions at a level I get when I speak at universities.

I read these essays and was most impressed by the way they could have been written to me in my prison cell. Some of them would have accused me. Others would have admonished me. Still others would have called me to reform my ways and join their optimistic community. All the essays promote the theme that we should do to others what we would have done to us. The Golden Rule.

I think you too will find much in these startling, bright essays to be moved by.

INTRODUCTION

by Ravon Anderson, Angela Colon-Chin, Miguel Espinoza,
Victor Greene, Josué Henriquez, Dorrian Lewis, Sylvia McClain,
Jorge Pinto, Justo Reyes, Johnny Valencia

While the world today is divided by race, religion, and politics, we, juniors and seniors at Mission High in San Francisco, have used our diversity to come together to write a book of essays and stories about the Golden Rule. We come from different countries and backgrounds. Many of us speak different languages. Some of us have only been speaking and writing in English for two or three years. We don't always think the same and we have different opinions but as we began to write this book, we began to unite.

The Golden Rule is about realizing that even though we are all different, we all want to be treated the same way. Writing this book gave us a chance to talk about our experiences. Some of us used to think, *You don't know what I've been through.* Writing stories from our hearts about what we did and who we are let us open up. It led us to ask each other, "You went through that too?" The similarities between the stories, between us, came out and we met new friends. We came together and we ended up working together even though we might not have everything in common.

Our stories are not all the same but they have things in common. They all share the struggle of being young and trying to be heard. These are stories of family, friendship, hardship, politics, and pain. Some stories have people doing good, and some doing bad; some are about the government and politics; some are very personal. We wrote about leadership and integrity, which are part of the Golden Rule in our terms, and about dishonesty and lack of respect. But what our stories have in common is a quest—a quest for a better future. We're all on a journey to find acceptance, truth, compassion, trust, happiness, and change from what's going on right now.

As we were writing these stories and essays, we thought much about how to be heard. We wanted people to get it, but we didn't want to preach. We had to write something that was real, that would be history. The recent election of Barack Obama is big. The failing economy is big. This *time* is big; it feels historical. For readers of all ages, we hope our stories can provide a lens through which to view current issues.

For that reason, it was especially difficult to write, in terms of how we wanted people to perceive our pieces and understand them. Though different people could see different things in them, we wanted to say what we wanted to say and show people what our opinions were, but more than that, we also wanted to be correct.

We wrote during eight weeks, first with pen and paper, then typing and editing on computers. We worked with tutors from 826 Valencia who came to our school, revising over several drafts. We even sent our drafts over email to volunteer editors who would comment on our stories and send them back to us. It was all a learning experience, even when some of the editors didn't understand our points of view and asked us to make changes that we didn't like. In those cases, we would ask the tutors about what the markings were supposed to mean. Then we understood better and fixed the problems. When we look at our early drafts, we can see where we put the present and past tenses in the same sentence, where we mixed up ideas. But now, after all the help we got, we won't lose readers. They'll understand what we want to say.

When we were done writing, we met in the evenings at 826 Valencia and after school at Mission High to edit the different pieces into a book that really represents our work and our thoughts.

We hope you enjoy reading our stories. Not all of them have happy endings, but it is important for us to share them nonetheless. We hope they reach you. And that you understand what we have come to learn through writing them: not to judge people, to keep an open mind, to make good decisions, and not to regret one's life.

CONTENTS

DOING THE RIGHT THING
Mayra Ramirez

I f I could go back to when it all happened, I would choose to not be there at all. At that moment, I felt sad because he was just a young man stealing and showing no respect for his fellow human beings. At the same time, I was worried about him and wondered why he did it. My story is about how the world has changed, and how it is still changing every day. It was one of the moments in my life in which I felt disappointed about how we make this world work.

One day, I was waiting at the bus stop. I was bored, so I took my cell phone out and started to play with it. A young man stopped his bicycle in front of me. He was wearing a white T-shirt and blue jeans, but I don't remember his face. I remember that I wasn't afraid of him. I never thought he would do anything to me. I was just messaging with my friends.

After a few minutes, I caught the man looking at me and my cell phone. All of a sudden, he passed in front of me and took my cell phone. The battery of the phone dropped to the ground, and at that moment I thought, *What is going on?* I was confused, scared, and worried that my mom would get mad at me for losing my cell phone. I ran to grab my battery and noticed that the man had come back to take that too. Then he said, "Hey, give me the battery."

I said, "No, this is my battery!" and I thought, *And that is my cell phone.*

Then he said, "Hey! I need it, give it to me," like the battery belonged to him. I felt offended because it was mine. He took it from me.

I kept saying, "Hey, please give it back to me, please! Give me the battery, I need it!"

But he refused to do it. In his eyes, I saw that he was scared. I looked at him, but he never looked at me—he was looking at the street, and I saw he was scared. After the small amount of time I had spent with him, I pitied him. I said the magic words: "Please give me my cell phone. I know that you are not that bad. I know you feel something, please!"

Then he looked at the cell phone, looked at me, and said, "OK." He gave the cell phone back to me, got on his bicycle, and disappeared down the street. I think he gave me back the cell phone because he wanted someone to say that to him, because nobody had ever said that he was good or believed in him, and it made him feel like the good person that he could be. Or maybe he felt sad for doing something wrong, and he knew he would feel guilty. I felt scared, sad, and mad, but also like a hero, because I stopped him from doing something wrong. When the bus came, I got on and never looked back. Now, I don't even remember his face and I hope to never see him again. But if I did see him again, I would have only two questions for him: Why would you do something like that? And why did you give me back the cell phone? I thought about what our differences might be, thinking that the biggest would be our lifestyles.

I am from Puebla, Mexico, a little town where all the people know each other. In my country, people are very conservative. Since I was a child, my parents have taught me to try to be nice to others. If someone was carrying heavy bags, I should help them and carry some. And there is a strong tradition of saying "Good morning" to all the elders and treating them with respect. Here in the United States, I just say "Good morning" to my family, not to every elderly person in the street. In Puebla, if you see your family members across the street, you must go and greet them. The people are much friendlier and more respectful with others. I felt safe there because everyone knew what to do. When I came here, I realized there were a lot of people who never say "hi" in the street, or yell strange things instead.

There was another time when I was waiting for the bus, and an older man said, "Hi, how are you? Can you give me your phone number?" And I said "no" and started to walk away from the man, and he just stayed there. I thought, *Oh my god, you are the same age as my father, and you are saying that to me? That's disrespectful.* I would have never had that experience in my country, in my town. People are respectful there. Only classmates asked me for my number, and that was OK because they were my age.

Anybody can get robbed and it happened to me. That day, I started to think about how an innocent person's bad circumstances can make them a criminal. What factors make a person disrespectful? Someone without respect for humans, for themselves, for life? One of the most important influences on human life is family. Everything starts with the family. The world of a baby is its family. When you're born, you start as neither a good nor a bad person. If you don't receive lessons from your family on how to be a good person, then it will be difficult for you to learn. You'll have to learn from the streets or from your friends. In your house, your parents can make you a kind person or a person who will make bad decisions.

I agree with the thoughts of my mom. She says that a good person can come from a bad family. A guest came into class and he talked to us about his life. He was a man who had been living with domestic violence since he was little. He made bad decisions that got him sent to jail. Inside jail, he started writing. When he got out of jail, he tried to change his life, and he is now a good person. It was hard for him because he didn't have any support from his family in staying out of trouble. But he changed his decisions. No one else forced him to change his way of life.

It takes a long time to change from bad to good after trouble. This could take a whole lifetime. It doesn't happen instantly, because people have to learn the right way to treat other people, and they might make a lot of mistakes before they become better people.

If the person who gives you life treats you badly, or makes you feel like human trash, or like you don't deserve to live, other people could do the same. You might accept all the bad treatment, feeling like you deserve to be treated like that. This is why the world of a child must be healthy, with care, affection, attention, and other important things to help the child survive emotionally.

Do the right thing with others and apply the Golden Rule. Remember that children are like sponges, absorbing everything around them.

They respect you if you respect them. If you don't, they might treat people like they themselves expect to be treated. They might learn bad things in the streets, steal things, disrespect people, be violent, and fill the world with their selfish violence.

Some children grow up without money, but their parents make them understand that even though they are poor, their family can still be happy, and teach principles such as humility, responsibility, solidarity, respect, and tolerance. We need people with these traits to make society better.

People's morals must be instilled early by their families, because then they will never forget them and will use them for the rest of their lives. Many people think that school is where people learn disrespect, but I don't agree with that. We act the same at school as we do at our house. If our parents let us act with disrespect in our home, than we will do the same at school. But if our parents teach us respect for life and other people, we will take that with us to school. I think that in school, we practice our principles and adopt some of them from other people, but we have to be aware of the people we might meet who have different points of view. Those kinds of people can confuse us and make us act differently. We cannot let them change who we are.

My mom was the main person who taught me how to accept and love myself. She loves me and teaches me by her example. She has always told me that I'm a very valuable person—not because I'm her daughter, but because I'm a person with feelings. She told me that I have to keep the good comments for myself, that the negative comments will just make me feel bad and won't help me grow as a person.

If people could accept who they are and what they have, it would be easier to relate to them. Acceptance means being proud of yourself and loving yourself. When you accept yourself, you have self-respect and self-esteem. If you respect yourself, you can accept people without seeing their skin color or their nationality. You can just accept them, and at the same time, others can accept and respect you.

I experienced acceptance when I came to the United States. In the first months I was living in South Lake Tahoe—a beautiful place, but also a place where a lot of white people live. In my school, more than half the students were white. There were no other races, just whites and Latinos. In one of my classes, a friend and I were the only two Latino people in a class full of white people. I remember how the white kids were always trying to make me feel accepted or included. I felt excluded because of me, not because they were trying to make me feel uncomfortable. They never said anything to me about my skin color or about my accent. Sometimes we create our own limits, not the people around us.

When I lived in Lake Tahoe, I met a boy who was very friendly. He was always trying to talk to me in Spanish. He drew me a lot of funny faces when we were in class together. With my help, he was learning more and more Spanish. He was the person who made me feel most accepted in that world. This experience helped me to love myself even more. When I came to San Francisco, I felt like a better person, like I could do anything that I wanted to do.

The most important thing that I learned from him was that we can include different types of people in our lives. It doesn't matter if we speak the same language; it only matters if we want new friends. Maybe in his life, he moved to a new place and people did the same thing for him that he did for me. In the future, I will do the same with new girls or boys in my school. It is important to be conscious of what we do and what we can change.

Many people who come to the United States are affected by whether or not they feel accepted. You can feel the situation getting worse every day as people come to the United States. They miss their country, their family, their language, their culture, and the people who make them feel accepted. I know people who have lived here for many years and still don't speak English. This not only happens to Latinos, but also to people from other countries. The question is, how are we helping new people feel welcome?

In these times, we don't know who to trust. Kind people are few. The world is full of hate. We need to have respect for each other; we have to learn how to respect before we can have good relationships with people in society. But sadly, the number of people without principles is increasing. Each day, we lose a little of our principles because of the way society is. I don't think this is because of the president or because of specific parts of the country. We all make up the country, and we all choose the president. I could be unfair and say that the president is responsible for my mistakes. The president can inspire many children, but he can't live our lives.

Your relationships in society are important. Someday you could need someone's help, or be in a position to offer help to others. How will you act? Will you do the right thing? Will you be kind? These are important questions to think about. You have the choice to treat others as you wish to be treated. I miss the boy from Lake Tahoe, and I have good memories of him. I wish I could speak to him again. I wish that I could go back and be his friend. He was kind to everyone, just because he wanted to be nice. He was a model person. From him, I learned to be accepting of others even if you don't speak the same language or share the same nationality.

I don't have bad wishes for the boy on the bike, because he had his reasons for taking my phone. I want to ask him why he gave me back my cell phone and what was in his mind when I said, "I know that you are not that bad. I know you feel something." My experience helps me to be a better person every day. When someone gives you kindness, if you respond the same way, you will feel better about yourself. The choice is yours.

THE INNOCENT VICTIM
María Alfaro

On February 19, 2008, I fell victim to a horrid crime. Although the crime hurt me physically, the fact that no one helped me when I was in pain also ate at me mentally. I couldn't believe that no one would help me when I was assaulted. Most people don't know what it's like to have people walk or drive past you when you are afraid, bleeding, crying, and begging for help. I wondered if I was dreaming. I never thought I would be a victim, let alone a victim no one was willing to help. That day it was me, but next time it could be you. That is why we have to look out for each other.

I remember that day vividly. It was a sunny morning. I was happy that it was a holiday and that I didn't have to go to school. The night before, my aunt had asked me if I wanted to take BART with her to Hayward to visit the restaurant where my mom works. (She is an excellent chef.)

When my aunt was ready to go that morning, I was just waking up. I told her I would go later by myself. After I woke up, I had a feeling something awful was going to happen. My instincts told me that I shouldn't go.

During the journey I tried to stay passive and forget about my bad feeling earlier that morning. I called my mom to tell her I was on my way and that I was starving. I looked out the windows and enjoyed the sights. I arrived in Hayward at noon.

I felt scared as I left the BART station. I felt daunted by the two blocks I had to walk to get to my mom. A strange feeling came over me. I felt very alone. The other times I had gone to the restaurant I had never felt like this. I passed by an empty parking lot, crossed a thin pathway, and out of the corner of my eye I saw something move. A thin, old man with a beard, long dirty hair, and filthy clothing was walking towards me. I remember being calm. I didn't think to feel afraid of him. He said, "Hello," but I didn't respond. I just kept walking. I don't talk to strangers. The man followed me for about a block. All of a sudden, I got very nervous. My heart started beating faster and faster. I looked around for help, but no one was there, not a person or a car. It was just me and the man. He started getting mad and yelled at me because I hadn't said hello. He was swearing and shaking his fists at me. I didn't run or say anything. I continued walking calmly, to show him that I was not afraid of him, in hopes that he would stop bothering me.

Instead, he ran toward me, lunging at my throat. I didn't have a chance to escape his grasp. The first thing that came to my mind was that he wanted to sexually abuse me and kill me. I only felt him hit my back and push me to the ground. I didn't feel the edge of the knife crossing my back the two times he stabbed me. I couldn't accept the truth of what was happening. I tried to wake myself up from what seemed a horrible nightmare. I was helpless on the ground, wondering what I had done to deserve this. I wanted to stand up and go run for help, but I couldn't feel my feet. I watched him run away, as the blood poured out of my body. I prayed to God to help me and prayed that the man was not going to return to hurt me even more.

Nobody had seen what happened to me. The man who stabbed me looked on from afar. I wanted to take out my phone, but I didn't know how he would act if he saw me with it, so I decided to ask for help from the people who were driving by. Unfortunately, only two cars passed, and neither of them stopped to help me even though I was bleeding and crying. I didn't know what to do. I helplessly begged for someone to stop their car and help me. I heard the man who'd stabbed me laugh in the distance.

Suddenly, a Latina woman came walking towards me. "Excuse me," I cried, "Can you help me? A man hurt me and I don't really know what he did to me. I can't get up and I have too much pain in my back. I just want you to call my aunt. She is one block from here, and—just stay here with me until she arrives."

"I am sorry," she said, "but I'm late for work. I can't help you."

"Thank you," I said. But I was shocked that she wouldn't help me.

I felt like the world was collapsing all around me. I couldn't believe that people wouldn't help me. I didn't understand how people could be so selfish when I needed help. I was there suffering on the grey cement and my family had no idea where I was.

I waited and hoped that someone would come to help me, but a Good Samaritan never came. My back was causing me so much pain. I tried to touch the place where the pain came from, but it hurt too much to reach. I stared at the blood on the ground. It became clear to me that the man hadn't just hit me. He had stabbed my back. I was numb from the shock.

I couldn't see the man anymore. I immediately took out my cell phone and called my aunt. "Can you come to help me?" I stammered through my tears.

"Why? Are you OK?" she said.

"No," I said, "a man stabbed me and nobody will help me. Please come as fast as you can. I'm scared that the man might come back and hurt me even more."

"Don't be a liar. Come to the restaurant," she said.

I started to sob. Then she believed me. She hung up the phone and immediately ran to where I was. She didn't say anything to anyone in the restaurant. She just left everyone wondering what had happened.

Because I was only a block away, I could see my aunt as she came running. I felt so relieved to see her. Despite the fact that my aunt was coming, the nightmare was hardly over. People see these kinds of crimes every day, but you never imagine that you might be the victim.

When my aunt arrived she was very scared. She was trying to figure out what had happened. She didn't know what to do or say. The first thing I asked her to do was check my back. She got even more scared when she saw the wounds. She called the police but they didn't understand her English because she was so nervous.

A driver stopped to ask what had happened. He was white, and my aunt asked him to call the police. He called immediately, and the first people that arrived were the paramedics, who checked my back. I didn't know how big my wounds were, but I imagined they were big because of the pain I felt.

Many curious people appeared when they heard the ambulance, but when I needed them no one had been there.

The police arrived. A Latino police officer started to ask me what had happened. I couldn't answer clearly; it was hard for me. Another police officer called more police officers who were near to the area to find the guilty man.

I just wanted them to take me to the hospital to check my wounds so I would feel better, but they left me a half hour more on the ground while they investigated. I was so desperate. I pretended to faint, so that they would do something, and immediately they took me into the ambulance.

The Latino officer stayed with me to continue with the investigation. He was my protection at that moment. No one from my family could be with me in the ambulance.

When the ambulance was ready to go to the hospital, another police officer brought a man who had been near the area where I was stabbed. He looked like the one I had described. The police officer asked me if he was the man who had stabbed me, but I was not sure enough to blame him. The man looked nervous and scared, and he had different clothes on, which made me doubt that he was the guilty man. I could have blamed him because of my anger, but I would have felt worse doing that when

I wasn't really sure if he had stabbed me. I answered that I was not sure, and the police officer let him go.

I arrived at the hospital, and nurses and a doctor were already waiting for me. I felt so much better; finally they were going to check me out. I couldn't stop crying, and one of the nurses held my hand and told me, "Don't worry, honey. Everything will be OK." She couldn't believe I had been stabbed. I remember her saying that I was too young and innocent to have this happen. She thought about her own children in the same situation. She was with me until somebody from my family could enter to see me. The doctor finished examining me, and he let my mother enter.

When I saw my mother, I started to cry even more. She hugged me and told me, "Don't worry." This horrible incident made me love her even more, because it could have been my last day alive. She didn't understand why it had happened. She was so glad and thankful that God had only given me a lesson and let me continue to live. It would have been too hard for her to face my death.

The doctor said I was not seriously hurt. The knife had not reached anything inside, like a nerve or an organ, so they let me go home. It was hard for me to walk.

After I left the hospital, I realized that I was not alone. I had the support of my family, and it helped me get through what had happened.

The first night I couldn't sleep. I just thought about what had happened, and it made me cry. I thought my incident was not important to the police.

Three days later, a detective arrived at my home, asking for me. He showed me pictures of some criminals who had been arrested near the area where I was stabbed, but there were so many that I couldn't identify my attacker. It was difficult to pick out the right man; I hadn't seen his face.

The detective was very amiable with me. He did a great job helping people he didn't know, like me. Perhaps he did it just because it was his job, or because he really loved to do it. He came three times to show me pictures of criminals, but it was hard for me every time. I asked God to help me find the guilty man, but all the criminals looked so similar.

All this taught me a lesson in life. Now, I am here, but tomorrow, I don't know. You go out of your home, and you don't know if you will be lucky enough to come back later. Someone could hurt you, or a natural disaster could happen. You and your family have to be prepared to assimilate to the gravity of events.

This accident was traumatizing. Now I didn't want to go out if no one was with me, and when I was walking alone outside I was scared, thinking it could happen again. I couldn't get the attack out of my mind. When I heard someone coming behind me, I immediately turned my head to see if it was someone who wanted to put me in danger. I had to fight against myself to realize that it had happened to teach me something, that nothing is perfect and there is no guaranteed safety. An error can put us physically in danger, but it can help us to continue appreciating this strange and wonderful world.

Even now it affects me. When I go to see my mom I need somebody to pick me up. When I'm walking in that place where the accident happened, I start to shake. Although I try to end it, I can't avoid my fear.

Thinking about this, I also realized that in some cases, being a Good Samaritan could put you in danger, and sometimes that a Good Samaritan might even be more affected by the unfortunate events than the victim. Risking your life doing good and helping people is scary and hard, but you should always treat people the way you want to be treated. But you never really know if you are helping or not when you try to help someone you don't know, because you don't know if the person really needs help or if they are only acting needy to then do something against you. I think this was the case with the woman who wouldn't help me. She might have wanted to help me, but she also had to think about herself.

People just act this way. They think for themselves when it looks really bad. But we have to look around us and think about what we are doing to our society. Children, for example, look at what adults do, and that example makes them think they can do the same things. In my experience as an adolescent, I have seen that people sometimes want to cover the world with one finger. Because of this, in the streets you sometimes feel frightened.

Unfortunately there are people with mental problems who are suffering and also causing damage to other people. Maybe they don't get special attention or in the past they didn't receive enough affection. Just because it makes one feel better isn't a good reason to hurt each other. On the contrary, it makes one a person nobody wants to know about.

We have to stop all kinds of violence. We have to be united and stop criminals. They don't think how much damage they cause for something that is satisfying only to them. I still look over my shoulder in fear that I might be made a victim again.

And we have to be a close society, helping each other. If you are hurt one day and I am there, I'm sure you'll get my hand to help you. One time I was the victim, but next time it could be you. That is why we have to look out for each other.

MY GOOD DEED
Miguel Espinoza

Have you ever just had a sudden moment of kindness? Have you done something nice even though doing nice things is something you never do? Well that's what happened to me. Now, I'm not a very honest guy. If I saw someone drop their wallet or phone or something like that I would probably not give it back. I guess what I'm trying to say is that I don't like helping people or being nice to people I don't know. That's just not me. I am not the type of person who helps people look for lost items. I do not like to think of myself as a nice guy, as someone who likes to help others. I don't think it's worth my effort or my time. I mean if you help people, most of the time you don't even get anything in return, and sometimes people don't even appreciate the help. It's like you help them, and they don't care that you did. From my point of view, helping people sucks.

But this one time it was completely different. I did an honest thing. I'm not even really sure why this happened. It just did. It's probably because I felt sorry for them, but I'm not sure. For whatever reason, I just did a nice thing.

It was a sunny Saturday afternoon in July, and, while I was walking around the arcade at the Metreon looking at all the machines, I noticed a woman and little boy playing a game I wanted to play. It was a DJ music game. It looked really fun and I had my eye on it for a while. I was just waiting for the woman and the little boy to move. While I was there, waiting, I saw that the woman had her hands in her pockets trying to pull out more tokens. As she pulled out the tokens, a bill fell out of her pocket and landed near her feet. I thought she was going to pick it up, but she didn't. She just dropped the tokens in the machine and started to play again. I looked down and right next to her feet was a nicely folded twenty-dollar bill. As soon as I saw it I knew that I had to pick it up. That money was going to be mine.

I started thinking about how I was going to take it. What was good was that they were facing away from the bill toward the screen of the machine. I thought I could easily pick it up and walk away. As I neared the machine, I heard the loud music playing and felt the lights blaring. I could tell that the woman and the boy were completely distracted. They would never notice me. I moved right behind them. I looked around to make sure that no one was looking. If someone saw me they might tell the woman that she had dropped the bill and that I was taking it. They might think that I was a bad person. After confirming that I was in the clear, I bent down and quickly picked up the bill, shoving it in my pocket. While I was walking away, I pulled it out of my pocket and looked at it in my hand. A big smile came to my face. It's not every day that you find twenty dollars just lying around. Despite my joy, a slight sense of guilt made me think about the woman. Nonetheless, I convinced myself that the woman was dumb for dropping the money, and that I deserved to keep it. Then I started walking to the token machine, thinking that it was my lucky day and my new twenty-dollar bill was going to buy me some more tokens.

However, for some reason, as I was walking toward the token machine, I couldn't help but look back at the woman and the little boy. They were still playing. They were so into the game, moving their arms, vigorously spinning the discs, shaking their bodies trying to keep to the rhythm of the game. I looked at them for a minute, and then their game ended. The woman put her hands in her pockets. She kept digging, even pulling one of her pockets inside-out. I thought this was funny. I said to myself, "Tough luck, lady. You dropped a twenty and now it's mine." I kept looking at her to see what she would do. She continued digging in her pockets, pulling the other pocket inside-out. She shifted her attention to the ground. As time went on, the woman started to look more and more worried. She kept moving her head back and forth. I could see her eyes move from left to right, scanning the floor. She was nervous that she had lost a twenty. The expression on the woman's face made me think about what I'd done. It looked like she was about to cry. Her head was down and her face was motionless. She was lost in her thoughts. It made me feel bad, and I began to feel like I had done something wrong.

I didn't feel like it was really stealing, but I still felt pity for the poor woman who had lost her cash. I started thinking that maybe that was the only cash the woman had, that maybe she needed it for something more important than some tokens. Maybe the lady and the little boy needed that money to eat or to get somewhere—maybe to get home. I just felt worse and worse about myself as I thought about what the money might be for. Again, I looked at the bill in my hand, and I thought that if I'd lost it, I would want someone to give it back to me. I wasn't sure what to do. If I walked up to the lady and gave it to her, she might wonder why I had taken it in the first place, or why I hadn't given it back sooner. I thought it would be easier just to keep it and avoid having to go through the embarrassment of going up to the lady and giving it back to her. I just wasn't sure what to do. I mean, I knew what the right thing to do was, but I wasn't sure if I could muster the courage to do it. I didn't want the lady to think I was a thief or something for not giving the money back as soon as I had picked it up.

As I stood there considering what to do, my friend walked up to me. He saw the bill and said, "Sweet. Where did you get that? I thought you only had one twenty."

"Nah," I replied. "I found it. I think that lady over there dropped it." I pointed out the woman, who was still looking through her pockets.

He said, "That's cool, you just got yourself twenty bucks. Nice."

"Yeah, it's cool, but I think I should give it back. I mean, look at that woman. She looks like she's about to start crying," I said.

My friend said, "You'd be stupid if you gave it back. Dude, it's twenty bucks! Don't give it back to her. She lost it and you found it. Now it's yours. Don't give it back."

I said, "I don't know, man, I really feel sorry for her. She looks worried. If it was you, wouldn't you want someone to give the money back to you?"

My friend said "Do whatever you want, but if I were you I'd just keep it and enjoy it. But if you feel sorry, then do what you got to do."

My friend walked away. The woman, at this point, had walked away from the machine to some nearby seats where she had left her jacket. She picked it up, put it on, and sat down for a bit. She looked sad. She just sat there with this blank stare on her face. At that moment, my conscience kicked in.

I thought about my mom. I wondered what it would be like if that were me and her. I started thinking about that, and it made me sad because my mom would be sad if she lost twenty dollars. I mean, she would have worked hard to get it, and to lose it would really have made her sad. I thought about that. Maybe the woman had had to work hard to make that twenty. Maybe she doesn't get paid too much, or maybe she has to work really hard to make any money, and I just took their twenty. It made me think that I was an awful person.

I decided that I needed to give this money back. I looked back to where the lady was sitting and saw that she and the boy were getting ready to leave. Then I saw the woman and the boy heading toward the exit. I hurried over to them. I tapped the woman's shoulder and said, "I think you dropped this over there by that machine." She turned to me. I finally got a closer look at her. She looked like a woman of about twenty-five to thirty years old. She looked like she needed that twenty way more than I did. Her jacket was old and ripped in some parts. Her clothes looked dirty and her shoes looked old. The little boy had on dirty clothes, and his shoes seemed like they had been with him for a while. I felt sorry for them and thought that it was a good thing that I came to the decision of giving the money back to these people.

The woman's eyes opened wide and a smile grew on her face. "You found what?" she said.

"I found this twenty over there by the machines you guys were using. I thought you guys might want this back."

She looked at my face and said, "Thank you, I thought I lost this on the street."

"No," I said, "it was right over there."

She said, "Bless your soul. You're a very kind person, thank you so much."

I felt very good about myself. I felt like that was the best thing I had done in a very long time. If it had been any other time, I probably would have kept the money and been on my way, but this time was different. I felt remorse, and it made me feel pretty good to give the money back. As I watched the woman and the boy walking away, still happy from the unexpected act of kindness, my friend walked up to me. He said, "You gave it back, didn't you?" I explained that I felt it was the right thing to do. It felt good that I had done the right thing. I might not have twenty dollars, but at least I have a good feeling, and that's all that really matters to me. Really, at the end of the day, having integrity and honesty is way more important than twenty dollars.

Like I said at the beginning, helping people is usually just not for me. But through this experience I realized that I should help people because it's a good thing to do; it helps you to feel good and to feel that you have done the right thing. Another thing I learned through this experience is that I should follow my feelings. Throughout this experience, my feelings were telling me the right thing to do, even though I could not get myself to do it until it was almost too late. But I went with my feelings and I did the right thing.

I learned that I could be a good person. I learned that, under the right circumstances, I could be a really nice and honest person. This event showed me that I am an honest guy. I learned that honesty could occur every day. When I saw the woman's emotions, it made me feel like I had to do the right thing. I learned that I had to do this more often. I learned that I could be nice.

This experience taught me a lot about myself and I guess in some ways it changed me. I now feel that I would handle situations like this differently than I used to think I would. I now feel like I am a more honest person. I now feel like I would help someone who really needed my help, and I would do it gladly. Before, if I saw someone drop something or lose something, I really would not care at all. But now I actually do care. I put myself in other people's shoes and think how awful it would be to lose something. If I happen to come across something that someone has dropped or lost, I really do my best to try to get it back to the person it belongs to.

This experience really changed me. I became a caring person who looks out for people and thinks about their feelings. It's not just all about me all the time. I have to take what other people are feeling into consideration as well. I am not a completely different person, but I think I have changed for the better.

THE POORNESS OF RICHNESS

Josué Henriquez

I don't want to be rich. I don't want money and fancy things to define my life. I love how I am, and I love what I do even though I don't have many things. Why do I need a big house? I don't need a big house.

I prefer to live in a regular house because in a regular house I won't have a place for loneliness and sadness. I'm rich in dreams and poor in money, but I am happy and my heart is full of love. I love to dream. It's something that makes my heart beat because it gives me hope, love, and strength to continue living. I wish and dream to be a good person in this world by respecting others, helping others, and setting a good example for younger generations. I believe we need to give advice and guide everyone who struggles.

I don't want to be recognized by what I *am* but by what I *do*. I want to make friends, real friends. Real friends are people I know I can count on and who can count on me. I wish to request the things that many people are afraid to ask for. Many people are afraid to ask for their rights, for an equal voice, and for their own individual lifestyle. I wish to be a bridge of information for those who are looking but cannot find the truth.

I am seventeen years old. The government says that I am too young for a beer or a cigarette, but also says that I am a complete man and that soon, if I choose to enlist, I can be sent to war to kill other people. I am just a teenager. I don't want to hurt others. I prefer to fight with words of peace and kindness. I am just a teenager who dreams to be a father and to have his own family. But my biggest dream is to fight for peace, love, equality, and unity. I'll try to do whatever I can to be someone recognized for his hope.

In my short life, I have had some experiences that have shaped this path of hope. When I was younger, I used to discriminate against poor people. Sometimes I used to look down on them. I was someone who didn't have worries. I had money, and I didn't need anything. I believed that I had everything even though I felt alone, and no one was behind me. I thought that I was right because my family and the people I grew up with in my neighborhood taught me that I was different from others. That's what I learned *then*, though *now* I recognize that everyone is equal, that we are all people. I can say that most of my life I discriminated against others, even though a part of my heart used to tell me that I wasn't right and that I had to change. I did not understand the language of my heart, not until one day a few years ago, when I met a young boy on the street.

I was fourteen, on my way to the market from my house, when I found a little boy crying because he was hungry. It was a cloudy, hot summer's day with lots of cars on the street. This boy was crying, sitting on a rock with one hand on his stomach and one hand holding a stick, drawing on the sandy ground. I started to think about the boy, and a part of my heart felt that I should buy something for him. So I went to the market and I brought him a fresh hot dog and an apple juice. But as I was getting closer to the boy, I heard a voice in my head tell me, "Don't do it! He doesn't deserve to eat, he is nasty." This voice was the voice of every person who told me I was better than others. So when I heard that voice, I took the food that I bought for the boy and threw it in his face. He just looked at me with his reddened eyes. Then I started to laugh and shout at him, but the red-eyed boy didn't say a word. He just took his sandals and left.

The boy walked away slowly, indifferent to what had just happened. I felt confused because I thought that I would make him cry or maybe he would get sad, but he didn't tell me anything so I kept on laughing. At the same time I was wondering about him. Why didn't he do anything? Why did he just leave without saying anything?

I always wondered about that boy, but I was still doing bad things to poor people and those who were different from me. I went on with my life as if nothing had happened. Six months later, I turned fifteen years old, and I wanted to have a big party with all of my friends and family because I wanted others to see me and admire what I had. I made four hundred invitations. I was looking to hand out as many invitations to as many people as I could. Nearly five hundred people came, even more than I had invited, and I was happy. I said, "I am the most important person here. I don't need anybody. I can have whoever I want as a friend because everyone wishes to be around me."

We had the party. Everywhere I saw many people laughing and many people admiring the big house. People were eating *pupusas, carne asada*, hamburgers, pizza, hot dogs, and all sorts of other foods. There was dancing, people playing games; everyone was having a good time. The party ended at midnight and the dancers, the diners, and everyone else were leaving. I only got lonelier as more people left. I was getting sad, so I decided to go inside and sleep. The next day, my house and yard were completely empty. I didn't see anybody. I felt that the house was getting bigger and bigger, and I was getting smaller each second. I understood that I was lonely, and that was why I felt the house getting bigger.

Three or four days later, I was walking on the street and I heard someone shouting. He was selling fresh red strawberries, ripened mangoes, and clusters of bright yellow bananas. I didn't know who he was, but his voice sounded happy and excited. I was far from him and sad because I was alone with no friends or people near me. I walked up to this fruit vendor, with his big smile and shouting, and I recognized him. I thought, *I know that boy. That's the boy who didn't do anything when I threw the food in his face.*

As I got closer to him, he looked at me with that big smile, and I was surprised again. I thought, *How can he look at me with that smile knowing that I did something bad to him?* Then I asked him, "Why do you look at me with that smile? Do you remember who I am?"

"Of course I know you! You are the boy who threw the food in my face," he said. "How can I forget that?" His laugh was filled with life and a sense of peace.

I felt so strange. I didn't know what was going on with this boy. I thought, *Is he crazy or is something wrong with him?* He was in front of me, and I felt the peace and love that the boy had in his eyes. In his face I saw happiness that I'd never seen before in anyone's face.

With a big grin he asked me, "What? Why do you look at me like that?" I said, "Nothing, nothing. Don't worry about it!" I asked him, "Why are you so happy?" He just laughed and answered, "I am so happy because I am alive, I am healthy, and I have a job to earn money. I know that if I work hard today, I will have something to eat by tomorrow."

He just looked at me and said, "I know why you are surprised! Because you think, *If this simple fruit vendor has to work to earn money and to buy something to eat, and if I've got a lot of money and I'm healthy and I'm alive, am I not supposed to be happier than him!* But you know what? I don't have a big house. I have no money. But I am happy! I don't really care if I don't have money, because I can't buy friends with money. The only friends that I can find with money are those who are interested in looking for an easier life, without having to work hard. But those are not real friends; a real friend is someone who is with you no matter what the situation is. A real friend is a person who takes your hand and guides you in a positive way.

"With money you can buy a big house, but you can't necessarily build a home. A home is not built by materials. A home is built by dreams, hope, and unity, and it doesn't really matter how big the house is. The only thing that matters is how big the home is. You can't buy a light of hope with money. Without hope, how can I pursue my dreams and goals? Love, peace, and truth give me hope. I don't really care what other people think. Some people may think that I am crazy or something is wrong with me. But I'm not crazy. What is important is that I'm living and letting others live their own life. I don't care what they do, how they think, or what kind of life they have."

I didn't know what to say or what to do. I felt that I had to run away from him, but when I tried to walk I couldn't. My body was frozen, and my hands were sweating! I didn't know why I felt like that, but I loved what he had to say. I hadn't known that I could find something good in that boy. I don't know how to tell you because I can't explain what all happened there. I was so confused, I had a crowd of thoughts in my head. I didn't know what to do. That boy made me wonder about things that I had never thought about before. I didn't say much to him; the only thing I could say was, "I'm happy."

He looked into my eyes and said, "Are you sure that you're happy? How can you be happy? I can see the loneliness and sadness inside you! I can see that you don't have friends, only people who admire what you've got. You can tell me that you're happy, but your eyes are telling me that is not true. I'm not judging you. I am not laughing at you just because I'm happy and you're not. I could do that, but I don't want to because I know people like you can change. People like you think that they're happy only because they can buy whatever they want but their happiness is attached to money, and that happiness only stays for a little while, then they get sad and mad again!"

He just told me that and left! I never saw that little boy again. I don't really know what happened to him. I always looked for him, but no one knew him. But I knew that he was right. But I didn't know who he was, and I never learned his name, but I learned something from him. That boy helped me to change the direction of my shoes and put me on my path to discovery. I remember each word that he told me, and I remember how he looked at me.

Because of this experience, I'm not just a teenager. I say that I'm a dreamer, someone that fights for the rights of people and reveals the violations of people's rights. One of my dreams is to shout for those who can't speak for themselves, break the silence with my noise, speak out on the things that people are afraid to talk about, like injustice. Some people don't let others live their own lives, but who has the right to tell someone how to live? We all want to be happy, and if others are happy in their own way, what can we do? The only thing that we can do is live and let others live. What are our differences? It doesn't really matter what color or race you are, what culture or religion you practice, the thoughts you have, or the lifestyle you live. The only thing that matters is what we have inside of us, and to make our dreams real.

Some people don't understand the Golden Rule. The Golden Rule must not be a rule but a role. The Golden Rule means love and peace. Sometimes we do things that we wouldn't want others to do to us, such as lie, cheat, or be hurtful. We do those things even though we know it's not right. Some people don't practice the Golden Rule, but they want to change to be better people and to help others. They think that they can't change. Like me, they have to recognize their error and apologize to those who they have hurt and work towards doing the right thing. Change is not something easy, but it's something necessary. Change will help this world avoid killing itself with discrimination, racism, and ignorance. If we all practiced the Golden Rule it would help us to live better and to be free.

Alone in a Crowd

I walked on the street,
My soul was blind,
My heart was dark, without dreams,
And without life.
I was alone; no one was near me,
No one was behind me.
I felt my tears, I felt the darkness.
There were a lot of people, but I was alone!
People shouting, people laughing.
And I was crying because I felt nothing.
Dunes in my mind, fallen stars in my heaven.
Splinters of oxygen that helped me to survive.

There were just winters in my weather.
But suddenly and quietly a light of hope appeared in my life
That taught me the real way, a way that I started to make,
Sometimes with tears, but always with hope.
Sometimes I felt that I was wasting my time and wasting
    my tears.
But in the night, when I saw that the stars of my sky began
To shine, I knew that I was starting to live in a real world.
Now I am up in the stars, I make my own decisions
I fight for them!

THROUGH PINK-COLORED GLASSES

Catalina Almeida

One Friday morning I was at home watching commercials on TV and checking out MySpace on the computer. Everything was going as usual. Well, except for the fact that I was packing for camp. Yes, camp. "Boring old camp," as I had referred to it earlier that day. I wasn't really all that excited about going, but Derrick told me it would get me community service hours, and I needed the money. Derrick is a young man I have known for a while. He was my basketball coach in school.

As I lay in bed picturing my weekend and hoping I wouldn't have to go to camp, Derrick called to tell me that he was outside my house, waiting for me in the car with Jessica. Jessica is a friend I met through one of my passions, volleyball, a sport she also loves. I had known her for about a year at that time, but it seemed like we had known each other for way longer. It was only because Jessica was going to the camp that I was willing to go. I walked over to Derrick's car, climbed in, and we were on our way to San Jose, about forty-five minutes away.

Many thoughts were running through my mind as we got close. What are the people going to be like? What if I mess up? What's the place like?

What if I want to go back home in the middle of the weekend? Finally we were there. Getting out of the car, the first thing I saw was a lot of adults playing some game and laughing. They seemed nice and friendly. The camp had a lot of land and all the trees caught my eye. Nature at this place was so pretty. There was the sweet smell of the trees and almost no clouds. There were small plants everywhere, and most of the place was covered in grass, except for the rock paths that led to different places. There were basketball courts, swimming pools, a cafeteria, lodges, and at the top of a hill there was a path that gave a view of the camp and led to a horse stable. The counselors' lodge, where I would sleep, was pretty big itself; it had about eight beds in one room.

Little by little, the campers started coming in. They were kids of all ages and races, and they had many different types of disabilities. Some were in wheelchairs, others could not talk, and some had disfigured features. A good part of the group seemed very independent, while others looked like they would need more help mobilizing. While I was wandering around, the older counselors gathered in the cafeteria and started doing exciting paperwork, assigning each camper to a counselor and deciding who would stay in which lodge.

After I went to my lodge and put my stuff down, Derrick told me the first counselors' meeting had already started, so I hurried to the cafeteria and joined everybody else. Once the counselors had found out who their campers were, we sang a song to welcome the kids. When the song was over, I met all of the kids' parents, including my camper's parents. Some of the parents seemed to reject their kids for the simple fact that they had been born with a disability. I remember one couple; when it was time for them to leave, the father didn't even say bye to his daughter and the mom just gave a simple goodbye and left. You could tell that she was somewhat happy to leave her daughter behind. It was sad. Other parents loved their kids so obviously. It was clear they didn't care if their kids looked different, they still loved them for who they are. The mom of a girl named Erika gave her such a nice hug and kiss, told her she loved her and would miss her, and left crying.

Since it was my first time at camp I had only been assigned one camper to take care of—a girl named Karen, who was about my age, maybe a year or two younger. She was light-skinned, short, and had beautiful blue eyes that were hidden behind glasses. Karen was holding a big rag doll tightly. She had named the doll Gabby. Gabby had yellow hair made of strings and was wearing a dress. Karen's parents told me she would take her doll everywhere she went. She treated it like it was her kid. Karen was sweet and smart, gentle and kind. But I found that out later. When I first saw her I thought she would give me a hard time, but I had made that assumption only because she was disabled. She was drooling a lot. She also seemed kind of slow. Only after I really got to know her did I see that I was wrong.

Upon first seeing me she told me she didn't like me. Funny thing is, it was only because of my sweater. I had a bright orange sweater on. She said she only liked pink. There were two ladies next to me who appeared to be in their early twenties. They knew Karen from before, so they helped me. They just told her to pretend my sweater was pink, and then everything was OK. It surprised me how that little detail changed our relationship. After that she opened up, and that made our time a little easier for me. At first I had a hard time with her, but through the weekend she became a friend. After talking to her parents and getting her all set up (fixing her bed, unpacking her baggage) and resolving the sweater problem, I asked her to show me around the place. She said she didn't want to, that I'd have to learn my way around on my own. That just made me think the weekend would be even harder as it seemed like she didn't want to talk to me, and I thought, *How do they expect this to work out if she doesn't even want to talk to me?*

I asked her what she wanted to do, and she said she only wanted to go to the lodge and stay there. When we were in the lodge, I got to chat with her a little more. While we were chatting, I smelled the smoke of fire, and then I saw that a bonfire was going on outside. All of the counselors were already there with their campers. When Karen saw the bonfire, she didn't seem too excited by it. We were the last ones to get there. Jessica was already sitting with her campers, so Karen and I joined her and her campers.

Karen took a while to get into it, but when she did—wow! She was singing, "With a basketball in my hand, I will be Air Jordan," and dancing to all the songs. And me, I just watched. Since I had never been there, I didn't know any of the songs or dances. But then Karen taught me, and after she did, I started dancing and singing with her. Whenever I'd do something wrong Karen would laugh at me, then Jessica and I would look at each other and start laughing. The bonfire was so much fun. When it was over, Karen and I headed back to the lodge. On our way back I said, "Did you have fun? Thanks for teaching me!" She just looked at me and said, "Yeah, yeah. Can you read me a bedtime story?" Once we were back in the lodge, she quickly put her pajamas on and jumped into bed. I started reading *The Three Little Pigs* and when I looked at her she was already sleeping.

On Saturday morning, the second day of camp, I woke up early, still tired from the day before but excited for the day to come. Now that I had a better understanding of how camp worked, my mind felt lighter. I just lay in bed for a while, listening to the birds singing outside. Looking out through the window, it seemed to be a really nice day—not too hot, or too cold, just right. While getting dressed I remembered what Karen had said about my sweater, so I decided not to wear the same one again. As soon as I was ready I woke up Jessica and told her to hurry up if she didn't want to be late. At 8:30 AM, I started walking to Karen's cabin. It was quiet outside. Hardly anyone was out. I guess most of the campers were still sleeping or getting ready for breakfast.

Stepping into Karen's lodge I could tell all of the girls were still sleepy and didn't want to get up. So I walked inside singing, yelling, and playing around with them. When I saw Karen, she was already dressed and had done almost everything she needed to do, which gave me the chance to just relax a little bit more. Karen was wearing the same outfit as the day before, a pink jacket with blue on the hood, some pink sweats, and white shoes. She also had her tiara on (it was pink too). She loved pink! When she saw me, she gave me a hug and said, "Good morning, Cat! Could you help me get my doll dressed?" I told her she could do it on her own, so she just did it. I saw that my friend was having a hard time with her camper, so I asked her if she needed help. She looked so happy when I asked that.

Once all of the girls in the cabin were dressed, Melissa, the head counselor, told us we should head to the cafeteria for breakfast. Karen yelled when she heard that. It was a happy yell though—she seemed really hungry. Sitting in the cafeteria, I started looking around. I saw all types of people, and got to thinking. I remember seeing this one kid in particular whose face was distorted, his lips weren't straight, his eyes weren't at an equal height, and his nose was kind of flat. I wondered how his parents were with him, how his friends treated him, and how he felt about being how he was. Was he just like me, except his appearance? What if I were like that? I wondered how I would feel in his shoes. I still think about how his disabilities affect him and the people around him. I know it certainly affected me. I guess I wasn't used to seeing people like him. I don't know if I was scared, curious, or just felt sorry for him. But whatever it was, I got over it by the end of the weekend. I got to talk to him once or twice, and that changed my perspective. While I spaced out looking at him, everyone had already started eating, so I just joined in.

Breakfast was fun; all the little campers from my cabin were sitting together (six of us actually). They talked about everything. It reminded me of my friends and me. They were so curious to know more about me. They started asking all these questions about how San Francisco is different from where they live, where I went to school, and if people at school like me, and then they asked if I had a boyfriend. I thought that was so funny. We passed the entire time talking, and once we were done the campers helped me clean up and then went running back to the lodge. At the lodge one of the campers showed me her yearbook. She looked so proud of it. I asked her if I could hold it and look at it, and she told me to go ahead. As I flipped through the pages, she pointed out all of her friends, and even showed me the boy she liked. About fifteen minutes later she reminded me that we had to go to the arts and crafts lodge, so I called Karen and started walking up there with her.

In the arts and crafts lodge I saw many plastic hats on the counter, along with glitter, markers, feathers, and glue. Karen went running to one of the tables to sit next to her friend, and I joined her there. At first, she wasn't all that excited about doing whatever it was we were going to do. I tried cheering her up so she could get more into it. Derrick had told me that the most important thing for the whole weekend was to get the campers to participate in every activity. I walked to the counter and got supplies for my table. Since there was no pink, Karen made a yellow hat with a green feather. She didn't put glitter or anything on it though. The glitter was green and she doesn't like green. After finishing her hat she ran up to show me. I told her it looked beautiful, and she smiled. She told me she wanted me to make one for myself too, so I did. We agreed to wear our hats to the dance that night. Karen said she was going to put them in a place that was safe so no one could take them. She grabbed the two hats and put them on the counter. I told her that wasn't safe enough, but she just laughed and said, "Don't worry about it." I laughed.

We stopped for a minute and looked around. Everyone had already left the lodge. Karen immediately looked at me and said, "They're in the sports court." She ran out of the lodge and toward the court, and while running she looked back and said, "You can't catch me!" I chased after her and told her she'd better run. I ended up getting to the sports court before her. When I looked back to see where she was, I didn't see her behind me. I looked at the bench and there she was, sitting down. She looked tired. Karen told me she didn't want to join in on the activity, and I wasn't really up for it either. So we sat it out and just talked the whole time. I ended up taking a nap, and when I woke up Karen was staring at me. "Are you tired?" she asked. "No, but I am hungry," I said with a smile. She yelled out, "Lunchtime," and grabbed my hand. She started pulling me to the cafeteria. She said she didn't want to be late and not get to sit with her friend.

Our table was still empty by the time we got there. More and more people started walking in, until finally everybody was in the cafeteria. At camp, they have a routine for lunchtime. Before lunch is served, the kids are required to have a minute of silence. After that minute of silence, they find out what the lunch for the day is going to be. We went through the routine, then had lunch. It was macaroni and cheese. Karen loved it. She had about four plates. After that, she still wanted dessert, but I didn't let her have it. Her parents had told me she wasn't supposed to have more than two plates at each meal. I told her that that lunch would be our little secret, and so it was.

It had been a full morning and everyone was tired. So once lunch was over all the campers walked back to their lodge for their free time. Karen said she wanted to sleep because she was tired. So I dropped her off in her lodge and headed to mine. I would have about an hour before she woke up and we enjoyed our next activity, so I met up with Jessica, and we joined the rest of the counselors in the cafeteria. We had hot chocolate and talked to Derrick for about thirty minutes. We told him how fun it was so far and how we were so happy we went to camp. The hour had passed; it was about 3 PM.

When I got to her bed Karen was still sleeping, so I poked her. All she said was, "Ouch." She told me she wanted to sleep more. I gave her about five minutes, then told her she really had to get up this time. It was hard, but she got up. The afternoon went OK. Whenever we got bored with what we were doing, I'd take Karen and one of her friends outside for a while, and they would sit at the campfire and talk. I'd sit there and stare at the sky. It was so blue, and you could barely see any clouds. It went like that for the entire afternoon, just going in and out of the cafeteria and walking around the camp.

Then the people in the cafeteria started cleaning up. My legs were too tired to get my body to get up and help, so I just sat and watched. The other groups started coming in for dinner. Once again, the routine had to be done. Ugh, I just wanted to hurry up and eat. I said so to Karen, and she said, "Me too." She was about to get up and run to the front to get food, even though she was supposed to be sitting, but I told her to be patient.

After dinner, I headed back to Karen's lodge and helped her get ready for the dance. She said she wanted to wear her pink dress and wanted my help with her makeup. That took us about thirty minutes. When we got back to the cafeteria for the dance everybody was already there, dancing, having fun. Karen got into it quick. She wanted me to go dance with her, but I was too shy. I told Jessica to go with her, and I stayed with Christina. Christina was another camper whom I had met on Friday. When the dance was over, I took Karen back to the lodge and once more put her to bed. That night, I had the night shift, so I had to stay an extra thirty minutes in the girls' lodge to make sure they all went to sleep. I was so tired. Once the room was silent and I knew for sure they were sleeping, I went to the cafeteria, had hot chocolate, and headed straight to my lodge. The day had been awesome; my camper did well in all of her activities, and barely needed my help. It was that day that I realized that just because someone has a disability, it doesn't mean they're not capable of doing what everybody else does all the time.

Sunday came. There would be a talent show going on later. Karen was going to sing a song by Britney Spears—you know, the one that goes, "Hit me, baby, one more time." She said she didn't want my help with it, that she could do it all on her own, so I sat back and enjoyed the show. When it was her turn to go up, she grabbed her doll and ran to the front of the room. She danced and sang with her doll. She was great! After every camper had done their presentation we headed outside. Since the schedule didn't have anything else after the talent show, we could do what we wanted. Most people went outside and lay down on the grass.

Parents started coming in the afternoon to pick up their kids. After all the campers left, the counselors got in a circle and shared whatever they wanted to share with the rest of us. After that, we all got our stuff, said goodbye, and headed back to our cars.

In the car, Jessica, Derrick, and I talked about our weekend, about how much fun it was and how we couldn't wait for next weekend to do it all over! Jessica told me that camp had maybe been the best thing she ever did with her life, and I agreed with her.

This whole experience had meant a lot to me. I didn't want the weekend to end. At camp, I forgot about everything else. It was as if I were a whole other person. I could be me, and not be judged for it. Everybody got along so well. It was fun all the time. Especially because Jessica was there with me. Those kids brought me so many smiles and memories. After that weekend, camp turned out to be my runaway spot in a way. When I was there, I had no problems, no sadness. I was me in my calm, happy state. I could do what I wanted, when I wanted. I had more liberty. So I started going more often on weekends. It just felt so right. What had started out as a job turned out to be one of my best experiences. Karen had also had a wonderful weekend, and seeing that smile on her face made my day. She taught me a lot and became very important to me.

That weekend, I learned that appearance isn't everything, and people are capable of more than they appear to be. I learned more from those kids than they did from me. Before I got there I thought I would be helping kids, doing things like chores for them. But what I ended up doing was becoming a friend to a lot of them. I learned that they're just like everybody else, and I don't need to treat them differently just because they look different. Like everybody else, they have responsibilities. For example, some of them work, some go to school, and they all have friends. This changed my thoughts, feelings, and behavior toward disabled people.

Before camp, when I walked around my school and saw kids like that, I wouldn't say or do anything. Sometimes I'd even act like I didn't see them. What I did was wrong. Most young people discriminate, and I had to find out the hard way that there's no reason for that. People with disabilities are capable of doing everything I can do, and maybe even more. Now I don't judge anyone anymore.

MY CRAZY LIFE
Justo Reyes

Banging [bang · in'] *verb*—being part of a group of people causing nothing but trouble

punk'd [pun · ked] *verb*—getting bullied by a group of people or just one person

*   *   *

I've gone through this. Sadly, in my experience, the people who supposedly care about me are often the ones that really don't. People wear costumes. It's nearly impossible to know who's being real with you at first; sometimes it's the person you least expect.

I had a rough childhood. When I needed my parents the most, I didn't feel their support. They never got along, were always arguing and fighting around me like a bunch of cats and dogs, and got divorced when I was in the fourth grade. My folks and I have never gotten along. I always felt I was last in the family. Simply put, they didn't teach me the facts of life.

Back when I was still in middle school, I got into a fight with my older brother. He was boring, constantly unhappy, and greedy—a person you really don't want to kick it with. My parents favored him. He was gold to them. If anyone touched him they would be outraged. My brother and I got into it because I told him not to touch my stuff anymore. He didn't listen. I pushed him and spit out some words that would make most adults cover their kids' ears. He pushed back, so I laid a fat one into his face. We fought—throwing punches wildly, socking one another in a whirlwind of rapid rage. I left him with a blue-black, baseball-size bruise on his cheek.

My mom had just gotten home from a long day at work when she noticed the swelling on my brother's cheek; she knew instantly that I was responsible. She kicked me out of the house and I was left on my own. I called my friends to ask if I could stay with them. Most of them said no—except one: my oldest brother's girlfriend. She said I could stay over, but only for a night. As I walked to her house, my dad called me on my cell. I answered, but before I even got the phone next to my ear he was yelling at me about what I had done to my brother's face, and asking why I had hit my mom. I knew I hadn't hit her. I told him that I would never do such a thing. He said that my mom told him that I did. I hung up. I didn't want to hear any more of that nonsense.

I went to sleep thinking about how screwed up my life was. I was only twelve. The next day at five in the afternoon, my oldest brother arrived at his girlfriend's house. I told him to take me home. I didn't care what my parents would do to me. There was a police car outside when we drove up. I was nervous—I thought they were going to take me to Juvi. I stepped inside and saw two Sasquatch-sized police officers in my living room. They asked me why I had run away from home. I explained that my mom kicked me out, and they accused me of hitting her. I told them I didn't, and my mother and father just stood there, speechless.

Thirty minutes went by—question after question—before they finally left. I asked my parents why they lied about me hitting my mom but they didn't respond. I sat alone on my big, comfortable couch thinking, *Why do I live a life with so much tragedy?* I hated my parents at that time; they weren't there for me. Ultimately, they didn't show me how to survive in the streets, how to cook my own food, or how to be successful in school. I basically had to teach myself. Thinking about the past, I realize that I've gone through a lot. Although I suffered and struggled at times, I learned a lot from my experiences.

At the age of fourteen I was a freshman at Burton High School. I was always kicking it with the older guys because they were both popular and well-respected. I wanted what they had. I thought that by being with them, I'd become popular too. I did everything they did: I banged and I cut class. Eventually, I had a bad reputation that spread throughout the school. Everyone—students and faculty—knew my name. One day after school let out I was down the hill from Burton (where we all usually kicked it) with one other friend. We were standing around, chopping it up and relaxing on a cloudy afternoon. A blue Crown Vic drove by. Then it reversed, and I noticed that there were some guys in it that had funk with my friend.

They were staring straight at us. My friend seemed paranoid, and I knew he was scared. He was acting like he wanted to tell me something, but couldn't get the words out. He was stuttering, trying to get to second gear, but the clutch kept slipping. The guys in the car got out. They almost all looked the same: bald, black and white shirts, and baggy, Dickies-logoed pants. They started punkin' my friend. I asked them with a crucial tone, "Why y'all messing with him?" They told me the guy I was with was talking a lot of head about them. Shaking and nervous, I told the guys to just leave him alone, to drop any problems they had with him. They stared me down with vicious eyes that looked as if they could see right through me. Then they left like I wasn't worth their time. My friend thanked me. He said he would always have my back, no matter what. I felt good—strong, tough, solid as rock. I was unbreakable.

After that, my friend and I stayed close throughout the year at Burton. I transferred to O'Connell because my parents thought I was doing poorly and the school didn't want me there anymore. My friend and I lost touch.

Years passed. I was sixteen, kind of grown, with a little goatee and a thin moustache. I was still at O'Connell. It was after class, and I was walking to the bus stop at 22ND and Mission on a hot day—sun shining down, burning my head. Across the street I noticed some guys that didn't like me. A couple of years before one of them had thought I was trying to get at his girl, but I really wasn't. We were just friends. There were a few of them standing tall—two with hoodies and black jeans and another with blue jeans and a white tee. They looked ruthless. There was a lot going on in my head. I was tense and anxious, not knowing what to do, stuck in the moment. They came up to me acting all slick, and one of them said, "What up, got something to say to me, fool?" I stood quietly, because I'm not the kind of person that likes to start problems.

One of the guys who was trying to punk me was very distinct looking and seemed familiar. I thought to myself, *I know this guy.* I realized that he was my friend from two years ago, the one I had defended when he was getting punk'd at the bottom of the hill. But why wasn't he defending me? I knew he knew me and recognized me. He acted like he didn't know me. That said it all. In a low tone of voice I said, "Two face." It was the second time someone had turned their back on me. The guys that were bullying me kept on running their mouths like a non-stop flight to Asia. They finally stopped talking smack. I thought they were going to do something like stab me or jump me but they didn't. They just left.

The whole bus ride home I couldn't stop wondering how one of my good friends could turn on me. He was a chameleon, changing his appearance just to fit in. I couldn't get it out of my head. I didn't know what to do. I kept wondering whether I should go after him and do something or just drop the whole controversy. I let it go. After that, everything collapsed. I didn't care about anyone unless I knew for a fact that they cared about me and would be there for me when I needed them. I could have seen someone getting mugged and I wouldn't have done anything about it. Luckily, my girlfriend was there for me. She was and continues to be the only person I know who genuinely cares about me: short, sweet, and as beautiful as a rose. Without her I don't know where I would be. I think I'd go back to the way I was before I met her. My gratitude for her is eternal.

How'd she do it? When no one else was there to stand by me, she was. While others lacked it, she had the courage and compassion to tell me to get my head straight, to stay off the streets and do whatever it took to survive on my own. She told me she was always going to be there for me, no matter what. She gave me the courage to believe in myself, to overcome anything that stood in my way. She gave me power. She gave me confidence.

We met at the park years ago. I was supposed to meet up with her friend at the park. The two of us were just going to kick it, but she showed up with this other girl. The second girl attracted my attention with her smile and beautiful hair that waved from side to side. She was so quiet and nice, amused with everything I did. I just loved the way she acted around me. She seemed so shy but felt very comfortable around me. Daniela was her name. After I met her I started doing better in school; I wasn't kickin' it on the block as much as I used to. One day, while sitting on the stairs outside of my house, it sparked in my head: I wasn't damaging myself anymore. The illness was gone. She was—and continues to be—my cure.

My past has shaped me. I've learned to defend only myself and the people who really care about me. I had a homeboy who died in 2005 on the corner of 24TH and Alabama. He got shot twice in the chest and three times in his back. He was involved with gangs just like I used to be, but he was much older than me. His name was Brian Marquez, and he told me four days before he got killed, "Everyone goes through situations that we don't want to be in, but we got to be ready for those problems. We got to take the hits any way they come." That made me think a lot. Life is a steady struggle. The hits keep coming—big and little ones. I'm ready to take them. However, I've learned that living a life that involves putting yourself at risk for a gang or for people who call themselves your friends isn't worth it unless they will be there to show you care and support when you truly need it. Point period: you respect me and I'll respect you.

*   *   *

care [kair] *verb*—to be concerned or solicitous; have thought or regard

trustworthy [truhst-wur-thee] *adjective*—deserving of trust or confidence; dependable; reliable

FOUR YEARS

Victor Greene

I remember watching Sponge Bob early in the morning while getting ready for school. My grandmother and sisters were upstairs watching TV. My mom called me upstairs and said, "Look." On TV there was a building on fire that looked like a missile had hit it. I asked her what happened. No answer. And then we saw an airplane hit the building. All over the house it was quiet. We were mesmerized when we saw that. When I saw the building fall I was thinking, *That is not real.*

Right when I was leaving, an announcement said no one should go to school. I remember looking up in the sky. The clouds were looking weird, like they were going towards New York. President George W. Bush used that as an excuse to start a war with Saddam and Al Qaeda. Without evidence that Iraq was responsible for the bombings that occurred on 9/11, Bush sent troops to wage an unnecessary war.

*   *   *

My father served in the army in Iraq. I can't imagine my dad having close combat with another person, killing another person, or having to look in the people's faces when he took their homes for cover. He got into a car crash and then came back. Now he's retired, but I still don't see him much.

He has missed every birthday for the past several years. On my thirteenth birthday, he wasn't there. On my fourteenth, not even a call. My fifteenth birthday, no one answered. Maybe he forgot, or maybe he was really busy with the war he was in. Or maybe he really did remember and tried to call, but something happened so he didn't have time to. I thought he would at least try to call or have my stepmom call or send me a card or something. It felt like everything was going wrong. It seemed like this could happen to someone next door or across the street, but not to me.

My thirteenth birthday was the first he missed. He had to leave. My mom didn't care. They had been divorced for about two to three years at the time. This birthday was one of the most memorable because it was missing the one thing that my dad used to always do. Every birthday my dad would get me a carrot cake. The funny thing is I never used to like carrot cake. What really annoyed me were those chewy things that you got every bite you took. But since my dad used to bring me one every birthday, I began to really like it. Now I kind of miss it when he's not there to get me one. I didn't really know how I felt at the time. All I knew was that I didn't have carrot cake on my birthday. My mom bought a strawberry cake, and she knows that I hate strawberries. I was disappointed because my sisters are the only ones who like strawberry cake. I can remember thinking that it felt like one of my sisters' birthdays, not mine. On my birthday, there were always two cakes: a carrot cake and another one that I picked out.

At the time of my fourteenth birthday, my oldest sister's baby was almost due, and she didn't know what to name her new son. Our dad had a couple of ideas before he left for Iraq, but we didn't like them. My father named every child he had with a name beginning with *V*. My sisters are Valerie, Vikkie, and Vanesha, and there's me, Victor. My dad's name is Victor, too. Even my grandma, Valerie, and my mom, Vinell, share the *V*. My father wanted to keep the chain linked, but it was broken.

My nephew was born on May 17, 2003. My little sis named the baby

Kevon. We kept the *V* in there for Dad's tradition. On my father's birthday we called him and told him my nephew's name, and he was kind of mad about the *K*. He was happy to hear the *V* was in there, though. A couple of months later, my dad called us and said he was coming to our house to see us and the baby. Instead my sis went to him. I couldn't go because my mom wouldn't let me. I wasn't disappointed, but inside I was kind of sad.

Another thing about my dad: He really could not cook. He would make some of the weirdest combinations, like grits and broccoli. Come on, who eats that type of stuff? Or this other time he made this big pot of the most disgusting chili. He said that he made it himself—and I believed him too. It seemed like he just made it up as he went on and expected us to eat it with no problem. Although my dad was a really bad cook, I still tried to enjoy my time with him. Any time my dad would cook, we would just go out to eat somewhere. It would be kind of funny because we would just look at the food like, *Are we supposed to eat this,* and then laugh. One day, my dad had a friend over, and she cooked. She made some kind of meat with jerk sauce. It was the best, although my sister and I looked at it for a little while thinking, *Who cooked this?* We were like, *No, we're not eating this,* until he told us that he didn't cook it.

On my fifteenth birthday, we found out my other sister had gotten pregnant. And again we didn't know what to name the baby. My dad was the first to know. My sister called him. He was happy to hear the news. He was happy to hear that he was going to be a grandfather of two boys. We named the baby Avion. Again we didn't use a *V* as the first letter of his name, but we put the *V* in there.

The Christmas before my sixteenth birthday was alright. My dad came. My sisters, my nephew, and I all went out to dinner at Home Town Buffet. I like going there because my dad used to take us there after church. After we had dinner, we went shopping for the kids. When we got to the store, they saw all the toys and went crazy. They ran all over the place. Every toy they saw they wanted: Tonka trucks, Big Wheels, and especially action figures like Spiderman, Batman, Superman, Hulk, Iron Man, and Power Rangers. Just to see the look on their faces when they saw all that stuff—they were so happy. Then it was my sisters' turn. They went to other stores to get their stuff. My lil' sis and I are into games, so we went to GameStop and my sis went crazy. We didn't exactly get what we wanted, but we were satisfied with what we got. We got the new Guitar Hero, and she got a Nintendo DS.

My sixteenth birthday was the best because we did a lot of things that day. I had kind of gotten used to my dad missing my birthday by this time. My sisters took me to Olive Garden and brought my nephews. They go everywhere with me. They ordered some spaghetti and chicken. My mom and grandma never want to come along. My mom doesn't talk to my dad anymore ever since she supposedly caught him cheating on her with another woman.

For those four long years while my dad was at war, my nephews never knew they had a grandfather. I wonder if my father ever received the pictures my sisters mailed to him, or if my nephews know who my dad is. I remember one of my nephews asking me, "What's your dad's name?" I said, "Victor," and he said, "I want to see him." I told him he only had a year left before he would meet him.

I was there when he "cheated," but my dad and the other woman were just sitting in the car. He said that he was going to take her home. I don't know who to believe at this moment. I was really young. It was me and my little sister. We were going to pick up my dad from his job. We hit the corner, and we saw my dad in the car sitting there not doing anything. Then we saw a woman come out of the building and get into the car. And that's all my mom needed to see. She got out of our car, went over to the other car, and cursed my dad out because she thought he was cheating on her. My dad said he was taking the woman home, but my mom didn't want to hear it. So my mom moved out. She took me and my little sister. We moved to Oakland, and my mom bought a house there. We lived alone there for like a month or two. My dad came back a month later. It was all going well until my parents started arguing over dumb stuff. One time, they were arguing over ducks flying. My mom said that they could and my dad said they couldn't. My sister and I tried to solve the conflict by looking it up in the dictionary, but it was useless. Each thought he or she was right no matter what.

About two months later, my dad moved out, and my auntie Vickie and her children moved in. My cousins started to take over my house. They ate all of my food, played my games, and even took my room. I had to sleep on the couch. My big cousin took my room. My little sister slept with my mom, and my aunty slept on the floor with them. My dad hasn't come around in a while. The last time I saw him was the day before he left. He didn't say anything to my mom, just left. While my cousins were in the house, things started getting out of control. My mom was arguing a lot with my aunty. There was even a fight between my sisters and my cousins. I didn't know what was going on that day. A month or two later, my mom lost the house. My mom said we were going to move in with our grandma for a couple months. My big sisters were already there. They decided not to go with my mom to Oakland because they knew that they would end up with my grandma anyway. My grandma took us in even though I didn't want to go. I thought it was boring. It kind of made my grandma sad. My grandpa lived there with us. He was white. I didn't know him before I got there, but afterward it seemed like I had known him for a long time. For as long as I lived there, it seemed like my mom, grandma, and older sisters always had something against my father. Every time he would call my granny's house, she would pick up and yell, "Don't call this house!" She wouldn't tell us who was calling, but I knew. My little sister didn't understand at the time because she was too young. I really didn't understand why my grandmother had anything to do with my relationship with my father. If he called to speak to me, I don't see why he couldn't. My mom has gotten a cell phone, so he doesn't call the house anymore, but she doesn't even give him her number. My sister had to give my dad her number so he could call her to talk to his kids. He called and it went kind of wrong. My mom was asleep and was kind of angry so she cursed him out, hung up, and went back to sleep.

So my dad sued my mom for custody, and he lost, but the courts gave him joint custody. We get to go with him once a weekend. We decided on Sunday because we weren't going to church a lot. When we went with my dad, we could tell he was very happy. My dad is very silly when he gets around us. And when we get around him, we act as if we were all born on April 1.

One time my dad didn't take us to church, and we didn't know where we were going. He said he had a surprise for us. We thought we were lost, but it turned out he was taking us to Great America, the amusement park. We were so happy because it was my little sister's sixth birthday and we had to do something. After that, he took us home and my mom was waiting at the front door. We got out of the car and walked past my mom, and she started screaming at my dad because he brought us home late. He just drove off.

One time my dad had brought us home with my stepbrother in the car with us. He was like ten and my mom was waiting for us again. She walked to the car slowly, and my dad thought she was going to be nice for once, but she punched my dad in the face. My dad almost got out of the car, but he just drove off. After that, my mom thought she was so sick because she had done that. A week later my dad didn't mention it. Maybe he forgot, or he just didn't think about it, and we didn't remind him.

*   *   *

I remember once my dad did like 100 push-ups with my sister on his back, so I jumped on his back too. I was around eleven at the time. That was the best day ever. Now he's back from Iraq. His leg was injured, but my dad is just as strong as he used to be. But I still don't really see him that often. The last time I saw him was last week for my sister's birthday, but we didn't talk for that long because my mom was coming from the store, and he didn't want to get into it with her. I hope that my dad can come to my seventeenth birthday without my mom having a problem with him. Hopefully we can all go out somewhere where we can enjoy each other's company. Maybe he could bring me something other than carrot cake.

DADDY'S LITTLE GIRL MAKIN' HER WAY

Angelica Marisel Colon-Chin

I don't really know why, but I guess I was born a *fighter*! Ever since I was young, I've always been easily angered. As a child, I had a temper that no one could calm—except for my dad. You could say that I'm an imprint of my dad. When I was younger I was always with him. Wherever he went and whatever he did, I was there.

I remember my dad having medium-long, brownish-black hair with little bits of copper color. He was medium set with a light caramel skin tone and brown eyes that would change with the light of the sun. He always dropped me off at preschool on his Harley. My days in preschool were, so far, the best school years of my life. I was teacher's pet. I never really got in trouble for much that I did. Once I got into a fight with this funky lookin', mean starin' girl who thought she was Lil' Miss Thang and reached out to pull my hair.

I didn't get in trouble, at least from what I can remember. I do remember that when my dad came to pick me up that day, my teacher talked to him, and then we went on our way home. My dad talked to me about what had happened right when we got home. My dad always said that

I shouldn't start fights, but if someone hit me first, then I was allowed to hit that person back.

When my dad was still living with my mom, he was always in the garage working on cars. Go figure, I was right there underneath the car with him while my older brother was busy playing with his toys or watching TV. My mom and dad separated when I was about three or four years old. I always wondered where my dad was. I was told he'd come back some day. When he did come, a few years later, he didn't come back to live with us, but came to pick us up for the weekend. He also picked us up every summer. Although my dad was always working, I enjoyed every second I was able to be near him. I love my dad. No matter what I'm doing, my dad is always somewhere in my mind.

My dad knows me very well—maybe a bit too well. I guess it can be a good thing or a bad thing, I'm not sure. My dad and I have a bond like no other, allowing us to understand each other and to know how we're feeling. My dad trusts me in every way; I have no reason to lie to him. We are always truthful with each other, and this makes our relationship even stronger. Even if I try, I just can't lie to my dad.

As I grew older, not having my dad around really affected my actions. I held in all of my emotions (mostly my anger), and I started taking things out on other people. I didn't exactly go out looking for trouble, but I was very defensive towards people I didn't know well. I remember one time in second grade, when this one girl was bothering me and asking me if she could be my friend. I told her that I didn't want a friend right then and to leave me alone, but she kept bugging me. I went and told a teacher, but the teacher didn't do anything about it, and the girl kept bugging me. I got irritated. I grabbed her by the collar of her shirt, threw her up against the wall, and walked away. I didn't get in trouble for doing this because I had followed the procedure and told an adult first, before deciding to take it into my own hands.

My dad always told me that fighting won't solve anything, that taking your anger out on another person will only make you feel better for a little while. Furthermore, he told me that I was not to hit anyone unless I was hit or swung at first. My dad always tries his best when it comes to me, my family, and my friends. I've always admired that my dad doesn't drink, smoke, or gang bang. My dad is a man of many talents, and with the right tools, he gets the job done.

You're probably thinking, "What about your mother?" Well, yes, I *love* my mom, but it's with my dad whom I have a better bond (clearly I am "Daddy's little girl"). My brother has a better bond with my mom (he's a "Mama's boy"). My mom is usually working, trying to support my brother and me as a single mother of two. And sometimes she goes out with her friends, kicking back and taking a break from all the hard work.

Frankly, I'm glad that I'm not a "girly girl." If I was, I'd most likely be less independent and worried about how my nails look, if my hair is too frizzy or has enough volume, and my body shape—whether my butt is too big, if my boobs are the right size, or if my stomach sticks out. I wouldn't play sports, and I'd be less brave.

While living with my mom, I didn't do too well in school. I got pretty bad grades when I was about ten and eleven years old. I remember that I was told by a few family members that I wasn't going to make it far in life and that everything I did was leading to nowhere good. Once my sixth-grade year was over, I was finally allowed to go live with my dad in Sacramento. The court ordered that my brother and I were to live with my dad for a whole year. After that, we had to decide if we wanted to stay with him or go back to live with my mom. Another rule for me was that if I did better in Sacramento "school-wise," I would be able to stay and live with my dad as long as I kept improving. I was so happy that I was moving and that my brother was coming along too. Moving to my dad's house was a very exciting moment for me although I knew that I was going to miss my mom and my family no matter what had been said or done. Once I got to my dad's house I was so excited. I wanted to see what my room looked like. As time went by I started to improve academically, emotion-ally—pretty much in every way.

After a year went by, I stayed with my dad while my brother went back to live with my mom. I was devastated that my brother moved away. My brother and I had never been separated in our lives, and I was going to miss him so much. But I didn't let that affect me; I just kept doing the best I could.

As time went by, my grades in school kept improving. I learned a lot from my mom and dad, and a few other things from my stepparents. They and my aunties really gave me a boost to keep up the good work I was doing. They encouraged me in everything that I did and never let me quit at anything that I started.

Though my brother is two and a half years older than I am, I was the one who stood up for him when trouble came creeping around the corner. Throughout elementary school my brother was always teased about his way of expressing himself. At a young age, he knew that he was gay. His peers would ask me why he was different and why he acted the way he did, but what was I to say? My brother has always known that he could count on me to be there at any time and any place. When he needed me, all he had to do was yell my name and I would come running. First, I would scan the person bothering my brother to see what I was dealing with; then, I would chase them away and make sure they didn't come back. If they did, I would keep chasing them until they gave up. I was never really scared, even while I was chasing the big kids, because I knew that they weren't going to hurt me. Now that I think about this, it's really funny how when we're younger, we do the first thing that comes to mind without thinking about what the consequences are. But as we grow older, we always think, think, and think before we even start to do what we really want to do.

In high school, someone once told me that it's good to be respected, but what good is it if that respect is earned out of fear? This made me realize that hurting others and making them feel bad didn't make me a better person. From that moment on, I have based my way of life on the Golden Rule. By the end of my freshman year, my attitude towards people changed in a positive way. During my sophomore year I gained a lot of patience and became a more honest and respectful person.

As the years went by, I noticed that my overall GPA was 3.0. As long as I wasn't failing, my dad was always proud of me no matter what grade I got, and that's how all parents should be. My dad knows that if my grades start going down, there's a reason for it.

I never thought I'd move back to my mom's, but I did. I call my dad and talk to him every now and then. I tell him pretty much everything that's going on in my life and the things I do. I'm grown up enough to make most of my own decisions without having to inform my parents, and they don't worry as much as before because they know what they've produced.

Right now I'm just a junior in high school, and I'm making sure that I get all of the credits I need to graduate and be prepared for college, where I'll be heading soon. I was thinking about going to a community college and then transferring, but my counselor wants the best for me, so she's going to make me aim higher. When I'm done and ready to go out into the world, I'm going to help people in the community. I want to make a difference in people's lives. I want people to smile, knowing that there is someone they can count on. I want to be that helping hand for those in need. I'm Daddy's little girl, all grown up and ready to make a difference.

LOST & FOUND
Daarina Berry

There are a lot of nice people in the world. Sometimes it's possible for a stranger to be kind, but you just don't expect it. You don't know if a person is kind. When you're walking down the street, you don't just look at a person and say, "Oh, that person is nice." You have to talk to them if you want to know more about them. Normally, your parents would tell you not to talk to strangers, but sometimes a stranger can help you out with your problems. When I was a little girl, I never would have thought I would need a stranger's help.

Here's a story of when I was six years old at the California State Fair in Sacramento. I was with my family on what felt like the hottest day it could be. Back then, I loved to go to the fair. The things I liked most were the rides and the nice hot sun. When we went to Sacramento we would stay all weekend. We would go to the fair on Saturday and the mall on Sunday. Early that Saturday morning we got dressed, had breakfast, and then were on our way. When I opened the door to the van it was blazing hot, and I didn't want to get inside. To make matters worse, I burned myself trying to put on the seat belt!

The fair was only a short drive away from our hotel. After only a few minutes of listening to music and to my mom and grandmother talking about what they were going to buy, we arrived at the fair. As soon as we walked in, I saw all kinds of rides and big buildings with a lot of people coming out with shopping bags. I saw and heard the train that went all the way around the park. There were a lot of different smells. I smelled tons of roasted corn, cotton candy, and pool or lake water. When I saw the rides, I wanted to get on one right away. I saw a ride with bears that had red and blue shirts on. I saw two different kinds of car rides—one that was for little kids and one for bigger kids. There was also a red and green caterpillar ride. It was like a mini roller coaster ride for kids my size and looked very fun. But the ride I couldn't wait to get on was this cool-looking, upside-down ride that went from side to side and stayed in the air for a couple of seconds, then went around in a circle while it twirled. It looked like it was more fun than any of the others.

When we go to the fair, we start in the back and make our way to the front. That day we walked to the back of the fair where the big warehouse was. On the way I saw this big water fountain where kids were playing and getting wet. *It does look kind of fun to play around in that water, and it's hot out here,* I thought. *Maybe I should ask my mom if I can go in the water too!* But before I had the chance to ask, we were past the big water fountain.

We stopped at a cart where a guy was selling hats, and my grandmother bought a pretty straw hat. Then my little sister and I spotted colorful foot massagers. We asked our mother if we could take a go at it, and she gave us fifty cents. As soon as the massagers came on it shook my whole body, and I jumped off and broke out laughing. At that time I had four silver front teeth, and when I was laughing everyone in my family saw them and they started laughing. Moments like those are why I love going to the fair.

We continued to walk to the back. When we reached the entrance of the warehouse, we saw all these carts selling goods. The one I remember most was the cart selling the fan with the spray bottle. We actually bought one, and it was green.

Once inside, I saw a lot of people and stands where people were selling various things. We were shopping and looking, and we stopped at a stand selling jewelry. Across from it was a stand selling toys. I asked my mother, "Can I go over there to look at all the toys?"

"Where is it?" she asked.

I pointed and told her, "It's right over there."

"Yeah, sure, go ahead," she said.

I said, "Thank you," and walked over.

I saw all kinds of toys. I saw skate shoes, Barbie dolls, hula-hoops of all colors, jump ropes, and many other toys. As I was looking at them, I saw a pink plastic princess jewelry set. I went crazy because it had Disney princesses on it, and I thought, *I just have to get it before someone else does.* I ran over to ask my mom if she would buy it for me and tell her that we needed to hurry up and get over there. But when I got across the path, my mother was gone!

Normally, children in this situation would go crazy, but I didn't panic. I looked for her in a very calm manner. But then I still couldn't find her, and I started to panic and cry. I walked back to the toy place and stayed there just in case my mother came back looking for me. As I sat there, I cried even more. Then all of a sudden someone stopped in front of me. It was a black lady with short black hair and dark eyes who was about five feet, three inches tall. She was also alone. She bent down and asked me my name.

"Daarina," I said, trying not to cry as much as before.

"What's wrong, Daarina?"

I told her my story, and she said, "Come on Daarina, let's go and find your mother."

As we walked around the warehouse to look for my mother the lady asked me questions like, "How old are you? Where do you live? Who else did you come here with? What's your mom's name? What does your mom look like?" We walked and walked and walked, and I still couldn't find her. I looked up at the woman and saw that she was starting to look worried. She said, "Daarina, let's look for a police officer or something. Maybe your mom is looking for you, too." Seeing her worry made me a little worried too, and for a second I thought I had no hope of finding my mom or anyone else in my family.

We walked out of the nice, air-conditioned warehouse, back into the hot Sacramento weather to look for a police officer. Even though we were looking for help, I was still nervous and a little bit scared just thinking of my mother leaving me in this big unfamiliar place. After about ten minutes of searching, we found a police officer, and there was a woman standing with him. As we got closer, I recognized the woman's white T-shirt which had the names "Redwine" and "Craig" on it. I realized that it was my mother. I screamed, "Mommy, Mommy, Mommy!" She turned around and shouted out my name, and with the lady's hand still in mine, I ran to my mom and gave her a big hug as if I hadn't seen her in years. Seeing my mom was like watching the sun rise again on a new day. I felt a huge weight disappear off my shoulders. The feeling of being reunited with my mom was something I had never felt before.

While my mother and I were still hugging, the lady told my mom how and where she found me. My mom thanked her a lot and asked if there was anything she could do to repay her for finding me. The lady said, "No, it's okay," because she would've wanted someone to do the same for her.

I think about that day a lot. I think about it to this day because that lady took time to help me—she didn't have to, but she chose to. I am still grateful that she did. Sometimes I wonder what would have happened if I hadn't found my mom. What would the lady have done? I think she would have stayed with me until I was with my mom again. She was really nice and didn't get irritated.

I think about that day and wonder, "Wow, would people do that to-day?" I don't think that many people would. There have been other times, as I got older, that I got separated from my mom and nobody took a second glance at me. Thinking about this makes me very upset because I see people with their children, and they are happy, but if their child went missing they'd be ready to turn any place upside-down. Even though people don't always show strangers that kind of respect, I would show it to them. If I saw a child who needed help, and I was just randomly walking somewhere, I would help that child and stay until the problem was solved. I think that the woman who helped me that day was thinking the same thing I'm thinking now.

I still carry that lesson with me. Recently I went to Target with my mom and my two little sisters. Like always, I had gone to look at CDs and games for Nintendo DS. As I was looking, there was this little boy who had that lost look on his face. My first thought was, *Should I help him?* Then I thought, *Yeah, I should because it's the right thing to do.* I walked up to him, and I asked what was wrong. He said he was looking for his grandpa. I thought, *Okay, so here's a little boy who needs help.* I started to think back to the fair. I grabbed his hand, and we walked around until we found a Target worker. The Target worker announced his name on the intercom so his family could find him. We waited and waited. Finally, his grandpa came, and he thanked me and began to pull out a ten dollar bill. I told him, "No, it's okay. Just getting your grandson back to you is good enough."

"No, no, no," his grandpa told me. "You deserve it because I can tell you're a very kind person, and you have a lot of respect for people. A good job deserves some kind of reward so here you go, young lady."

It felt good doing something for someone else. When I do something nice for someone I feel like I just won the lottery. I like it when people do nice things for me. That feels good also.

In life, it goes to show that some people have respect for other people. People have that control over who they respect. It has to start in you. Some things you do can have an impact on others. I know that lady at the fair, a stranger, impacted my life in a good way. Now, if I see a child crying who is alone, I'll take time out to help them. I hope people will take this lesson and start doing good for others because later on in your life something good just might happen to you.

THEY NEED YOUR HELP
Jesus Henriquez

Dear Mr. President,

My name is Jesus and I am an eighteen–year–old senior at Mission High School in San Francisco. I came to this country from El Salvador when I was sixteen years old. The reason I'm writing this letter to you is because the lives of poor and undocumented people are too difficult. In El Salvador salaries were not enough to provide basic needs. When I came here things became a little easier, but it was still not easy to find a job. Immigrants are not safe in their jobs because of ill health or documentation problems. For that reason I would like you to help undocumented and poor workers. They just want to get money to support their families. They are not criminals. They just want to get out from where they were and get a better future for their families. I feel bad each time I think that I have to buy my food and it's more expensive than yesterday, and the money is not enough because I have to pay the rent and other bills. You can be compassionate with undocumented people. That's what it means to have character, to fix the economy.

I want you to have the integrity to change this country by being brave and honest in how you deal with important issues concerning poor and undocumented people. I know you can do it. I trust that you will make the right decision. The president is honest when he sees problems and makes them public. He is brave when he develops a plan to fix the problems. It is important that the president shows his integrity because he is a role model for the people who live in this country. A brave person tries to be strong. He shows it doesn't matter what happened before. What matters is your present and your future and what you can do right now to improve your work and your life.

I think, Mr. President, you have these characteristics and can help people, like a family that I know. I want you to be compassionate, and I want you to help them get a job. Four people are in this family. They are in a bad situation because all of them are undocumented.

The father is fifty-five years old, and he is the only person that supports the family, but he can't find a job because he can't compete with people who are younger than he is. The mother is forty-five years old and she does all the work in the home. She cooks and takes care of the kids. But the most interesting are the children, eight and ten years old. They are always playing at home, but in school they are different because they are disciplined, quiet, and they are eager to learn because they are good students.

The dad is always worried, and I feel compassion for him because I can see it and feel it. He is always trying to get money and trying to find a job. When I see that—I feel even more sad. I know that it's not so easy for someone to give him a job because of the way he looks. This man looks so stressed and worried and tired. He is gray-haired. His hair is like cotton. His eyes are tired and frustrated. His clothes are very dirty. His black pants are full of paint and they have holes in the knees. His shirt is a faded green T-shirt with white letters across the back—LA CASA LUCAS, THE FRESHEST VEGETABLES IN THE UNITED STATES. When he is standing on the streets he looks bored or tired, but when he sees that someone can give him a job he acts happy because he knows that's his chance and that's why he has been standing there.

He looks so anxious because he knows that his family depends on him. This is a really sad story, and I get sad when I think that this man is standing on the streets waiting for someone who can give him a job, some money for something.

The mother is another case. She always does all the cleaning at home. She is not older than the father, but her appearance tells everything. She has black hair. She is a good person, but I feel bad when I see her because she looks tired and she is always busy. I feel sad when I see that she is always wearing the same clothes and the same dirty apron. She is always wearing the same green dress that has flowers and looks like an old dress for an old woman, and her shoes are in really bad condition. They are supposedly black, but they look grey. The right shoe has a hole on her small toe. The left shoe is very thin in some parts, but she can't buy a new pair because she prefers to use the money to buy something to cook.

She is always doing the work at home like sweeping or mopping, if not cooking or taking the kids to the school. I know that she is tired because she sometimes tries to smile, but you can see her nervous smile. She can't hide the pain, or the things that hurt her.

The little boy is named Jorge. He is always playing with all the things that he finds, like kicking a bottle or climbing up trees. He wants a toy car but his father can't afford it. The little boy looks like a common active kid. Jorge has brown hair like his father had when he was young. The little boy looks happy, but he knows all the things that his family is going through. When you see this little kid, you can see the poverty and necessity of his family because his clothes are very dirty. His black pants are very dusty and his white shirt has brown parts, but he still wears them to school. His black leather shoes are damaged because he likes to play soccer. He wants to be a professional soccer player.

The last one is the baby girl of the father. He loves her. She is the smallest of the family because she is only eight years old. She is a very cute girl. All the people say that she is the portrait of her mother. Her brown eyes are like honey and her brown hair complements her eyes. She has beautiful smooth hair, and she always puts the same red clip in her hair. She always brushes her hair at night before she sleeps. She is always walking around and looking for something to do. She looks innocent. She has no blame for anything. She just wants to grow up close to her family in spite of everything.

This family lives in the city, where houses are close together and the streets are busy with cars. It is very sad. The neighborhood is not really a good place to live. It's a very dangerous place because you feel scared. You feel that someone is spying on you or that people are hiding something. Everybody looks suspicious and that is not an environment for children. They have to live in a peaceful place without any concern that something might happen to them. When the night comes, they can no longer go out because it's very dark. That's why they are left to wait for their father in the house.

They wait anxiously to see if their father was able to get some money to buy something so they can eat. When they see their father they get happy because they know that he will not let them die of hunger. If their father could not get money, they become sad and have to endure hunger, but if their father brings some money, their mother gets happy and goes to the store to buy a little something to cook. While she is at the store, the kids clean up the dinner table. They take off papers and food from an earlier meal and wash the dishes. After cleaning, and when the mother is done cooking, they sit at the table using buckets as chairs. The table is very uneven, and you see that it was made of very old wood, but when they are seated at the table they try to ignore the reality and try to be happy. The father begins the stories that he likes to tell the kids and distracts them from everything that's happening. He also wants a distraction because he feels tired. The father only wants to enjoy the time with his family.

When the mother says the food is done, everybody gets a plate and makes a line. The mother always serves the food. The common foods are eggs, beans, rice, and cheese, and maybe the traditional coffee of the father, but that's not all the time. It depends on how much the father got because the mother is always going to buy the most available things. When they are eating, they talk about economic problems, or they dream about being in better conditions in the future, planning a way to get out of that situation. The parents also ask the kids how they are doing in school.

This family is an important case because you can see the economic crisis that they are living. Sometimes these problems are caused by despair because the family has obligations, and they don't know how to respond to them. This is a patient family; they know that they need help but they also know that their case is not the only case. They try to do their best to survive. I feel sad because I know that I can't help them. I don't have enough money to do it.

I want this family to get ahead and that's why I wanted to know if you, dear President, could help all people who are in similar situations: because they need it, because they can't find jobs, and because they are discriminated against and treated badly. I think that you could create programs that would help all these people and at the same time help the economy of the United States. Instead of wasting money on war or other problems with other countries, you could figure out how to fix the economy.

In addition to economic aid, the health of these people is also very important because they don't have medical control. If they feel that something hurts or if they just feel pain, they can't go to the clinic or hospital because they don't have money to pay for the appointment or to buy the medicine. They are afraid and the way that they are living is not healthy. They don't have a good, balanced diet and are not eating enough vitamins that the body needs. They need psychological help, or something that makes them go out of their everyday life, something that makes them feel different or important in society, like festivals or community parties. For children it could be a fair or games. The main thing is that they feel like someone is thinking of them.

That's why I wrote this letter to you. That's the only reason. There is no other way to get your ear. All these people need to be heard and they also need an answer to their situations. I know that you can't fix it all, but everybody is going to do their part. I wrote a hypothetical example for you to know how these people survive and all the things that they have to suffer to get the money to buy food. The thing is that I got this inspiration when I started to think about how unfair their lives are, why that situation is happening, and what I can do about it. There are so many similar cases in this country and in this world, and the only thing that I ask you, dear President, is to be compassionate because they need your help and you have the resources in your hand to do something about it. You can do it. I hope that you're going to read this letter and that you're going to make the right decisions. I know that you'll be the person this country needs. The only thing left to say is thanks, dear President, for reading my letter and for listening to the people in need of your help.

THEY ALWAYS THINK THEY KNOW BEST

Cindy Tuala

I come from a confusing family. My parents are divorced, and I am an only child. I'm spoiled by my father; he owns his own business, a grocery store in a pretty bad neighborhood on 6TH Street, in San Francisco. He is very protective of his store, and he works there alone. Sometimes it makes him a little crazy. My mom is a certified nursing assistant who works all the time, except on weekends. Every weekday, I go to my dad's store and work. I try to pack up stuff and clean everything. Then I close the store at 5:30 or 6 PM and go pick my mom up from work. I also work at the store on weekends, from like 8 AM to 6 PM, and then go visit my dad afterward. It is the only time I can see him because I am so busy on the other days.

One Friday night in September of 2008, my dad was at the karaoke bar above his store. The bartender told my dad that one of the men there didn't want to pay, so my dad and the man fought, and the guy threw a table at my dad's leg. When I saw my dad the next day, he was hurting. He told me he got into a fight and that he could not walk. I called my cousin, who is a nurse, and told her to come to the store to see if my dad's leg was all right. She wanted to take him to the hospital, and he refused—I think he is afraid of doctors—but we forced him to go. While my cousin took my dad to the hospital, I opened up the store and worked. Later on, around noon, I got a phone call from my cousin. She said my dad's leg bone was broken and he needed surgery, but his leg was too swollen. He would have to wait about a week and a half until the swelling went down. I was so sad when I saw my dad in a hospital bed. I didn't cry, though; I wanted to be strong. After that, things weren't the same. My father said he didn't want to be at the store any more. He just wanted to go back to the Philippines and rest. He told me and the rest of my family to clear everything out of the store and to make sure to take out all of his expensive belongings.

When I opened the store the next day, it seemed so quiet. When my dad was there, a lot of people would come by just to visit with him. That day, the people stopped by and asked where my dad was. When I said, "He's not here," they just left. On September 24, 2008, my dad came home from the hospital; he hadn't had the surgery yet because his leg was still swollen. He wanted to come home because it was his birthday the next day, and he wanted to celebrate at my auntie's house.

That next Monday, my cousin brought him back to the hospital to have the surgery on his leg. He was there until Thursday morning. Now he's at my cousin's house. I am happy that my dad got to stay with my cousin because I thought they were just going to stop helping him out.

I get mad sometimes when my auntie tells me that I need to work at the store, since my dad can't anymore because of his condition. She tells me I need to start thinking about my future because I'm getting old, and my dad can't help me out anymore. She says I have to help him out now. She tells me that I can't go out anymore and I can't buy the things I used to, like clothes and shoes.

When my dad got back home from the hospital, I didn't see him for about two days, but I called him to see how he was doing. I told him I couldn't visit him because my cousin was using the car. I was complaining that my mom got me the car for my birthday, but she let my cousin use it even though I needed it. I feel that's not fair, it's like she bought the car for him and not me. My dad said he was going to get me a car.

The next day, I got to use the car, and I went to go visit my dad at my cousin's house. A lot of my family was there, and all I kept hearing were lectures about how I need to snap out of my old life, stop hanging out with my friends and my boyfriend, and being out and about. They said I didn't care about my dad because I didn't visit him and I didn't check on him. But my cousins all go to work and are barely at the house. No one was there to see if my dad ate or if he needed something—he was in a bed all day. I was trying to explain myself to them, but they were not hearing me. At that moment, I felt like cursing my auntie out and telling her to stay out of my life. But I held myself back and thought about how my auntie took time off of work to help at the store; she cooked for my dad and helped him out with other things. All I wanted to do was cry because I didn't know what else to do.

All of my clothes and everything are still in boxes because I had to move from the loft above my dad's store to my mom's house. When I want to find something to wear, I have to go through the boxes. I have to share a room with my mom. Soon I'll be moving into the room in the backyard that is currently used for storage. My mom needs to get all of the stuff out, clean everything, put new carpet in, and paint the walls. All of my clothes are in boxes until then. And it sucks because every morning I have to open all the boxes and pick out my clothes, then put the boxes back in their place. All that takes about twenty minutes. I find my life very complicated because of all my duties. I try to do my best to live my life well, but I still am having a hard time multi-tasking with all my responsibilities.

I am juggling a lot in my life, between this tribulation and that tribulation. I have to deal with my friends, my family, and school. Right now I am unsure about my trust in my friendships. I am struggling with my parents because they put so much pressure on me to work at my dad's store and drive my mom everywhere, and I have so many responsibilities that it is hard for me to focus on schoolwork. Even though it's hard, I am trying to make the best of my troubles by taking one step at a time.

I try to deal with everything that is thrown at me. I want to be able to finish what I have to do in one situation before I go on to the next thing. I am learning that the pressure is hard and that there is really no one there, like a sibling, to give me a hand. I am therefore becoming more confident. Sometimes I start feeling down because of the struggles in my life, but they are also challenging me, and I am treating them like tests. I am proud that I have not fallen flat on my face. I have not given up, but have done what I can to be a good friend, help my parents, and get good grades. I am trying to get the most out of my life.

*   *   *

Teenagers talk about each other—a lot. When you hear them talk about someone else, you have to wonder if they are also talking about you behind *your* back. All this he-said, she-said makes it hard to figure out who your real friends are. I think I have finally learned my lesson, but it hasn't been easy.

I go to school at Mission High in San Francisco. I like it here. I have very supportive teachers who listen to what I have to say and try to help me out. I get pretty good grades at the beginning of the school year, but then I slack off at the end. School is fun when I understand how to do stuff, but when it's hard, I tend to just let things go and not even do them. That's bad. I'm going to have to stop losing hope for my education.

I have numerous friends. One best friend of mine is Tania. Tania has big brown eyes and straight black hair. She's shorter than me, maybe four-feet, eleven inches tall. We see each other at school, and on the weekends we go to the mall, shop, eat, or just hang out. We've been friends for four years. We used to cut school together *a lot*, but don't tell anyone. One of my favorite things about her is that she catches on to things slowly. It's like watching someone tell a joke before they understand it. Her slowness makes me laugh, and even when I am already feeling good, she makes everything more fun.

One of my other friends is Lena. We talk a lot over the phone and hang out sometimes on the weekend. Lena is tall and dark-skinned. She has really long hair with blond highlights. Lena makes me laugh. She's funny and she talks a lot. I guess I'd call her feisty. I've known Lena for five years, but Tania and Lena have known each other for six, since middle school. Tania and Lena were best friends back then, way before Tania and I became close. Sometimes we all hang out together, but mostly it's just me and Tania, or just Tania and Lena, because they live close to each other.

One Thursday, Tania and Lena hung out at Tania's house on the front porch. Lena was talking about some girls that go to her school who are jealous of her. The next day at lunchtime in the second floor hallway, Tania and I were standing by my locker. She was telling me how she doesn't like Lena's attitude and feels that Lena is a bad influence on both of us. Lena lies a lot about little things. She will say that she got me and Tania a present but then she never gives us anything. We know it's a lie because she uses the "um" word a lot when she's lying, but we let it slide because we just don't care that much. Sometimes Lena is aggressive, lies, and talks about people, but she is still my friend.

The next day, Tania asked me if I wanted to go to the mall with her and Lena. I began to think that Tania was a backstabber because she was saying all that stuff about Lena the day before, but then she was standing right in front of Lena's face being friendly and all that. I felt confused. It made me wonder if she talked about me behind my back the same way she was talking about Lena. I wondered if Lena talked behind people's backs the way Tania did. We were all friends, but it didn't really seem that friendly if people were talking about each other. I decided not to go to the mall because the situation really made me question my trust in Tania and Lena and my friendships with them.

I wondered, *Are they really my true friends?*

True friends are people you can trust, people who won't talk about you behind your back. True friends are there when you need them, and don't act funny toward you when other people are around. True friends understand you. The thought that my secrets were being let out to other people bothered me so much that I thought about our friendship and wondered if we were true to each other.

That night I called my friend Kelly to tell her about the situation with Tania and Lena. I told her how I felt it was really mean of Tania to talk about Lena behind her back and then be with her the next day. Kelly said she could understand where I was coming from and that it wasn't right of Tania to talk about Lena that way and then hang out with her. Kelly told me to watch out for Tania, and to keep my eyes open and be aware. I took Kelly's advice into consideration and watched what I said around Tania.

I thought Tania was being two-faced. She could have just told Lena how she felt about her attitude instead of telling me. I felt like I needed to tell Lena what was going on. It was creating a bad feeling, and it was breaking the trust in our friendship. I felt it just wasn't fair to Lena if I didn't let her know what was going on.

I thought long and hard about it, and realized I was doing the same thing Tania was—running my mouth. I was telling Kelly how I felt about Tania instead of telling Tania herself. It was a self-understanding moment, and because of it, I am changing my behavior and learning to keep my mouth shut in situations like that.

*   *   *

At the beginning of the school year, I thought I was going to be dedicated to school and not miss any days, but then these things happened with my family. Now I float in and out of school. I am stressing because I am trying to please everyone else and not myself. When I try to talk, no one listens to me because they are older. They always think they know best.

I'm always putting other people first, but I'm realizing that other people do not do the same. It makes life harder when I try to do the right things but no one seems to care or recognize my efforts. If we treated others the way we want to be treated, life would not be such a blur, because we could all understand each other a little better.

RESPECT IN
THE WORLD'S EYES

Johnny Valencia

Everyone has had an experience that taught him or her the Golden Rule. Mine happened when I arrived at my elementary school. I didn't know anyone there, so I felt anxious and alone. As I sat at my desk, my teacher introduced a classmate. His name was Michael, and he was the first person I ever met who didn't judge me or discriminate against me. He was a real friend, and unlike the other students, he was able to cooperate and offer support. He helped me with schoolwork and was there when I needed someone to talk to. He stood out from the rest in that rather than ignoring me he stood up and talked to me. He helped me get acquainted with students other than the ones in my classroom. Michael was the first genuine friend I ever had.

After meeting Michael, I realized I wanted to reach out to other people the way he reached out to me. I learned from him why integrity and leadership are characteristics needed in a person and in a leader. I have always helped others in any way I can, from translating a book for a student who could not read English to giving advice to a friend in need. We all possess the ability to understand each other, but what matters is how we use this ability.

Our leaders must possess good judgment and perform to the best of their ability. Without unity, we run the risk of disorder within our communities and our country as a whole. Our government is essentially a two-party system. One side is the Democratic Party. Its presidential nominee, Senator Barack Obama, was the first black president of the Harvard Law Review, and is the first African-American to have a realistic chance at the presidency. The other side is the Republican Party. Its presidential candidate, Senator John McCain, served in the military for twenty-two years. Upon his graduation from the U.S. Naval Academy in 1958, he became a naval aviator, and was a prisoner of war in Vietnam.[1] While their backgrounds may be dissimilar, both candidates must prove their integrity to the voters of America.

Our next president will need integrity because the United States has been through hard times in the last seventy-five years. The country has struggled through the bitter Cold War, the harsh fighting in Vietnam, and the controversial wars in Iraq. One tremendous blow against the nation, and the world, arrived on September 11, 2001, when the Al-Qaeda terrorist attacks occurred on the World Trade Center and the Pentagon. The country subsequently lost a great deal of security and stability, as well as respect in the world's eyes.

In addition to global troubles, we have domestic ones. Over the course of the current administration, many Americans have lost their jobs and fallen into economic distress. According to the Illinois Gas Association, the price for oil has skyrocketed from $23 per barrel in 2001 to $105.22 per barrel in 2008.[2] According to the *New York Times*, American citizens are now paying twice what they paid for health care and taxes in 2001.[3] It seems the Bush administration provided a misleading solution to these crises in the invasion of Iraq. President Bush insisted that fighting terror-

---

1. http://www.johnmccain.com/About/McCain-Palin 2008
2. www.ioga.com Illinois Oil and Gas Administration
3. http://www.nytimes.com/2008/10/24/opinion/24beane.html?ref=opinion

ism was our primary reason to go to war, but I believe the government's motive was to forcefully obtain oil from Iraq.

The United States needs a true leader who will guide our people and provide the answers we need. I've seen Senators Obama and McCain in countless television and print appearances, and I have concluded that Obama is the one who will change the country for the better. The immediate impact of Obama's election will be one of cultural acceptance, for Obama would be the first president of color in United States history. Obama's election would demonstrate that the middle and lower classes understand that our country is represented by the character and integrity of our leader, regardless of race or color. Our diverse country depends on people of many races and religions cooperating on a daily basis. Obama's election would change how we view the politics of presidential selection.

The candidates have different ideas about how to change the government and economy, and the American people must choose the candidate who will best lead them in these areas. The president will not have an easy job. Each candidate must perform to the best of his ability. Obama and McCain can first establish the authenticity of their leadership by keeping their promises to the American people. For example, the next president will need to offer solutions to provide shelter to the less fortunate, end the war in Iraq, and admit that the previous administration's central motives were racism and profit.

Also, the president should provide a solution to the problem of oil addiction—namely, the excessive, widespread use of oil that I see damaging the environment. One example of this is the gasoline used in automobiles, which is responsible for carbon-based emissions. These emissions are one of the many factors in global warming[4], which leads to the depletion of the ozone layer and makes the earth more vulnerable. Our oil addiction must be impeded before it causes more damage to the environment, resulting in further deforestation and greater endangerment of wildlife.

Another promise I believe the president must keep is the provision of jobs and economic assistance for the working class. Our country should

---

4.   http://www.fueleconomy.gov/FEG/climate.shtml

create more manufacturing jobs within the United States so the government can finally stop exporting jobs, which contributes to the country's national debt.

If I had no ideals or common sense, I would not even consider who has the right stuff to become the next president of the United States. I would not even think of the words *Democrat* or *Republican*, nor would I try to understand why it's so important to vote. If we did not have individual ideals and opinions in the United States, most of us would give up making decisions and let the government choose for us.

The issues that affect us range from economics to politics to everyday life. It's so important to retain our individuality, especially when it comes to government. That is why I support Obama: I've seen him demonstrate his ideals as a U.S. Senator. Obama's strong sense of leadership is shown through his campaign's idea to create a website where anyone can see how his or her tax money will be spent, so as to ensure that citizens have confidence in their government. That's a positive step toward making sure that taxpayer money does not go directly into the government's wallet, to be spent on weapons or the military. Obama's tax plan will help the middle and working classes in America because his plan will provide tax cuts for ninety-five percent of workers and families. They will receive tax cuts of $500 for single workers, and $1,000 for working couples.[5] With this plan, citizens will be able to save more money and the crumbling economy will be rebalanced. Obama has provided other plans for health care, the economy, immigration, and even civil rights.[6] All the plans and ideas that Obama supports show that he is able to lead this country. He knows what the real issues and crises are. I believe Obama is dedicated to serving this nation.

McCain also has strong leadership skills. He has demonstrated them by visiting foreign countries, such as Iraq, to support the U.S. soldiers who are sacrificing themselves and restoring order in that country. McCain actually visited Iraq before Obama did. He also wants to create a proper

5.   www.barackobama.com/taxes
6.   www.barackobama.com/issues

retirement plan for the veterans who served in combat.[7] I think this demonstrates McCain's strength and valor, because while many veterans come home unharmed, some are physically or mentally ill and receive little respect or assistance from the government. Anyone fighting for our country should be treated with respect and dignity when they come home, because it takes true courage to answer the call of duty.

McCain has also shown integrity by visiting neighboring countries like Mexico, and is proposing immigration reform that will let many undocumented immigrants have a chance at residency and eventual citizenship in the United States.[8] I strongly support this because there are countless immigrants from all countries who work hard, most of them for minimum wage or less, and who have been treated unjustly or with racial prejudice.

Our next president also must have a sense of compassion. I may not come from a rich or financially stable family, but I make up for it by having compassion, participating in politics, and discussing the issues with teachers and friends. Many people do not come from a stable financial background but are nonetheless able to make their own choices. If the government made all of our choices, we would no longer be a democracy. Without democracy, people will lack compassion, understanding, and awareness of economic matters. The government should not underestimate the everyday citizen because many of us participate in community or nonprofit organizations that support many people.

I have grown to understand the true meaning of character as a personality trait. Whether a friend, like Michael, or a presidential candidate—everyone has some sort of character. Everyone is capable of compassion, regardless of race, gender, or background. Everyone is able to demonstrate integrity. Many of us may not help others in our daily lives, yet are able to communicate with others. As I've grown older I have seen so many people whose ideals and character have influenced my life. My family and my teachers influenced my belief in guidance. My family helps me in every way

---

7. http://www.johnmccain.com/Informing/Issues/9cb5d2aa-f237-464e-9cdf-a5ad32771b9f.htm

8. http://www.johnmccain.com/Informing/Issues/

they can, from providing me with school supplies to keeping me under a roof. My teachers help me by telling me what I need to know, and ensuring that I understand what I need to learn rather than what I "should" learn. Providing knowledge and compassion is guidance.

Obama and McCain must appeal to the kind of Americans I see represented by friends, family, and teachers: people who respectfully represent their ideas and actions for the good of the nation. Obama wants to end the war[9] and McCain wants to create immigration reform.[10] The candidates must keep these promises and not stretch the truth. A true leader must be faithful to his work and his actions. Ranting about a rival candidate doing this or that is not indicative of leadership. A leader must not complain, and should take action when the time is right.

And the time is right now! The United States' economy is sinking, and the mortgage crisis has affected the economy to the extent that President Bush asked for a $700 billion bailout, which was approved by the Senate and the House of Representatives in October, 2008.[11] The bailout will provide money to banks that have declared bankruptcy and help cover other debts in the economy, aiding in the stock market and mortgage crises. The problem I see is that the bailout does not ensure that the money will be spent properly. Because there is no guarantee that the bailout will work, I am somewhat unsure of this plan. In my opinion, the plan provides salvation to banks yet not much to the American taxpayers who are paying for it. Besides the mortgage crisis, the stock markets were hit hard on September 15, 2008, when Lehman Brothers Holdings Inc. filed for bankruptcy protection[12] on Wall Street, home of the New York Stock Exchange. Many other global banks also fell due to the mortgage crisis, and the Dow Jones industrial average experienced its largest single-day drop in history, causing the stock values to dwindle. This is known as a liquidity crisis.[13]

9.   http://www.barackobama.com/issues/iraq/
10.   http://www.johnmccain.com/Informing/Issues/68db8157-d301-4e22-baf7-a70dd8416efa.htm
11.   http://money.cnn.com/2008/10/03/news/economy/house_friday_bailout/index.htm?postversion=2008100309
12.   http://www.nytimes.com/2008/09/15/business/15lehman.html
13.   http://www.nytimes.com/2008/09/21/business/21qanda.html?em

Whoever is chosen to be the next president of the United States must represent our country to the very best of his ability, as the head of the Executive Branch. He must show leadership, tell the profound truth, and do the things agreed upon by Congress with the vote of the American people. He must lead looking forward to the future, creating changes along the way that will benefit everyone, such as stopping oil addiction and the global warming and pollution caused by "black gold."

Overall, I feel anxious about what the future may hold for our government, our economy, and the next presidency in America. I don't really know what the future has in store for me, but I think there will be many world events that will make me nervous. But this also makes me think about the strong leadership examples displayed by my family and my peers. Their educational values will benefit me as I finish up school and start my professional career. So even though the Golden Rule states "Do unto others as you would have them do unto you," I know from my own experiences that the Golden Rule can turn out to mean much more than that.

THE SHY DEFENDER
Ruben Gutierrez

I t was the first day of sixth grade. I was sitting on the field with my friend Tony during lunch time. All of a sudden Tony got up and started throwing food at a new kid and calling him names. The new kid said, "Who are you? Why are you doing this to me?"

I didn't understand why Tony was picking on this kid. I felt sorry for him because he couldn't defend himself. In a way, I saw myself in the new kid. I knew I needed to defend him.

I stood up and walked over to Tony. I wanted to say the right thing to make Tony stop hurting the other student. Surprisingly, I didn't even care that it was Tony, someone I once called my friend. I just wanted Tony to stop picking on this kid. I felt like Tony was only picking on him because he was an easy target.

I said to Tony, "Hey, stop it, man! Why are you treating him like that? You shouldn't be doing this to him just because he can't defend himself. You are taking advantage of him because he is smaller than you."

Tony said, "Back off before I kick your butt. This is none of your business."

Then I said, "I am not going to let you take advantage of people who can't defend themselves." I wanted Tony to understand that what he was doing was wrong and that good people don't hurt others. I decided right there that I didn't want to be Tony's friend anymore.

Tony is a bully. Even when he was in his country, Spain, he was a bully. He has told me stories about how he acted maliciously towards other kids. One day when we were in middle school, Tony told me the reason why he was mean to other people. When he was in Spain people always made fun of him. He told me how the older kids used to take his money and beat him up.

The people who were mean to him made Tony realize that he wanted to be stronger and tougher and meaner so people wouldn't be able to hurt him. He felt that if people were scared of him, no one would pick on him or beat him up. Now, thinking about this, I realized I didn't want to have a friend who hurt other people so that he could feel better.

In seventh grade Tony started to hang around me again. He kept telling me that I was too shy, that if I were tougher and beat up on people, I would have more friends and girls and people would respect me. Tony still hadn't changed. He still thought that hurting people and making people afraid of you got you respect.

I never wanted to be like Tony—someone who needed to beat up on other people to make himself feel powerful. When I was little, I was shy—so shy that people used to call me names and make fun of me because I didn't like to talk. I don't know why people tried to make me feel bad. Maybe they didn't have anything else to do. Maybe it was because I was different. People used to take advantage of me because they knew I wouldn't stand up to them. I was an easy target. But I realized it doesn't matter what people think of you. It matters what you think about yourself.

I feel like a lot of people are afraid to stand up to bullies. People think that if they stand up to a bully, they will become a target and get picked on. They don't want to get beaten up, or worse, end up dead.

Before this incident with Tony, I wasn't able to stand up to people because I was so shy. I was always worried about what people thought about me. I would get nervous around other people and feel like I could do nothing right. The worst thing about being shy is that when people know you won't stand up to them, they take advantage of you, just like Tony did to the new kid.

When I saw Tony bullying that kid, I realized I didn't care what other people thought of me. I just wanted to protect the new kid. What I did was impressive because most of the people who were there were so scared of the bully. I was able to defend that kid because I mustered up the confidence to defend him. I realized that making sure he was safe was a reason to speak up and stand up to Tony.

After this incident, I knew I could stand up to others, but I went back to being quiet even though I couldn't stand someone getting beat up by someone else who was covering up for their own insecurity. I was still afraid to talk a lot. After the incident with Tony, I continued developing my courage.

Three years later, I met a wonderful girl who changed my life. I was sitting in class when she stood up and started to talk confidently in front of the entire class. She wasn't afraid, and her personality was so confident. I wished I could be more like her. After that day, I tried to speak up a little bit more in class. It wasn't easy for me to start speaking more and to be more confident in myself, but thanks to her, I was able to do it. We're still friends.

She is so outgoing. She inspires me to talk more. It is because of her that I am getting less shy. I am not afraid to speak out anymore. Because of her and the incident with Tony, I have become more confident. She was the one that convinced me that it took bravery to stand up to Tony.

At the time, I didn't feel brave, but I knew I couldn't just sit back and watch Tony hurting that new kid. That is why, in my personal opinion, standing up for him was the right thing to do. I wish someone would have stood up to the bullies that picked on me and made fun of me for being shy. When I grow up, I will teach all my kids how they can live the Golden Rule in their lives and actions and to treat everyone the same way they would like to be treated.

TRANSITIONS: GOOD OR BAD

Dorrian Lewis

As an African-American woman, I see that life today is something else, and I don't mean that in a good way. Society and my community, especially the youth, are different. It's like the people have changed for the worse. When I say worse, I mean to a violent state of mind, not a bad person. In certain situations people are forced into violence because they have no other option. It's either violence or face the consequences, which may be death. In my community, I see a lot of African-American people, especially young men, killing each other like it's a law. Some laws are good, but the one I'm talking about isn't one of them. The one I'm discussing is the violent retaliation towards other gang members or just your everyday enemy. Such violence is wrong because if you get into an argument or disagree with someone, you shouldn't take what you think is the easiest or "coolest" way and say, "You know what? I don't like what you said, so I'm going to take your life. *Bam!*" I'm not saying that's what they say, but from the outside looking in, that's what I see. Why is life like that? We can think and analyze all we want, but I don't think we will ever know. People should stop trying to brush over reality and speak up about this worthless violence.

I can relate to this issue very well. May 24, 2007, was a life-changing and devastating day for my family, friends, and the community. His name was Jamar Anthony "Bear" Lake. Bear was my cousin, but for most of our lives we weren't close. That changed when I entered high school. Bear was a senior and became the big brother I never had as I tried to fit in. May 24TH was the day Bear was fatally shot, and I, and many other people, lost someone very special. It was as if time stopped.

When people heard the news they had no idea what to do or think. I tried to stay strong until they said he was gone. At that point I couldn't hold on any longer. It was so overwhelming that I just fell to the ground and cried. It felt like a part of me departed with him; it was gone and it wasn't coming back. Eventually I had to stand up, wipe my tears, and be strong for my family, seeing as I was really the only person who could keep everyone sane. Yes, it was difficult, but I did it with God's help. If it wasn't for God, I don't know if I would have been able to fight the battle with the pain that everyone suffered from in their own way. In life, you feel pain, but when you lose someone who was really special to you for something as worthless as twenty dollars, it hurts more than words can explain.

It was so hard to believe because the day before me and him were talking about his graduation while sharing Subway sandwiches. To come to school the next day and not have him there was something that I never expected. Honestly, I didn't know how to handle it. I didn't know whether to cry, scream, or hit something or someone. My mind went totally crazy. It's an emotion that overtakes your whole mind and body. It's something no one should have to feel. It's a pain that you wouldn't wish on anybody, even if you hated them. But through faith, my family and friends and I were able to make it through. I thank God for bringing us through that pain and that battle and taking care of Bear. He might not be here physically, but he will always be in our hearts. That feeling is so powerful. There's nothing like it.

That day and moment meant so much to me that it's almost unexplainable. It was so powerful because it taught me that, in certain situations, you have to learn to stand on your own. You can't always depend on someone else to be your security blanket or shield. Sometimes you have to be your own. Before that day, Bear and I made a promise that we would both get good grades and graduate from high school and college. When he went home, I kept thinking to myself, *Since he couldn't finish, I will.* I will always keep that promise, no matter what. I'm walking the path we paved together. To some people it may sound strange, or people might think, *Well, why would she want to do that?* Well, I'm glad you asked. When you have a special type of bond with someone, like I had with Bear, when it really comes down to it you will do anything for that person, even if they're not physically there. Even though he's not here, the bond is still there. That's why the promise we made to each other means so much to me. I've never had this type of bond before. It feels good because it's like a little piece of him is still with me. Sometimes I can hear him cheering me on. I don't want that feeling to ever leave. It keeps me going and keeps me motivated to aspire for the best. With that promise in my mind, I will always strive for the highest in life and nothing can stop me. I'm too determined.

Unfortunately, incidents such as Bear's happen every day. Actually, a few years before, another person who attended Mission High, my school, was fatally shot around the corner from where I live. His name was Raymond Bass. I don't know much of his story, but from what I do know he wasn't a target—it was a case of mistaken identity. That's a huge problem: Someone's life is taken for no apparent reason. To make matters worse, these aren't adults that are committing all these murders, they're teenagers! They are teenagers killing teenagers. I'm tired of hearing about someone being shot or murdered.

I don't want to say that the shootings and murders are all the fault of young men, but many men are very territorial and will go to the highest extent in retaliation if they feel they have been disrespected in any way. They weren't born that way. They're just doing what they think they need to do in order to get respect.

Young men today are judged and stereotyped so quickly that they're not given a chance to express who they really are. Instead of branching out on their own, they do what they think is easiest and follow what they see, which may be good or bad. In some cases doing the things you see around you can be good, but it depends on the type of influence it is. It's so easy to follow what someone else is doing. Sometimes you won't even know that you're starting to act like those other people. You can get so distracted by what's going on that before you know it you're just like them. I remember I used to hang around my guy friends, and they have a different walk than girls do. After a while I happened to catch myself: I was walking just like them and didn't even know it. It's that easy.

Life can be so confusing sometimes. It gives us choices; some are difficult and others simpler. Being human, we want to take the simpler path, but sometimes that's not the best choice. In certain situations choosing the easiest path can cause a lot of problems and even cost us our lives. In life sometimes you have to challenge yourself, try new things, branch out on your own.

I have a friend who is very smart and knows right from wrong, yet he wants to make himself seem cool or bigger than everyone. He wants to "fit in" so he does things he knows he's not supposed to be doing. He's taking what I like to call the path of danger. The path of danger can lead to violence, robbery, homicides, and death. For some reason, people think that's cool. Some young men are prime candidates for this path because they think it's easy, cool, or a way to get respect. Honestly, the path of danger won't get you the right respect; it will only get you respect out of fear. I don't know about you, but I would want the right respect. In order to get respect, you have to give it, and you have to earn it.

I learned a lot about respect from my teacher, Ms. McKamey. She taught me that you won't just be handed respect on a silver platter. She didn't have to tell me she was respecting me. It was through her body language and her facial expressions that I knew. Her overall appearance showed me that she was actually listening to me and understood what I was saying. Since she respected me, I wanted to respect her, because in a way respect is a privilege, not a right. And that's what I'm trying to clarify; respect can be something powerful, but respect out of fear is basically meaningless. I say that because the only reason they are respecting you is because they are afraid of you; they're being driven by fear. Some young men confuse gaining respect out of fear with actual deserved respect. Some young men who think they are "owed" respect will go to the extent of using a gun to make themselves feel powerful and respected.

Guns to some young men are like gold, and they will do anything to get one or find any reason to use it. These young men are killing each other for worthless reasons. It can be the smallest issue or discord and *bam*! There's a shoot-out, and in most situations there aren't many survivors. Even some innocent bystanders end up caught in the crossfire; my uncle is a victim of that. One night my uncle was coming home from work and was minding his own business, and I guess these guys were having an argument. A few of the guys were in a car and were just shooting in the air trying to scare the other group of guys, and well, what goes up must come down. The bullet came down directly through my uncle's shoulder, pierced his lung, and crossed over his spine. Thank God he is still alive, but he is temporarily paralyzed from the waist down. He had nothing to do with what was going on, yet he has to pay the consequences for someone else's actions. It goes to show that violence isn't just affecting the actual targets, but also innocent people who have nothing to do with what's going on around them.

Where did all this violence come from? Do you ever ask yourself that question? We innocent people shouldn't have to. We should be able to live our lives the way we want to. What's worse is that this violence happens in school. I'm one of those victims. That's why I'm at Mission actually. While in my freshman year, I was threatened with a gun for no reason at all. I never did anything to the guy. I didn't know what to think or do. I was so scared that I didn't even move. He had that much power over me. He thought since he had a gun that he could do anything to anyone. The fear I felt is unexplainable. To some people, guns or any type of weapon can be powerful, but they will abuse that power if they feel they can. Some people will use guns to get respect. People think that guns are a mandatory tool or a way to seem cool, but in reality, they make you look weak. If you were a real man then you wouldn't resort to a gun for self-defense. If you want to feel respected or want to defend yourself or whatever the situation may be, don't resort to a gun or other weapon. If you feel you have to fight, fight with your fist, not from your hip.

Shocking to see what's going on in the world, huh? Yeah, that's what I said too, but it's life, and we have to deal with it. But I'm tired of being scared to walk outside my own house, afraid that it may be my last day of life, and I know I'm not the only person who feels that way. It's a shame that we have to live this way, but there's nothing we can do. I wish there was. All we can do, honestly, is pray and hope for the best. I can say, though, that if we had more peace and harmony instead of all this violence and all these homicides, then this world would be a better place. And that's real.

NATIVE AMERICAN INFLUENCE

Idalia Beltran

My life in El Salvador was very fun. I grew up on a ranch where my grandparents taught me how to do all the necessary things to take care of the animals, like giving them food and water. School was a friendly place and the teachers were great—they did what they could. In my country, there was not that much money to give the children a better education, especially in rural zones like mine, but the people still had hope that they could achieve their goals. My grandparents were like parents to me; my mom left my brother and me when I was seven years old. My grandparents raised me in a beautiful way that was similar to Native Americans because we lived from the earth and only took what we really needed. I would love to go to back to my country and see the beautiful sunset from my balcony. When I see the sunset my soul feels free, clean, and relaxed. I feel so good. I feel so beautiful. It makes clean all the bad thinking. I forget everything. The red and orange colors remind me of the beauty of nature, the importance of keeping the sunset clear and beautiful. The sunset reminds me of my family and a time when we were all together. I remember the unity we shared, me and my brother and my grandparents. There are so many memories in my heart that I will never forget. They will be in my soul forever.

My grandma told me stories about her experiences in life. She was raised in an Incan tribe and she said that in her time, the Spanish did not give the Incas the same opportunities they gave themselves. For example, they did not let the Incan kids go to the same school as the Spanish kids. I did not have the same experience that my grandma did in her childhood. I didn't even know I was from a native tribe until my grandma told me about seven years ago. Now that I do know, I feel so proud to be part of that weird and marvelous culture. I love being a part of Native America.

My main connection with Native Americans is through their love for nature. I know they love nature the same as I do. I think this is a beautiful thing that I have inside myself and that I have studied for a long time. It is just that beautiful feeling that makes your soul rest, relax, and think about the future—about the good things and the bad things. I think I have their spirit of meditation, too. I love to meditate on my problems and figure out why and how to fix them. Another thing that I love, and I really would like to try, is their rituals. They perform them when something good happens in the tribe and they want to give thanks to the gods. It is like appreciating all the good things they receive. Another thing that I feel connected to is my spirit. I am very enthusiastic, and I have the valor to do things like stand up for someone or defend myself if someone is offending me. I feel sad because Native Americans did not have the opportunity to defend themselves completely like I am able to, but they did what they could. Giving a new world a welcome is not easy, and I understand that.

I came to the United States because my mother decided to be with us again. I never wanted to leave my country, but my mother thought that it was better for me to come here. She said I was going to have a better education and more opportunities to complete what I want to study, medicine.

I arrived in a city called Oakland, where most of my family now lives. From the beginning of the trip to Oakland, however, it was so difficult. There was my mother, brother, and cousin, and we spent one month traveling. At the beginning it was good. During that month we left El Salvador on a bus and then walked for ten days. We slept under trees, huddled together to stay warm. We saw bears all around us, and we were scared, but they never hurt us. The last three days we had no food, for two, no water. This is when my mom got sick and almost died. Something pushed me during that time. Maybe it was my mother's words or maybe it was my Native American ancestors, or it could have been my courage. That experience made me strong and taught me not to be lazy. I think that if I had the opportunity to do it all over again, I would have it the same way, even though it was a difficult journey.

My family and I went through a hard time in Oakland. We didn't have a place to stay or a job to get money from, which was a big issue for me. Our family here did not want to help us, and we were suffering in a hard way. School was horrible. Everyone hated me, and all the girls wanted to fight with me. I did not understand English and I felt so lonely. Everything was going so badly and my life was destroyed. I didn't care about my education or about my future. I was just doing ignorant things, like cutting classes, going to clubs with my friends, and doing stupid things in the street. I didn't like living there because it was a bad example for young people like me. All the young boys and girls just didn't care about their futures. On my block, I knew a couple of boys who were killed by policemen. They were selling drugs and got caught. The only thing the boys could do was run, but they were killed anyway. When I saw that, I realized how short life is. They were only teenagers and had not even finished high school, but they were dead.

In those hard times, I was going to do something very bad to affect my future. My cousins were acting in bad ways. I was considering doing the same things even though I didn't want to. I felt like it was all I could do to help my family survive. My cousins laughed at me because I didn't want to do what they were doing. Then I said, "I deserve better than this," because I was young, and I felt that I had a lot of opportunities to make my life better. This decision gave me more inspiration to do good things for myself. I started looking for a job. It was hard because I didn't have experience, and people said I looked young, but finally I got a job in a card store. I started to be more responsible and learned how to be economical with everything. The problems in my neighborhood gave me a better way of thinking and I realized that I have to appreciate life and do as many positive things as I can. These situations have given me inspiration to do something with my life—to go to school every day and to do all my work in class and at home.

What Native Americans lived through was horrible and inhumane. They were the most beautiful and peaceful nation until the Europeans came and destroyed everything in their way. They stole the Native Americans' land and made them move west, forcing them to leave their homes without food or water to sustain themselves. This path became known as the Trail of Tears.

The impact that my move to a new world had on me was big and somewhat different than what the Native Americans experienced because when I came here, everything was supposed to be so nice and kind. But slowly it got harder. I was living through experiences that marked my life in a way that no one could forget easily. However, from real situations in my neighborhood, I learned to be aware of everything and to respect people. I had a lot of bad and good experiences, and from those experiences, I learned things just like the American Indians did.

One such experience I will never forget. My cousin almost lost her trust in me for a stupid reason. She believed that I was with her boyfriend. She really offended me with this accusation. After she made me feel bad, she came to me and said, "I am sorry. He is a jerk and a liar." In that moment, I knew that the unity with my family is stronger than anything else. I really made an effort to forgive her, and after I forgave her, it felt good. I felt free of something that was pressing on my heart, and I chose to be noble. From this experience, I learned how to forgive people and how to understand people's lives. I learned how to be strong through tough situations with other people. After that, my life took a whole new turn. Every day, I wake up and see my life as more interesting, and I feel the strength to complete all that's on my agenda. It's like when you eat breakfast and you have energy all day.

The way Native Americans inspired me was so interesting. I didn't know that much about them until one day, I listened to a story my grandma was telling. I learned a lot of history, and from that moment, I was so curious to know more about them. It made me cry. It made me want to help people. It really affected me in a way that made me stronger. I started thinking of all the bad things that I experienced, and with that, I learned how to have hope when I have hard times, just like Native Americans did. During their lives, they had to have courage to do all the things that they did. They were not afraid of anything because they knew they were strong inside and had the ability to defend themselves. This understanding helps me succeed in life, and I feel so fortunate to have the chance to know more about them. It has improved my life.

In terms of nature and pure spirit, Native Americans have made a positive mark in the world and have taught us that the most important thing is for us to take care of our planet—to save it and to be connected with it. I love and admire nature. I love nature more than anything else because it is so good to have that unique and beautiful system that gives us life. The way I follow Native Americans' examples is by treating the earth the way they have, taking only what I really need. I love to conserve and not just waste.

I have learned that Native American culture is full of love, honor, and courage. They respected love. They were very united and helped each other when they needed it. The courage that I had during my hard times stemmed from their example. I kept my head up and didn't give up for anything, just like the Native Americans.

I have not just been influenced by Native American culture but also by my grandpa's European culture. My grandpa's side has been Catholic for two generations. I love to learn more about this beautiful culture even though it is hard to accept what the Europeans did to the Native American people. Both cultures share certain values though. In Native American culture, they have a chief or elder who holds a lot of knowledge and tells them if something bad or good will happen to the tribe. My grandfather always told me that listening to old people was good for me because they can help prevent us from making bad decisions. I think this is true. My grandpa's influence also changed my life by teaching me how to make better decisions in my life. All the values I have learned from my grandparents help make me a better person.

My Native American culture is very special to me, however, because I feel I am a part of them. All of the things that I learned from the Native Americans have led to marvelous experiences in my life. It's like I was born to learn about them, like this was my destiny—to have that deep connection with them. They have influenced me to live my life the way I want to. Sometimes I even feel jealous because I can't experience exactly what they did. I know that not everything they experienced was good, but I love everything they stand for. I especially love the warriors, the ones who fought for their nation and defended their origin. They are very special because they inspire me to be a respectful person, an honest person. With all their examples, I make my life like one of theirs. Native Americans make me look at life with a different perspective. I used to be the most ignorant person you could ever know, and in the moment I discovered their influence on me, I became so happy to have something that inspires me to change my life. It's so different now, and I love it.

After everything that happened in Oakland, my mom found a job and started working in a restaurant. Two months later, we moved to San Francisco because my mom felt we would have a better life here. I decided to come, and I have been here since 2006. This is wonderful city. It has so many opportunities for young people like me, and I love it because it has a lot of Native American history. School is great. I have never felt as comfortable as I do at Mission High School. It feels like home to me because there are more people here like me. This is my senior year, and I am so happy to graduate from high school. When I was in Oakland, I never thought I could feel this positive.

A big part of the improvement in my life is the result of Native American influences in my life. They have taught me how to be responsible with my work, my school, my job, and so many things more. They have helped me improve my character. I am learning how to talk with people, how to answer, and how to control myself in difficult situations. I have learned that when you don't have valor, everyone can use you as a tool to obtain their own goals. I have learned how to have courage in my life, how to treat people well, and how to treat myself. Everything I do is because of them. They inspire me in a way that I never thought could be. I feel that I am like those Native Americans that never gave up when they had problems. I feel proud of myself because I know I am trying to do the right things in my life, for me and for the earth.

TEN SECONDS
Jayson Icaro

This is about what happened to me. I named this "Ten Seconds" because whenever I remember this story, I always feel like I'm in the last ten seconds of a basketball game. There are two different things that I'm going to share: first is the bad thing that happened to me, which I can't forget, and second is the good thing that happened, the ten seconds that changed my life.

When I first came to the United States, I felt so happy, but kind of bored. I was happy because my dreams of coming to the United States had finally come true. I could enjoy the weather, meet people of other races, and make new friends. But it was boring, because it was the summer before school started, so I asked my mom if she knew a place where I could play basketball. She told me there was a park six blocks away from our house. The next morning I tried to find where the park was; I took a train and walked a couple of blocks to get there, but had no luck. I kept searching and searching because I really wanted to play basketball. Finally, I saw the clean and beautiful park at 6TH and Folsom Street. A lot of people were there walking their pets or jogging through the park. It was kind of noisy, but I didn't mind; there were rock, rap and hip hop performances, and people reciting poetry. It was better than a quiet park, because quiet parks are like dead zones. I watched the people who were playing. I couldn't play that time, because my shorts were kind of ripped out on the side, but no one noticed because I was wearing jeans. I thought to myself, *Maybe I can play next time, maybe on the weekend*. So I planned it.

One week later I woke up early, bought some Vitamin Water and went to the park. There were a lot of tall players that day, so I found a court that was open where nobody was playing. While I was shooting around, making moves, a guy about my age came up to me. He asked me to play one-on-one against him. I impressed myself with the way I played, and when I won the game, the guy came up to me and congratulated me. He said good things to me and showed me respect. I would have liked to have had a conversation with him, but I couldn't, because I couldn't speak English. I had a lot that I wanted to say to him, but all I ended up saying was, "Thank you," because that's all I knew how to say. I treated him with great respect, because he was different from the other people. Although I couldn't speak English, he was respectful toward me. On my way home, sitting on the train, I thought about joining the basketball team at school.

Two months later, school started. My mom woke me up at eight in the morning. I was so tired and afraid to go to school because I did not think I was ready yet. I was scared because I couldn't speak English and didn't know how to introduce myself. When I got there with my mom and my younger brother, I felt really nervous because I saw the school was really big. The school's name is James Denman Middle School. It's a bad name because it sounds like the word "demon" and our school mascot looks like a devil. The school was so big, I thought I could practically build a mall in there. My last school was actually bigger than this school. I was in high school in the Philippines. The building there is as big as a college here. The difference is that in the Philippines, one room has more than sixty students; here, there are less than twenty in each room.

When we went to the dean's office for registration, there were a lot of students in the hallway. They were playing and hitting each other, and

I was kind of scared. I asked my mom if I could start next week, but my counselor wouldn't let me. She said I had to go the next day. When I arrived the next day, I was late because I had been playing Playstation the night before. When I walked into my classroom, the teacher called me over to her desk. Walking to her desk, I felt kind of hated—some of my classmates were laughing and I didn't know why. Maybe they were laughing because of the way I was dressed. I just ignored them because I didn't understand what they were saying. After my teacher talked to me, she introduced me to the whole class. They didn't say anything, so I felt a little more comfortable. Then I looked for an empty seat. When I found one, there was girl sitting next to me who looked pretty. I didn't notice at first that she was Filipina. I only found out when she talked to me in Tagalog to tell me I was doing the assignment wrong. I am kind of shy; when girls talk to me, I put my head down. After that day, every time we saw each other, she came up to me with her Filipina friends and said, "Hi!" So we became friends. When I went home and told my mom and my siblings that I had made a new friend, all of them thought that I liked this girl, but I just ignored them because it wasn't true.

The next morning, I asked my friend if she knew where I could find a place to play basketball. She said that she was going to introduce me to her friends, because they liked basketball too. When the bell rang, she just ran out, and I thought, *She's going to leave me, even though she promised to introduce me to her friends.* I was wrong. She just went to her locker and put her things in it. Then she brought me to the backyard. When I saw it, I wanted to play basketball right away. There were eight basketball courts, a football field, and a track too. When I was looking around, a whole bunch of students came up to me and asked me what my name was. I told them my name and they introduced themselves in Tagalog. I didn't realize that they were my friend's friends, but I figured it out when they asked me to play basketball. I was surprised and said yes. When we were playing, I was so excited to get the ball and shoot it; I made a couple of shots and a lot of passes. When we were playing, I felt a little tired because the wind was so strong and it was really cold, but one of my friends asked me if

I wanted to keep playing. I told him I would keep playing until the game was over. They said that I was a good player. I played well and felt that I deserved their praise. I thanked them because they were good to me. I think they knew that I was a good friend.

The next morning when I was in class, my friend said that I was a good basketball player. I asked her if she had seen me playing, and she said she had. She was so kind and good to me. She asked me if I wanted to play basketball for our school, and one day I told her that I was going to play for the team. I didn't realize that I had already fallen in love with her. I thought she was going to be my inspiration, but I didn't want to lose our friendship, so I just kept what I felt for her a secret. It was better to just be friends, because if I were to show her what I felt for her, everything would change. I was scared that the next time I saw her at school she would ignore me. It was important for me just to be her friend; I didn't want to hurt her or myself.

Two weeks later, I went to the dean's office and asked who was in charge of the basketball team. They asked me if I wanted to play for the team, and they brought me to the gym to look for the coach. The coach was a gentleman who looked kind. He was white and really tall, about five feet, eleven inches tall, and thirty-five years old. His hair was kind of long and he talked with a booming voice. He introduced me to the whole team. After the practice we talked about the game. I was upset because I wasn't going to be in the team's starting five. I thought maybe they would keep me on the bench.

Two weeks later, one of our games had just started. The players on my team and on the opposing team were really good. The other team made a lot of shots and so did we. I was on the bench, but I wanted to step onto the court and play. In the last quarter, in the last two minutes, one of my teammates hurt his finger when the point guard's pass slammed into it. My coach called to me and put me into the game. I was really nervous and scared. Every time I got the ball, I passed it to my teammates. Even when I was open and all I had to do was shoot, I passed it or called a timeout. I was just killing time. There were about thirty seconds left when a guy stole the ball from me. When he took a shot he made it, I was shocked because the guy was so fast. They were up by two points and my coach called a time-out with about ten seconds left. My teammates checked the ball from out of bounds and passed it to me. I was dribbling the ball; I didn't know what to do. I looked to see who was open, so I could pass it, but no one was, and my teammates said, "Just shoot the ball!" I was nervous and when I tried to shoot the ball, there was a big guy blocking me. When the ball got loose, I ran after it and got it again. There were about three seconds left in the game. I shot the ball again, but missed. I was mad at myself because I put all of my effort into that one shot, but I couldn't make it.

After that game, when we were practicing, three of my teammates came up to me and said some insulting things. They said that I was a weak person and I couldn't handle the ball. I was so mad—I couldn't stand up for myself because I couldn't speak English. If I could have, I would have said something to make them regret their words. I wasn't going to make trouble or start any fights because I didn't want to be suspended from a game. I didn't care about them; I cared about the team and the game. I just ignored them and pretended that I was OK, even though I was not. When I went home, I talked to my cousin about how badly my teammates had treated me. I told him that I was going to quit, but he stopped me and said that if I understood basketball, I could do better next time. I listened to what he said and decided not to quit. I just waited until the season was over. One month later, the season was over and school was almost out. I graduated on June 11, 2005. When I graduated, I thanked all of my friends who gave me love and respect. I didn't want to play basketball in high school, because I didn't want to be reminded of what had happened to me on the middle school team.

My family usually spent vacations visiting my uncle, auntie, and cousin in Las Vegas. But that summer our trip was canceled because my mom had graduated from nursing school and needed to work for two months. Even though my mom said we could still go with my dad, I decided to stay at home and hang with my friends. While I was home playing video games, my cousin called and asked if I wanted to play basketball. I dressed, ate quickly, and he picked me up. When we got to the park, no one else was playing. My cousin decided that we would practice and he would teach me all day. When we played basketball, he taught me how to dribble left, how to shoot, how to crossover, and how to defend. I learned a lot from him. When we were on the way home, he asked me if I was going to play basketball during freshman year. I told him I didn't know yet. He said that if I believed in myself and played hard, I could play on the high school team. He also talked about our uncle, who was the best player in our family. Our uncle had worked so hard at basketball and been a member of the big basketball team in our city for many years before he quit. He got drafted in our *barangay*, which means city in Tagalog, so he played against other cities and was a representative of our city.

When high school was close to starting, my mom asked me which high school I wanted to attend. I told her I wanted to go to Balboa High School, but she pressed me to make sure that I really wanted to go there. I thought about whether I would be happy with my decision. I knew that the teammates who had treated me badly were going to Balboa, so I changed my mind and decided to go to another school. I remembered that my sister went to Mission High School, so I told my mom that I was going there. I wanted to meet other friends and nice people who would be respectful to others and treat me well.

On the first day of school, my sisters and I were late because we couldn't sleep the night before. We were excited about going to school. When we got there, I couldn't believe that the school was really a school, because it looked like a church. I thought students in this school would be nice and kind, because it looked like a Catholic school. Three weeks later, I had made a lot of friends. I had Filipino friends and friends of different races. They were so nice and kind to me, even though people said that Mission High was a violent school. I didn't believe it, and it turned out it wasn't true.

When I was in the cafeteria, I asked my sister where the gym was. When I got there, I saw the coach of the basketball team. He was talking with some of the students. I talked to him and told him that I wanted to play basketball for his JV team. He said I'd have to come back after school to practice. When classes ended, I went to the gym and saw a lot of players practicing. I looked for the coach, and saw him with another guy, who he introduced me to. He said he was the JV coach (JV means "junior varsity"). After that, both of them introduced me to the whole team, JV and varsity players. The teams talked to me and they were so nice and kind. Some of them told me what to do.

Last month my team was playing a game. We were up by twenty points, and I was ready to play. My coach called a time-out and put me into the game. He told me to shoot the ball every time I got it. I shot a lot, but I missed. The next time I was open, I made sure that I was going to make it. A lot of people were cheering for me. My teammates were trying hard just to cover me, so I could get an open shot. The background around me was yellow and brown while I was running. Finally, I shot the ball and made it.

All the fans were screaming; I saw my principal and both of my coaches clapping and cheering for me. My teammates ran out and hugged me. I fell because there were so many of them. I cried because I realized that there were so many people who loved and cared about me. When we were in the locker room changing, my coach came in and said, "Give it up for Jayson!" They all clapped and some of them made jokes about me. My coach said I had the potential to play basketball. I felt like I was an important person because everybody respected and loved me. I will never forget that day.

I learned that the last ten seconds can make a difference, and I can make a difference. When people encourage me and believe that I can do better, I push myself harder. When people cheer for me, I feel powerful, and realize that it's more than a game. This is the world and my life. Sometimes when I remember this experience, I compare it to the love between couples. When you are attracted to somebody, you'll try to do anything to make that person see how hard you are trying to get to know her. You try and try until you succeed. It was just like what happened to me with basketball. I tried and tried, until everybody appreciated what I was doing.

This time it was different, because I made the effort to be good in class, and my friends treated me well. I was a good student and I felt love from my family. These things helped me to be courageous and gave me the confidence to play basketball. I learned that there were people out there who would cheer me on and push me to play basketball. I felt the love that my teammates gave to me and the love my fans gave to me.

CUTTING SCHOOL
Jae-Del Nazareno

When I was six months old, I did not see my mother because she moved to San Jose, California, to live with her mom. She left me with my father because she wanted to make money to send food and money to help pay for my education. I started to speak when I was four years old, and it was then that I started talking to my mom for the first time. I only knew her through the phone. I was a little kid holding a phone, and I would use two hands to put it up to my ear to hear my mother. I would always say to her, "I want to see you, Mama."

My mom would say, "Yes, baby, I want to see you too. I miss you so much."

The memories of those conversations stick in my head because they happened a lot, and it was always the same; I always told her that I wanted to see her, and she always said she would be there soon. Now, I always see my mom when she talks on the phone to my family in the Philippines; she sits down in a chair—she never stands up. When I was young, I used to imagine her sitting in a chair while she was talking to me, and I was laying down in a bed, hugging my pillow like a baby. I wore a T-shirt with a cartoon character on it. I remember that all of my T-shirts had cartoon characters from Disney on them.

From the time I was five until I was fifteen years old, I just saw my mother in pictures, and I never knew her moods or personality. I didn't know how to love her because I didn't grow up with her. She would send pictures of herself at her house with her family in the United States, but those were only pictures. I didn't know what her skin felt like or how tall she was compared to me.

Because I grew up with my father only, I am close with him. He cared for me when I was a baby. I never felt love for my mother because she was not by my side when I was a baby. I wanted to love my mother, though, because when I was a child, I saw my friends had a mother. I was jealous that I didn't have a mother, and I wanted to see my mother in person.

When I was fifteen years old, my mother called and said, "I am coming to the Philippines."

My father said in shock, "Are you really coming here?"

I took the phone from my father when I heard him, and I said to my mom, "That's true, Mama? You're coming here?"

My mom said, "Yes, baby, I will be there this month. I am going to get you, and I am going to bring you here to the United States."

Inside myself I thought that I did not want to leave my father and that I did not feel love for my mother because I did not know her. I said, "No, Mama. I don't want to leave my father."

My mom said, "Jae, you don't want to see me and you don't want to live with me?"

I replied, "No, Mama, I grew up with my dad since I was a baby. I don't know if you are a good mother or not because I have never seen you since I was a baby." I had taken the phone from my father, and I talked to my mom. I was sitting on the couch when I talked to my mother, and my father was just looking at me. After I talked to my mother on the phone, I talked to my father and I said, "Papa, what is Mama's personality like?"

My father said, "She is a good mother, Jae. She left you with me to feed you and to give you an education. She loves you so much, Jae."

Tenth Grade

One day, my mom and I were in the office with my counselor, Ms. Jordan.

My counselor said, "I had a son, but he passed away. But if my son was still alive, he would be in school because he had ambition. You, Jae, you also have ambition, and it is my wish that you will graduate. I called this conference with your mom because you need her support to succeed."

My mom asked me in Tagalog, "Why do you not want to come to school? I give you everything you want."

I replied, "You know what my problem is? My problem is with someone who lives in our house. He continues to bother me when I am sleeping, and he intentionally slams the door to express his anger and resentment towards me. I choose to ignore him to keep peace in the family." As I talked, I was face-to-face with her, showing the seriousness of this matter. As I talked, the image of the guy flashed before me: he looks like an old man with big eyes, dark brown skin, and salt and pepper hair.

My mom replied, "Is this your problem and the reason why you do not go to school?"

I said to both Ms. Jordan and my mom, "The other reason is you, Mom, and Dad." My mom and dad don't understand each other, and I want to fix this situation. Unfortunately, I don't know how, and that's why I cut school—to get attention from my mom. While I talked, I was sitting on a chair facing my mom as my counselor watched. I felt mad and guilty. I felt mad because my mom wouldn't support me and take my side. I felt guilty because I did not go to school. I continued to say to my mom, "Why can't we find another house to live in, so we can stop the arguments?"

And my mom said, "I can't because I can't pay the rent of one thousand dollars per month on my own, not to mention the grocery, phone, and electric bills. I need help to support all of you."

I said, "You can pay."

My mom continued, "Yes, I earn money, but I also need to save." My mom looked angry.

I said, "You are saving money for what, for land in the Philippines? But what you earn is more than enough—to pay for the land and still support our needs here in the United States."

My mom got mad at me when I talked to her like that. That's why I started rebelling—because she can't give me a valid reason when I know my argument makes sense. Whenever we had this kind of heated discussion, my mom usually sat in a chair while I remained standing. I remain standing during these conversations so she knows I am serious.

My counselor asked me, "Do you want to graduate?" My reply was always, "Yes, I want to graduate."

My counselor said, "Why don't you go to school then?"

I told her over and over again what my problem is. This was always the same conversation with her—I sounded like a broken record. When I started rebelling with my mom, I always cut school. I went to my friend's house and sometimes chilled in the park. But I never joined a gang because I knew that, if I joined in a gang, it would be like I was selling my soul to the devil. Yes, I was a rebel, but I was not taking drugs or robbing people. If I was not in school, I could not stay at home because the guy I hate lives at my mom's house.

My counselor said, "Oh, but you want to graduate. How can you graduate if you don't go to school?" At this point, I became speechless because my counselor was right.

I said to myself, "How can I graduate if I don't attend school?" I started to think to about what my counselor said.

She continued, "I know you have a problem at your house, but if you want to live on your own to get away, you can't do whatever you want because you need your education. Finish school first, then get a good job."

What my counselor said left a mark in my head, and I said to myself, "Yes, my counselor is right again, for the millionth time." As I looked at my counselor, I saw in front of me this African-American woman, who really did not have any connection to me whatsoever until the time that I started to mess up. She wasn't my relative or my teacher. Never in my wildest dreams would I have thought that I would have had a relationship with a woman like that and that she would help a Filipino like me. She has always shown genuine care for me from the start. She talks to me constantly, and she calls me at home to check on me or to wake me up so I can be in school on time. Now I was here, face to face with her, my mom watching my reaction, and all I could do was look down and say nothing. Ms. Jordan is always right. I didn't know what to say. I just scratched my head.

Eleventh Grade

When eleventh grade started, on the first day of school, I stopped by my counselor's office to check in. When tenth grade ended, she had said to me, "In this coming school year, you will be in eleventh grade, and on the very first day of school, you need to report to me so I know you are here."

Back then I had replied to my counselor, "OK, Ms. Jordan, I am going to report to you on the first day of school." I clearly remembered that conversation, the last day of school when I stopped by in my counselor's office.

I kept going to school from that first day. I was always present in all my classes. Every day I stopped by my counselor's office to give a progress report, telling my counselor that I attended all my classes. During that time, I looked good. My counselor said, "Good job, Jae, keep going until you reach success and get a good life." When my counselor saw my grades, her face was so happy because of me. And me, I always had a smiling face because I knew I didn't have a problem in school. But in my house, I never forgot that I still had a problem. That's why when I was home I had a lonely face.

In first semester I didn't have a problem in school, and I was so happy during that time. I did not miss a class. I was happy because my counselor cared for me; I felt that. I had good grades in first quarter, but not in every subject. In four classes I got *D*s because I didn't do my assignments, and when I went to my classes, I just sat and didn't do anything.

During that time my counselor talked to me, and she said, "Why did you get a *D* in these subjects?"

I replied, "I did not do the assignment and quizzes in those subjects."

My counselor replied, "Why did you not take a quiz or do your assignment?"

I replied, "I was lazy during that time and I was sick. Not like physically sick but I have insomnia. That's why I can't concentrate in my other classes." When we had this discussion, I was sitting in a chair and my counselor was checking my grades on a computer. My counselor was tall and big with a braid on the right side, and she was wearing glasses.

In second semester, I started missing school again because I had insomnia. I tried to go to school, but I couldn't because I couldn't sleep at night. I just laid down on my bed and I tried to sleep. Sometimes, if I couldn't sleep, I wasted my time on a computer to get sleepy.

And if that was not effective, I just laid down in my bed and closed my eyes. I just closed my eyes and thought of anything. I was rolling in my bed to find a good spot. I finally could sleep in the morning; sometimes that's why I missed school at that time.

I called my counselor and I talked to her on the phone, and I said, "Ms. Jordan, I missed school because I have insomnia."

My counselor said, "You need to report to me because you missed a lot of school days."

When my report card came, I saw my report: I got a GPA of 1.0 only. I was so sad when I saw my grades. At that time, I was so stressed that I could see it on my own face. This was because of my insomnia and because my grades were lower. When I came to school, I went straight to my counselor, and she was there and talked to me.

My counselor asked me, "Why did you not attend school?"

I replied, "I can't sleep at night. I can only sleep in the morning, but I have been to my doctor and here is my note."

My counselor said, "OK, Jae, don't be absent again because you have been missing a lot of work."

I replied, "OK, Ms. Jordan, sorry for missing school."

My counselor said, "No problem, Jae, I know you want to go to school."

Again, I was sitting in her chair in her office. I showed her my note and explained why I was absent. My counselor was sitting in her own chair, looking at me and asking me this question.

After that first semester I missed a little bit of class. But in second semester, I started cutting school. I did not go to school again, but this time it was for no reason. I was not attending school for almost a month; that's why I was failing my classes. My counselor was calling me on my phone, but I did not answer the phone.

My counselor, she left a voice mail on my phone, and she said, "Hey, Jae, why are you not attending school again? What's the problem with you?"

I ignored her voice mail and I kept cutting school for no reason. At that time, I looked bad because I was not attending school. Every day, I was not in school, and I did what I did in tenth grade. I always went to my friend's house to chill. My counselor kept calling me because she worried about me.

One day my counselor called my mom, and my counselor said, "Your son is not attending school, he is always absent from his classes."

My mom replied, "I thought my son went to school every day because he always leaves early to go to school."

My counselor said, "He's not going to school. We need to talk to you in person, Ms. Manaois."

My mom said, "OK, see you on Thursday, and we will talk about Jae again." After that, my mom was so mad at me because she was so upset. She thought that I always went to school and that I was lying to her.

My mom asked me, "Did you go to school?"

I replied, "Yes, Mom, I went to school."

My mom said, "Liar, I know you did not go to school because your counselor called me and said you did not go to school for almost one whole month." I did not say anything to my mom because I knew I was wrong. At that time, when my mom was talking to me, I sat on a chair, and my mom appeared mad at me. I went straight to my bed and slept.

When they had a conference again in my counselor's office, my mom and my counselor talked first before my counselor called me from my class. I was thinking, *What are they going to do to me?*

When I went to my counselor's office, I saw my mom in the office and she looked like she was crying.

My counselor said to me, "Jae, why are you not attending school?" I became speechless because I didn't know what I was going to say.

My counselor kept asking, "Jae, why did you not answer my question?" I did not say anything to her because there wasn't much to say. The image of that conversation—of my counselor talking to me and me not answering her questions—made my mom cry some more. My counselor kept talking to me, but I was speechless.

My counselor said, "We are going to put you in juvi because you haven't been going to school."

I replied, "Ms. Jordan, please don't do that." But she said, "Why did you not go to school?"

I replied, "No reason, I am tired of going to school."

My counselor said, "I thought you wanted to graduate."

I replied, "Yes, I want to graduate, but I did my best in all of my classes, but I am still failing."

My counselor said, "That's a simple problem, Jae,"

I replied, "Yes, I know, but for me it is a big deal."

My counselor said, "Oh, I am going to put you in juvi because you don't want to go to school."

I replied, "Don't put me in juvi. I beg you, Ms. Jordan." I saw my mom was crying. I didn't want to see my mom crying because of my stupidity. When I saw my mom cry, I said to myself, "What's wrong with you, Jae? You see your mom crying because of stupid things that you did."

I talked to my counselor and I said, "Give me one more chance?"

My counselor said, "One more chance, again? Jae, for the last time, I will give you one more like you ask."

I replied, "I promise, Ms. Jordan, that I will never do this again! I don't want to see my mom crying because of my stupidity."

My counselor said, "OK, Jae, I will give you a last chance."

I replied, "Thank you, Ms. Jordan. I appreciate you giving me a chance."

My counselor said, "But you need to do this progress report, and if you miss a class, you are going to report to me, and you will explain to me why you were absent, clear?"

I replied, "Clear, Ms. Jordan."

My counselor talked to me, and she said, "I want you, Jae, to graduate because I know you can do this, and because I remember your problem at your house. That's why I want you to graduate."

I replied, "Thank you very much, Ms. Jordan, for caring."

My counselor said, "So, what is your plan?"

I replied, "My plan is to go to school every day, starting now, because I don't want to see my mom crying, and I want to graduate and to get a good job."

My counselor replied, "That's good, Jae. Make a goal in your life and hold on to it."

I replied, "OK, Ms. Jordan, thank you for everything."

My mom was crying, and I said, "Don't cry anymore, Mama. From now on, whenever I can, I will try to never do that again because I don't want to see you crying."

My mom wiped her tears and said, "OK, Jae, don't do it again, OK?"

I replied, "Yes, Mama, I will never do that again, promise!" I hugged my mom while I kept making her that promise, and she hugged me, too.

Why did I do bad things when I was in eleventh grade? I went back to being lazy when I was in eleventh grade, and I wasn't going to school. I did better things again, after I saw my mom cry in front of my face, and I realized I needed to go to school. In that very moment I said to myself, "I need to finish school to get a good life."

When I saw my mom crying, that was the first time I saw my mom crying in front of my face. I thought she didn't care about me because when I did bad things in our house, she always got mad. But if I did good things, I thought she never saw it. It's hard for me to love my mom, because I grew up with my father. When I moved here to the United States, I didn't know what attitude to have about my mom. But when I saw her crying in front of me, I said to myself that my mom loves me so much! I feel better now about my mom and my relationship with her. My mom's love is very important to me because she is my one and only mother, and she does everything for me to get a good life.

The lesson to learn from my story is to not mess up my life because of stupid reasons. I realized that if I continue cutting classes, I will be in juvi. But presently, I go to school every day, and I study hard in all my classes. I learned how to make goals in my own life, because all people need to have a goal in life. I need to make it all the way to the top to have a successful future, and I want to be successful. In my story, I learned what it is to regret because I regretted all the things I did when I was in tenth and eleventh grades. But now, I want to finish school as a gift to my mom, because my mom wants me to finish my schooling to get a good life and a good future; that is what I want to achieve for her. In tenth grade, when my counselor told me that if her son was alive that she would want him to be going to school, I said to myself I want to have that too. That's why I go to school. My counselor cared for me by treating me like a son. I appreciate that caring from my counselor. Don't make the mistakes I made in school and with my mom because, in the end, you are going to regret it. If you see your mom crying in front of your face, and if you don't go to school, then you may lose what is in your future. That is what my story teaches.

ONE MORE TEAR
María Zapotecas

When I was a little girl, I knew that everything was good. My mom said it was, and I believed her because my mom is perfect, and always tells the truth. But now that I'm older, I understand what is good and what is bad, and I have discovered that we are humans who make mistakes that affect others, even though we don't mean to.

Seven years ago my father decided to come to the United States because his job wasn't paying well. My family and I were living in Mexico City, but my father couldn't find a job to provide us with enough money for school, food, clothes, and all of the necessary things at home. When my father told us that he was going to leave us and move to the United States, my heart broke into a million pieces. I remember that morning. My father sat on the sofa with me, my mom, my brother, and my seven-month-old little sister. He told my mom: "I love you. Take care of our son and daughters." My mom started crying and he gave her a kiss on the forehead. Then he kissed my little sister, and then he did the same with my brother and me. When he walked out the door, I had a sour taste in my mouth and tears started to fall from my eyes. My heart broke again. I kept thinking of his last movements and words. He opened the door and each step that he took reminded me that we wouldn't see him for a long time. The tears poured from my eyes like there was a tsunami, and it seemed like they would never stop. I felt that everything was over and my heart was broken into millions of pieces, so small that even a microscope couldn't see them. And even though it happened seven years ago, I cry when I remember it—especially because five days after my father left us it was my birthday.

For some months after my father went to the United States, everything was nice because he sent us $100 per week. When he had a lot of work he would send us more for food, school, transportation, clothes, and all of the necessary things. But then everything changed. He also started to send money to help support his parents. When my father started doing this, the money wasn't enough for my family, so my mom had to start working. If she didn't, we would not have had enough food, and we would have had to leave school. When my mom was obligated to work, she started selling shoes to her friends and to the family. She supported us with that money.

With each passing month, my father began to forget about us. He called us less often and when he did call, he wanted to discuss money with my mom. After some years, my mom decided to follow my father to the United States because she thought she could change my father back into the person he had been in Mexico.

My mom always seemed like a strong woman. She has physical and spiritual strength. I say physical strength because it was not easy to argue with my father just to protect us, and spiritual strength because even when she couldn't hold her tears back, she never cried in front of us. She wanted us to be strong when the biggest problems hit.

Two years ago, my mom, brother, sister, and I moved to New York from Mexico. We arrived at different times, but we all came with the same goal: to be with my father. At the beginning, everything was perfect and my father was the same person that he was in Mexico. The first day I saw him, he acted like he really loved us and liked to be with us. It was the family of my dreams where everything was good. And at nighttime, the family was together and there was always a new conversation to have. But then, everything went bad, and then terrible.

When my father started treating us badly, something inside me changed. That good person who had a lot of love to share was now an ogre. He took for granted that we had traveled from Mexico to New York to be with him and to keep the family together. And I was a little scared because the woman that had been strong and was my hero was now destroyed. She was losing the war. She would never let anybody hurt us, but faced with my father, she needed help. It still makes me sad to think that my mom was the only person who fought for us all of the time, and we could not help her when she needed us.

When my mom and sister went to New York, they were the ones who first discovered how much my father had changed. My mom discovered that the good relationship they had was falling apart, and my sister realized that the loving father who always used to have time to play with her was now gone. The two people who I love most were the first to be treated in a way that I could never imagine. My mom felt alone, even though my sister was there. She didn't have anybody to talk to and she didn't have the love that she thought she would find with my father. My sister was a baby, and like she said to me during my childhood, my mom told her that everything would be OK. At the time, my sister believed it. But when she saw how my father treated my mom, she knew that something was bad. She was scared of my father and I was not there to hug her when she most needed it.

Now my family and I are here in San Francisco. The love between my mom and my father had grown a little, but even the best efforts of the whole family couldn't make him the person he was in Mexico. Now I see a smile on my mom's face and she is happy more often. I am not saying that it was completely good for us that my father stayed in New York, but his absence gives us a moment to breathe, and think with brightness. And we realize that love and the meaning of family is kindness, respect, and understanding.

I believe I did the right thing for my mom once. It happened one evening, around 6 PM, when my mom and I were having a big argument.

I told her that my brother was always doing whatever he wanted, and that he didn't respect my privacy and my things.

"I can't do anything!" she said. "I'm working every day and most of the time I come home late and I can't just start fighting with your brother about what he does."

Then she sat on the bed, put her face in her hands, and started crying. My heart shrank. Half of me wanted to help my mom but the other half of me was angry. I felt alone, because my mom wouldn't stand up to my brother. I didn't know how to hold my tears back. There were two or three minutes without sound, just a lot of thoughts in the air. My mom was always a strong woman, but that day she was being destroyed.

The tears came out of her eyes and she seemed without consolation. I thought that it was my fault, that I should never talk to my mom about these things. I thought that what my mom needed was someone's support, and in this case she was waiting for my help. At that moment I realized that my mom is human. Her heart is not made of rock—she is a person with feeling and emotions.

Then she said, "I need your help." She paused, cleared her tears with her hand and then continued, "You are the oldest and I count on you all the time... I can't control your brother." And her voice broke up. I felt like I should hug my mom and cry with her, but at the same time I wanted her to think I was strong. Then she continued and her voice was weak and smooth. "I can't count on your brother," she said. "You know how he is, and you are more mature. You know what is good and what is not."

I couldn't hold my tears anymore and I started crying. It seemed like it was only me and my mom, and no one else in the world. I gave my mom a hug and at that moment my aunt called me on the phone to invite me to go to church. I asked my mom and she said, "No."

I asked why and she told me that the answer was "no" just because she said so. I thought that wasn't fair because my brother had more liberty than I did. Also, I was going to the church, not a nightclub. And I was going with my family, not with friends. Many memories came to my mind, like when my brother came home at 8 PM, although his classes ended at

3:20 in the afternoon. But when I asked for the same thing he got, she said no. I couldn't understand why she was like that, but I had to try to.

I realized that if it was hard for me to be a good example for my sister and brother, it was worse for my mom to play two roles at the same time—mother and father. I felt closer to her because we had been through bad situations, like the time right after my dad left Mexico for New York and hadn't finished putting the windows in our house. The whole family had to sleep in the same bed to keep warm when winter came. Again, we worked together to try and keep the family together.

Now I realize that the base of a family is communication and the support we give each other. I remember the scene of my mom and me fighting; I was angry and I was acting in a bad way. But she is my mom and I should support her no matter what. It's like when people say, "Don't do to others what you don't want others to do to you," and, "If you want respect you have to give respect." Now I know that I did the opposite and made my mom cry.

I also feel bad for being ungrateful one Christmas after my dad left for New York, when my mom didn't have any money for presents. I was too young to understand that my mom couldn't afford the bicycle that I wanted and I didn't appreciate the presents I did get. I have made a lot of mistakes over time, but now I know that I reacted poorly because I didn't understand how much my mom sacrifices for us.

Now I can say that I have matured a little bit, and I think before I do things. If it is necessary, I think twice. Now I know that happiness is not focusing only on ourselves, but it is about what good things we can do for others. It is about the people we love and appreciate

Living in San Francisco, the relationship between my mom and me has become stronger. Now we are the base of the family; we work together so that my sister and my brother can grow up without bad memories of our past. My relationship with my brother is hard to describe because even though I want the best for him, he always makes me furious. I think it's because of the age he is at. He is not mature enough to understand reality.

At this point of my life I can say that all of my experiences, good and bad, help me to understand that life is not always rosy. At some point in our lives we cry. But there is always a reason, a reason that spirit knows even if we don't. Our spirit feels, understands, hears, smells, and touches the feelings inside of us. When your spirit doesn't support those feelings, they come out in tears, in a volcano of emotions. I know; it happens to my mom and also to me.

I know that we have hurt each other without always knowing it. I just wonder if my brother and I can overcome all of the bad moments and forget the bad things that my father did, not only for our own good, but to help our family to recover. All humans make mistakes. Sometimes adults think that they are doing the right thing, but their actions can affect their family more than themselves. My brother has hurt us sometimes, but I believe that he is going to mature and understand that we need to be more positive, and not disappoint each other.

Looking back, I can say that when I was a child and we were in Mexico, my father was an excellent father. When we were in Mexico, my father was my hero because he helped me solve my math problems. He would always tell me that I should never give up, that I should fight for my dreams no matter what the barriers are.

Maybe it is true that distance makes people forget the feelings they have for one another. In my case, the distance made my father forget that he had a family and that his family needs him. Even though my father didn't care about us while we were still in Mexico, we continued on with the dream that he would come back and continue with our happy family. I am not saying that it was only his fault. I know that it was not. I think that when a family breaks down it is the fault of all of its members. A family is like a tree. The trunk of the tree is the parents and the branches are the sons and daughters. If the parents fail then the branches fail too. In this case my mom, brother, sister, and I try to keep the family up. I think that my mom has fought very hard to keep the family happy. She has tried to keep the family together because of her religious ideas, even though it can't be the way my mom wants it to be.

Maybe this story will have an impact on many lives. Many of you may think that I am lying, but let me tell you something: This is my story and this is the story of many families. I wrote about my life because I know there are many others out there like me. Like my mom, there are many women who let their husbands control them and make decisions for their lives. If you are one of these women, stand up and fight for your happiness, and don't let others choose for you. Never, ever let a man scream at you or hit you. Just remember that if it happens one time, it will happen again. Remember that you are a special and unique human, and only look down when you are helping another to stand up.

DOUBLE LIFE
Juan Luis Omar Villamar

I t was my sixth birthday party. My mother, father, sister, and I were together and happy. Those times were incredible. I remember my father
giving me my first soccer ball and a T-shirt with my favorite team's logo.
Many pictures were taken at that party.

As I grew up, I began to change. Now I had a secret. Back in Mexico,
at the 68TH, where I used to live, I had double life. At home with my family I was a good boy who got good grades, followed directions, and was
obedient. In the streets with my friends I was in a gang—a bad boy with a
fake image who provoked fear, fought, and was aggressive.

Lying was the only way to balance this double personality. Omar
was my real name, and Omar was a real person—the real me. However,
I often felt lonely. I had no communication with my family, not even with
my mother. Pantera was my nickname in my gang family, and it was there
that I felt protected, dangerous, and able to survive. Today, my parents
cannot imagine my story—they only look at me with love. They don't see
a bad child. That's why in the past I didn't ask for their opinion, or other
people's opinions. Only my girlfriend's opinion mattered.

Three years ago, when I was about thirteen years old, my dark life began. I met friends in the streets who gave me bad advice; to me everything seemed like a joke, and I just wanted to play the game and have some fun. I joined a gang and began doing bad things and sometimes fighting. Living with risks and danger, breathing as if every day was my last—that was my daily life. My family didn't know what was happening to me because they were resolving other problems. By that time, my dad had left us to go to the United States. It was his third attempt to leave Mexico. The problem was that my father was lost in the United States, and my mother was looking for him while also working really hard to sustain my sister and me.

I don't mean to say that my father is responsible for my bad decisions, but I do think that his absence through my childhood affected me. My secret didn't affect my family because they didn't know about it. The only person who knew about me and the gang was Mónica, my girlfriend. She was so beautiful. She had long black hair and pretty eyes. I would like to see her again one day; she was like a model woman. She used to give me advice, telling me to change and to take the good way. One of the phrases I can't forget is, "Your family is more important than some friends who could stab you in the back." She loved me with all her heart and worried a lot about the double life I was living. I didn't listen to her advice because I didn't want to acknowledge that she was correct. Eventually, I ended our relationship.

I'm slowly telling my parents the truth in order to clear my conscience. They may ask themselves, "How could that have happened without us realizing it?" I now know it is better not to keep a secret. It is really hard; the burden on my thoughts and conscience is so heavy. It's not worth keeping it secret, because someday someone is going to find out the truth. Secrets hurt you, but they also hurt the feelings of others—sometimes the people you love the most. I have not yet told my parents everything about my secret, and when they read this essay, I hope they can understand that I'm sorry for not telling them earlier. I want to say to them, *Papá y Mamá, yo sé que se van a sorprender mucho, por todo lo que pasó en mi vida sin que nadie, ni ustedes, se den cuenta de mis problemas. Y, otra vez, perdónenme, papás, y nunca olviden que los quiero mucho.*

Late one night, I was at home and everyone else was sleeping. I went out to the patio to look at the sky. I felt alone and sad. I started to remember the beautiful days and moments with my family and my girlfriend. Their love was the key to my getting out of the gang. My mother worked in the morning and at night, and never stopped looking for my father or looking after us. She loved and cared for us. Mónica also did everything she could and never lost her patience. The love of my family is very strong, and the love of my girlfriend was also very special; she was the other half of my heart.

Mónica was really the person who convinced me to leave the gang for my own good and that of my family. When I decided to get out of the gang, I was confused and scared but at the same time happy and thankful to be starting a new life. I asked myself: "What are you doing? What happened to you, Omar?" I opened my eyes and made a good decision; I saw the person I really wanted to be, a person who wasn't lying. I saw the real Omar. I completely changed my life and started over.

I started a new relationship with my family. After a while, my mother found my dad in San Francisco, and we all began living together again. In America, we began a new life, with new opportunities. The day I saw my father in San Francisco, I knew it was a chance to change how I felt and communicated with my parents. I wanted to forget all of the horrible things that had happened and to thank God.

Looking back, I see that gangs are no substitute for family and love. Many people have lived in situations similar to or even more horrible than mine. My sad and hard experience can be an example to many sons and daughters who need to have a better relationship with their parents. Trust means love and sharing. Any time you face a problem or are keeping a secret like I was, go to your family and ask for a little time to talk. You can always find an exit if you look for it. If I had an opportunity to go back, I would change almost everything about my time spent in the gang—I destroyed my life. But now I understand the people around me. I know that it is important to tell the truth so that everyone knows who you are and can believe in you.

PART DREAM, PART NIGHTMARE
Dewayne Davis

As the plane headed towards my house, I could hear parts hitting the top of my roof. The next thing I knew, the plane crashed and exploded right in my kitchen. All I could hear were people screaming, "Help me!" I quickly grabbed a picture of my mom and my sister. My grandma, my sister, and I ran as far as we could. The plane burnt down a few houses and the firefighters took thirty minutes to come. By then our house was long gone. I was surprised that we even survived this tragedy. I wanted to express my emotions to my grandma. I was scared, but I tried to be strong for my sister, who didn't have a clue. Tears ran down my cheeks, while all of my clothes and my bed burned to the ground. Though I was only seventeen years old, I was almost grown, and this tragedy changed my thoughts and feelings. I was lucky to be alive.

I had this dream for years.

In my dream, I thought only of myself. I didn't care about my grandma and sister. I ran out and left everything. I would wake up every night sweating and terrified that I might actually let my family down, full of fear of being alone. Even though it was a dream, my integrity seemed to go up in flames. Everything was lost in fire: my character, my feelings, my personality, and my goodness.

For a split second after I woke up, I would think my life had ended when the plane hit. Something came to me like, *What did I do wrong? How could I have lived my life a little better?* I guess that my pride got in the way of things.

Afterwards, me, my sister, and my grandma ended up at my great-grandma's house. Remorse flowed through my head and I thought to myself, *What's my purpose on this earth?*

As we were getting ready to go to bed, my great-grandmother came to tuck me in and told me to imagine a happy place. I wished I could escape to that place, a place where you wouldn't have to worry about living to see the next day. I wanted to go to a place where it was just me, and people who understand me. No one could understand my thoughts or anything that came from my heart. I made mistakes in my life, but who hasn't? I felt like my karma came back to me but I knew there was still more to come. When would something good happen, and how could I be more prepared for the bad things that were bound to happen?

Good things started to happen when I got introduced to football. Before that, I thought I was going to be a drop-out or in jail. When my mom died, I was probably on my way to becoming a drug dealer or a gang banger. Football kept me off the streets and in school. My dad inspired me to play football. He loved the game so much that he had me practice almost every day. But that was before he walked out on my little sister and me. Sometimes I wondered if we were bad kids. Why didn't he have any interest in us? If I have a kid someday, I will take care of him or her with all my heart. Not having a dad is like having a body with no heart or brain. It's just a body that's very cold. It's hard not having anyone to look up to, or someone who can teach you how to be a man. It's pretty selfish to only think about yourself and leave your family behind. That's why I'll always cherish my sister and she knows that she will always be taken care of while I'm on this earth.

My sister, Wayniece, is really precious and she has the exact same smile as my mom. She is a very intelligent young lady. It's hard to look at her sometimes because she reminds me so much of my mother. She sings, dances, and talks to her dolls. Sometimes she gets scared at night and sleeps in my room. My sister is always looking for her mom and dad and it's too hard to tell her that they're not coming back. But secretly I hope that someday we will all meet again. Looking out for her in the future is going to be hard, but I'm up for the challenge and I've got her back.

My grandma had to raise us without any help from our family. She had to learn how to be a parent again. That is very unselfish and I hope that someday our family will come together and put aside our differences and dislikes. We can't let time pass this way, because I know that my mom is probably turning over in her grave right now. Every night I sneak a look at my grandma while she sleeps, and I whisper to her that everything will be all right.

Now, I have a new dream.

In this dream, I am living with my great-grandma. Tomorrow is my birthday and I'm about to begin a football scholarship at USC. The scholarship has changed my whole outlook on life. Life without family is a messed-up life to live. Personally, I think that you're lost without family, because there's no one to talk to and no one to give advice. Moving away from my family will be very hard for me, but in four years, and in the long run, it will be a positive change. For me, going to college is a big step. To be honest, it is something bigger than me: I'm doing it for my family. I hope that my mom is proud because I am the first person to go to college in my family.

Today is my first day of school and my heart thumps, as I realize what I'm here for: football, English, and engineering. I also remember what my grandma told me: that I need to be grateful, thoughtful, and intelligent—that those are the main characteristics you need in life. Many months pass and I'm doing pretty well in class and especially on the field, where I do my thing. I think about my mom, who was very intelligent and beautiful. The picture that I grabbed is in a frame on my dresser and every night before I go to sleep, I hug and kiss it. I remember when my mom used to make my favorite: fried chicken and macaroni. I can picture her buying me my first bike. Her smile lit up the whole world. I am proud that she's my mom and that we have the same traits. My mom wanted me to go to college and she wanted me to live a good life. I know that she's watching over me and loves me.

We beat Stanford, forty-nine to forty-two. I told you that it was going to be a nail-biter! We are now national champions and I'm so proud. A week passes, and I am now in the NFL draft room with my sister and grandma. I am the first person picked in the draft; the Oakland Raiders offer me $70 million to play for the black and silver. As I watch my grandma's eyes water, I finally realize my purpose on this earth—to love my family. As I look up to the sky, I can picture my mother's eyes and that's when I realize that I have made it. I finally understand that if you keep aspiring to do good, you can make it.

In this dream, I do the right thing.

MY BROKEN HOME: EL SALVADOR

Kenia Vanegas

No one wants to be discriminated against, but there is discrimination around the world. Everyone wants to be respected, but there is disrespect. All people want to be free, but many people all over the world do not have choices. People want a good education, they want jobs, and they want their health, but there are many uneducated, unemployed, and sick people. Every human wants to be safe, but there is so much violence in the world that many people feel fear. The Golden Rule states that we should all treat others the way we want to be treated. If the Golden Rule could be followed by everyone, all these problems would disappear, and the world would be a better and beautiful place to live. If the governments of countries or people in power used the Golden Rule, citizens could have the chance to live in a perfect country. However, this is not the case with my country, El Salvador. My country is broken and will never be fixed until the government listens to the people and treats them with respect and compassion.

My country is a beautiful country with many things that make me love it more now that I'm here in the United States. I miss my culture and those of my family who live in El Salvador. I can tell you many things about my country. I'm from La Unión, El Salvador. La Unión is always hot; if you woke up at 9 AM, you would want to take a shower or go to the river that's close to my house. I love that river because the cold water makes me feel fresh. When I am swimming in the river I feel relaxed because the water is not too cold and not too hot. The people love to go to the river to wash their clothes and swim. It is so wonderful—you would love it like I do.

Also, there are a lot of fruit trees. There, you can pick fruit from the trees at any time you want because these trees always grow along the river and the fruit is fresh. My favorite fruits are the mangoes. I take a mango from the tree and peel one piece. I look to the right as I bite my mango, and I can see beautiful flowers of many colors, like yellow, orange, red, and purple. These beautiful flowers grow by the river. If I look to the left, I can see Honduras across the river, another beautiful country in Central America. Looking north I can see the mountains that have many trees and animals living in the forest. When I see the mountains, I feel something inside me that makes me want to be close to them. When I am with my friends, we like to run to the mountains and play there by the trees. The rabbits and birds are so beautiful that they make me feel freedom, like a bird that flies in the air. These mountains are so beautiful that they easily get the attention of anyone who passes by. In the fall the trees lose their leaves, and it is so beautiful when the new leaves are growing in the spring. The flowers and new leaves of the trees smell so good, like the perfume of candy. People don't climb these mountains because they are too rocky, but you can go and walk all around and see the beauty of the trees and animals.

The people from my country are friendly; if they don't know someone, they always try to make a friendship with that person. For example, in the morning if going to the river, they always say, *"¡Hola! ¿Cómo está, amigo?"* and people want to answer because they are happy about how friendly and nice everyone is. When you wake up in the morning and you go out of your house, you can see people in the street, always doing something. Sometimes they go to the river to take a shower or go and wash their clothes. Women like to wash their clothes in the river because the clothes get cleaner than if they wash them in the washing machine, and they enjoy the feel of the cool water, and they get the company of their friends rather than having to stay at home. While the women are washing their clothes, their children are playing around or swimming in the fresh water.

It is a beautiful sight to see people wash their clothes in the river. They take a pair of pants, put soap on them, and beat the pants against some rocks. Then they push the pants forward and backwards on the rocks, and after that they dip the pants into the water, rinse them, and wring them dry. When they get home, the women hang a rope from one pole to another to dry their clothes in the sun.

The people also go to the river because they love nature. They prefer lives in the fields because the air of the city is so contaminated and there are just buildings and buildings. In the fields you can breathe the fresh air and the perfume of the flowers.

Along the side of the mountains are fields and plantations of corn where some of the people of my village go to work. They also go there because they have to watch that the animals don't destroy the corn. There are pigs that like to eat the corn. The pigs have their owners, but sometimes their owners are not at home, and if the pigs are by themselves, they escape and go to the plantations to find corn to eat.

El Salvador is a beautiful country with beautiful people, but there are a lot of problems. Problems that the government has not solved. I think that the government has to make a lot of changes in my country—changes that we all need. For example, a lot of people do not have health care. If I were the president of El Salvador, I would give all the people health care. Sometimes the people who live in the valley have children, and if their children get sick, they have to take them to the hospital or to a clinic. If they don't have health care, they have to pay for their medicine, and that's where the problem is, because if they don't have the money, they cannot buy the medicine. Sometimes the people stay sick longer because they can't get the right care. In the valley where I was living in El Salvador, there are many poor people. I know a woman who really needs help because she has five children and she is poor. The reason she has five children is because she doesn't have the knowledge about methods to prevent getting pregnant. There is not too much information about these methods available to women in the countryside. Because they have many children and cannot provide for their families, many people from my valley depend upon their relatives who are here in the United States to send clothes or money to provide for their children.

To give more jobs to all the people who live in El Salvador and who need jobs to support their families is very important. There are some families who, if they don't work a day, they don't eat. I know someone who is in my valley, and he needs a job. He was here in the United States, but he was deported, and now he is in El Salvador. He has been in El Salvador for one year, and he cannot find a job. He just works in the fields in the plantations of other people, and he earns money for that, but it's not enough to buy personal things that he needs like clothes, shoes, and food. That's the only job that he can find in the valley. Even if they want to work, there are no jobs for the poor people. The government should provide jobs with the companies that control building or repairing the roads. Also, the women sometimes go to the city to work in houses as servants, but they get paid only seven dollars a day, which is not enough money to provide for their families. The people work so hard and so long to try to get enough money. Some go to the city to sell the typical food of El Salvador like *pupusas*. *Pupusas* are filled with beef and beans and are delicious. The women get on the buses and take long rides, sometimes over an hour, to the city to sell their food. They also sell clothes that they buy from a company to try to get some money to take back to the valley. The people of El Salvador are hard workers, but they cannot find jobs, and that is why they come to the United States. The Salvadorean government needs to provide jobs to every person in El Salvador who wants to work.

Another big problem in El Salvador is that there are too many gangs and criminals, and we have to deal with that problem and solve it. The people are afraid to go out at night in the cities. The gangs are on almost every corner of the streets. If people go to the market or somewhere else outside their houses, they don't like to wear their jewelry because they don't want to be robbed or killed for that jewelry. That's too bad because people like to go to parties at night, but it's so dangerous that they prefer to stay at home because in their homes they feel safe. The members in the gangs are there because they have a lot of problems. Problems that they cannot solve. Many of the gang members are young people, and sometimes they don't have their parents and they live by themselves. They join the gangs because there they make them feel like they are at home with their families. Even if they have their parents, sometimes members join gangs because their parents don't give them the love that every young person needs. I think that people who have children must teach them about what is good or bad for them, because if they don't give them values, their children never will know the right way they can live their lives. Without good guidance, they might join gangs or do other criminal things. For example, there is a big gang called *La Mara Salvatrucha* that's one of the most dangerous gangs in El Salvador. This gang is also here in the United States. The government in El Salvador is trying to stop this gang and solve that problem, but the gangs are getting bigger every single day. If the government stops the criminals, the people would be happy and proud of their country and their government. This is an important change that the government has to make in my country.

I chose to write about the government of my country because it is something that makes me feel sad. The reason I'm here in the United States is because my country doesn't have a better future for me and can't provide the opportunities that I and everybody else need. If we all get together and speak in one voice, we can make a change in our country. If the Salvadorean government listened to what we want or what we need, we wouldn't have to come to a country where we are discriminated against by white people or by others who are racist against the Latin American people. When I was in middle school and I didn't know how to speak English, some students laughed at me. Often people make fun of those who don't speak English. On the bus one day, I saw a woman from Mexico sitting in a seat. An African-American woman got on and started yelling at the Mexican woman saying she had to get up and give her the seat. The Mexican woman didn't speak any English. She was sad and scared, and finally she got up and got off the bus. The government of the United States does not want us here. I don't think that we are doing bad things to this country just because we weren't born here. I give thanks to this country for letting me be here because now I'm studying and looking for a better future and making my goals to make a better life come true. But if we are here in America, it is because in our countries we don't have the opportunities that we have here in the United States.

People who live here and are born here don't know the needs that we have and the poverty that we have in our countries. They think that we are here just because we want to be here. They don't know what is happening in our countries. Even though I want to return to my country, I love the United States because for many of us it is like our second home, where we can live and have a better life, a life with *lujos*—luxuries. But it is not just *lujos* that we want because some of the money that the people earn working hard here is sent to their families in their countries. For people in the United States who think that we don't want to be in our countries with the love of our families, my answer is that we all really want to be in our countries—the countries where we were born and saw the light for the first time. That's the reality of what we feel and need, and it's also what people in the States have to know about Latin American people.

The Salvadorean people are fighting for a decent life for themselves and their families. The government is unable to help them reach this goal, so the people must find ways to help themselves. Let me tell you about the sacrifice that my family has made to bring happiness and opportunities. When my mother and my father were in El Salvador, they didn't have a job to support my brothers, sister, and me. I have two brothers and one sister. My brothers' names are Wilson and Jorge, and the name of my sister is Andrea. I love my family, and I love my mother because she works hard to give us a better life. My mother, named Edy, came to the United States ten years ago, but my father, Javier, came before her. He worked hard to earn the money to get my mother to San Francisco, California. When she came here, she started to work like my father. They left us in El Salvador with my grandmother. I was five years old when my parents left me with my grandmother, and for eight years I only spoke to them every once in a while on the telephone. Every month my grandmother went to the post office to get a letter filled with money that my parents sent to us.

One day I heard my older brother talking on the phone to my mother, and he was very excited. I realized that my mother had asked him to come join her in the United States. At that time I was eleven years old. I was so sad because he was my brother and my best friend, and he was leaving me. It was two years later when my mother asked me if I wanted to come join her and my brother. I didn't want to leave my grandmother and my sister and my little brother. I thought of my grandmother as my mother, and I thought if I came to the United States all I would do was study, and I thought that would be hard and difficult for me. I also never spoke English before, and I thought I would never learn to speak English because it was very hard for me. So I told my mother, "No, I want to stay here in my home." But my mother told me I had to come because she wanted a better future for me. If I stayed in El Salvador, I would never get a good education or opportunities that I would get if I came to the United States. So I kissed my grandmother goodbye and my sister and brother goodbye and came to San Francisco.

The first month I just stayed in my house with my family. The second month I went to school, and it was very hard because I couldn't speak English. Sometimes I cried myself to sleep at night. We talked to my grandmother once a week, but sometimes I preferred not to talk with her because it made me sad. After three years, I am doing OK. I have friends, and I know more English than before so I am doing well at school. My mother plans to go back to El Salvador to take care of my younger brother and sister. My grandmother is getting old. She is always sick and cannot take care of them. When my mother leaves, I will probably go live with my brother. I prefer that my mother goes because my grandmother needs help, but I will miss her.

People are willing to make very big sacrifices for a better life. It's too bad that they leave their families and their country to come here to work to support themselves. Why can't the Salvadorean government understand what we need? Why can't the world make it easier to live a happy life in our country?

I hope that my country changes, and that the government can listen to us and understand what we want. I'm proud of my country, and I love my country, and I want to be there with my family. My country, El Salvador, my home, is broken right now, and my dream to return has to wait. If the government or people in power in El Salvador used the Golden Rule, it would be a perfect country. All government officials have excellent health care. They need to share this with the people. All government officials have many opportunities to find jobs. They need to give these opportunities to the people. All government officials are educated in the best schools. They need to make it possible for the poor people to study and improve themselves. If people in power treated others the way they want to be treated, El Salvador would be a better place to live, and I could go back to my home.

TO GET RESPECT, YOU HAVE TO GIVE IT

Alejandro Flores

O ften, figures of authority in and out of school, such as teachers, security guards, and bus drivers, treat students disrespectfully. Although many of us are fairly mature and trustworthy, we are treated as though we are young children. It seems as though these figures of authority think we are not responsible when really they may not understand our cultures, problems, or personalities. I think that people with authority want to be treated with respect, but if you want respect you have to give it.

On multiple occasions I have seen security guards either threatening or making false assumptions about my friends. They often assume that my friends are trying to leave school just to have a good time or cause trouble, when in reality they are trying to deal with legitimate problems. For example, one of my friends had to leave school because he had a medical appointment. He went to the office and told the secretary about the appointment, but the security guards simply accused him of lying and assumed he was cutting class. Situations like this are constantly occurring.

A year ago my brother Rafael called my mom to tell her that he was sick.

The security guard who was working that day didn't believe him and accused my brother of lying. Out of frustration my brother got mad and said that if they didn't give him permission to leave that he would leave on his own. Finally, the security guard called my mother and told her that Rafael was trying to cut class. My mother explained to him that Rafael was sick, had spoken with the secretary, and had permission to leave. After hearing the story I felt mad and frustrated because if the secretary had talked with my mom and given a pass to my brother, then the security guard didn't need to question him. It felt like the security guard didn't care. If I were the security guard, I would ask the secretary if the student had permission to leave, and when she said yes, I would let him go. By simply listening to my brother, the security guard would have been treating him with respect instead of assuming he was lying.

Many high school students work in addition to going to school. Whether it's because we need to help our families out financially or because we want to save money on our own, a lot of my friends and I have jobs and struggle to balance them with our studies. My father works very hard as an electrician, plumber, and general construction worker. I frequently work with him to earn money to go out with my friends or buy new clothes. One time my cousin Raul and I worked until late at night in San Jose. After working overnight we were exhausted, and fell asleep once we got home. We overslept and came to school an hour and a half late, and once again the security guards accused us of cutting class. If the guard had taken the time to talk to us, he would have understood how hard we worked the night before and behaved more sympathetically towards us.

For what seems like no reason, one of my teachers almost always seems angry and has a bad attitude towards his students. I think that he may have personal problems and tends to take them out on us. This is both unprofessional and unfair. Even when we have legitimate reasons for being late or having to leave early, he doesn't believe us and punishes us.

Recently, I came to class late because my mother had asked me to wait to walk my younger brother to school, and even though I explained to him what had happened, he made me do twenty-five pushups. Even if his intentions are good ones, his method of teaching is too severe. By refusing to trust us, he lowers himself in our opinion.

I've also had negative experiences with adults in authoritative positions on public transportation. This past year I was taking the bus home, and as I boarded, I accidentally paid fifty cents instead of a dollar-fifty. While I was walking towards the back of the bus to find a seat, the bus driver got up out of his seat and asked me, "How old are you?" I told him I was sixteen and he called me a liar, pushed me, and demanded that I get off the bus. I refused to get off the bus because I was not in the wrong. I wasn't lying about my age. The bus driver could have asked me for ID or spoken to me with respect, but he didn't do that. He simply assumed that I was lying. Unfortunately, things like this happen to me all the time.

Collectively, I think this type of behavior is crazy. I often wonder why people treat others so disrespectfully. Perhaps they just don't know what respect is. Perhaps they were treated with disrespect in their past and therefore feel the need to treat people the same way. Perhaps their disrespectful behavior is the result of a generation gap. If this is the case, while they may not understand certain aspects of youth culture and technology today, they can't blindly assume that the majority of it is negative.

One teacher I had thought I was texting every time I used my calculator. Again, I tried to explain the situation honestly, but instead of listening, she said, "I know that trick." At a time when she could have put trust in me or actually heard me out, she chose to refuse me the benefit of the doubt. I know people stereotype me because I am Latino and I don't like it.

Certain teachers have treated me with respect. At Mission High, Mr. Waldman was kind and fair to me, which made me feel good. He gave this respect to all of his students, not just a few individuals. When I was in Mr. Waldman's class I felt comfortable. His class wasn't easy, and at first I was playing around. However, he showed me that he actually cared. He told me that I had to work hard and pay more attention because he didn't want me to fail his class. After he talked to me, I felt better, I started to work harder, and I passed his class. When I was in Mr. Waldman's class, I was satisfied because he effectively helped me understand the material and was genuinely interested in helping all of his students.

Before I came to the United States I thought it was the best place in the world because when I saw commercials on TV and in the movies, I saw only rich people who didn't have to work hard. It seemed like a place where we could get respect, but now that I am in the United States the situation is very different. Now that I am here, I see how hard it is to get a job. In this country, rich people treat those who have less money with little or no respect. I think that in the United States, the way I am treated is based on my race. For example, there was a time when I was with my father in his car and he was pulled over and didn't have his driver's license with him. The police officer was behind us and got out of his patrol car, came up to our car, and asked my father for his license. My father said, "I forgot my license at home." The police started laughing and told him, "That's what all Latin Americans say!" The police officer gave my father a ticket and then we drove home. I know that it was our fault because we didn't have the license, but the policeman expressed an anger that he has with Latinos. He said to us that all Latinos are the same. He didn't care that his expression was a stereotype.

When I first dreamed of coming to this country, I thought the United States was going to give me, my family, and my friends a better life. Now that I live here, I realize that life is not what I expected. I feel that schools should encourage their students and help them succeed in this country, not make assumptions based on their appearances, personalities, or cultures. If school employees took the time to talk to us or give us some advice rather than treating us like criminals, we would be more inclined to make a positive change. Ultimately, we would feel more comfortable and safe if they made an effort to understand us.

My parents instilled in me how to respect others, especially the people who have authority in my life. Thanks to my parents I know what respect means and what it feels like to be respected. For example, when I went to work with my father and I fixed a hole in the wall, he told me that it was perfect. He told me that I did a good job. I felt good because people, including your parents, don't always appreciate what you do. Another time I feel respected is every week when I help the priest in my church. What I do to help is carry the cross into the church past the communion wine. After that I feel comforted because people appreciate what I do. They thank me for being a good person and supporting my community. As a student, I feel that the way most people with authority treat us is not the way I would treat younger people.

GRANDMA & ME

Vicky Wu

Everyone should respect their grandparents. When I was child, I lived with my grandma in China. We slept together, played together, laughed together, and ate together. My grandma taught me many skills, such as how to be a good person, how to be obedient to my elders, and how to pay attention in school. However, despite her teachings, I'm not doing too well at all. Sometimes I cut school and, because of that, I have bad grades. Sometimes I feel like I cannot figure out the assignments, so I'm less motivated to do the work. Even though I have bad grades and I cut school sometimes, I do not feel like I am a bad person. My grandma has been around me my whole life. She knows that when I lived in China, I would try my hardest in school. At times I would do really well in subjects like Chinese grammar, but not so well in subjects like math. I have memories of my grandma sitting down with me while I did my homework. She was very supportive of me. She took the time to try her best to explain my homework to me. Doing homework together is a memory that I will always cherish. When I moved to San Francisco four years ago, she knew that I would have a hard time in school because I would be learning a whole new language. She understands my struggle, and because she knows my disposition, we don't talk a lot about my school situation when I call her on the phone. I feel that children should have a strong and respectful relationship with their grandparents because we have parts of them in us.

When I first moved to the United States, I lived with my parents in Sacramento. I did not like living there at all, so I decided to move in with my brother, who lives in San Francisco. My first two years in San Francisco were difficult. My brother is ten years older than me. He had already been in San Francisco for about two years. He's the one who takes care of me. Since I moved in with him, I have had to do much housework that I never did in China. In China, my grandmother always did everything for me. But now that I live with my brother, I have to cook dinner every night, clean the house, and do the laundry. I have to be patient because in China an older brother represents a father figure. When I first did the housework, I just thought I wanted to go back to China and let my grandmother do everything for me. It was hard to adjust to the American life. At first I had no friends or family except my brother. My first two years, I found myself not wanting to leave the house. I did not know how I could possibly communicate with people who spoke English when I didn't. In China, I didn't learn English that well. I found myself not wanting to learn because it was hard and I didn't like it. I soon found out that I needed to learn it in order to be successful in life. I just started speaking and writing English last year, and I am still working very hard at it.

As I get older and learn more English, I have started to communicate less with my grandmother and family in China. I thought that moving to San Francisco to live with my brother was a good idea because bilingual classes were offered in the city, whereas they were not offered in Sacramento where my parents live. Sometimes I feel alone because I have no one to talk to about what I am thinking or the hard things that I go through. I want to be able to talk to my brother about some of these things, but I can't relate to him because we are so different. There are many things he likes but I don't like, and that makes it hard for me to communicate with him. I have feelings in my heart, but I feel like I cannot talk to him about ·

them. That is why I miss my grandmother so much. She always listened to me and cared about what I was saying. She made everything easier for me because she was willing to help me with anything that I was stressed about. She helped me with school, chores, and personal problems. She helped me so much, and now I am struggling without her.

When I get lonely I find myself wondering how my life would be in China and how, if I still lived there, I would see my grandma. I try to go back and visit her as much as I can. When I do have the chance to visit her, I always go shopping with her. One time when we were shopping, we saw clothes that were fun and pretty. The modern and contemporary looks were new and unusual for my grandma, so it gave us something to talk about. When we lived together, we would also go to buy food, like vegetables, fruit, meat, and drinks. When we finished picking out what we were going to cook, we would go home and she would cook for me. I would just sit outside of the kitchen and wait for my delicious food to come. Actually, I would want to go help her, but my grandma knows I don't know how to cook. I would just be in the way if I were in the kitchen with her because she is such a better cook than I am. One time she let me cut the onions, and I just cried. When I cried, my Grandma laughed and wiped my tears with her sleeve.

We also love to watch TV together, especially the movies from Korea because they are so romantic. Although the movies are romantic, there are many sad parts which would make me and my grandmother cry. There are funny parts in the movies as well that made us laugh too. When the movies were over, we would talk about them together. I would make comments about the main character in the movie being so pretty, but then I would say things like, "Why did she always marry the ugly guy? That's so disgusting, far from perfect." When I said that, my grandma just laughed at me. She did not even say anything back to me.

When we watch action movies, she gets so excited. When a person in the movie falls from a mountain, she makes little sounds like "wah, oh!" My sister, aunt and I would laugh at her because her little sounds make it seem like she is in the movie herself. She gets so into the movie that she starts to believe that it is real. We even talk about the celebrities and know about their lives. We gossip about all the latest things that happen around them. We love to laugh together, and we joke around a lot. My grandmother and I always laugh together and cry together when we watch the romantic movies. I think that my grandmother and I do many things together that young people usually do not do with their grandparents. This is the reason for us being so close. She is always willing to spend time with me, and I love that about her. I hope to live with my grandma again because I miss her so much.

Because I have a very good relationship with my grandma, I do not understand why people would not respect their grandparents. For example, in China, there are many kids who live with their grandparents who are very disrespectful to them. It may be because some young people do not have a good relationship with their grandparents. I have a friend in China who once told me she hated her grandma because her grandma always said hurtful things to her whenever she did something wrong. Her grandma did not really take the time to teach her how to do the right thing; instead, she would just be violent.

To understand this situation, you have to know that boys and girls are unequal in China. The boys are favored so much more than the girls. Because of this, my friend struggled with the relationship that she had with her grandmother. Her grandmother would hit her with anything that she could reach and would say the meanest things to her. It is so sad because they did not have a relationship together at all. The girl hated her grandmother, and the grandmother did not seem to love the girl at all. I am so thankful that my grandma was different from her grandma. When I did something wrong, my grandma would talk to me, and she would try to let me understand how to do the right thing. Some kids are like me; they love their grandparents and they would do anything to show their grandparents that they love them. That is how I am with my grandmother. I would do anything for her because I love her. I wish that more people would respect their grandparents because youth have so much to learn from them, and grandparents do not live forever.

I remember one time I was disrespectful with my grandma. My grandma felt my mom didn't love her. I was eleven years old, and my grandmother still slept with me. One night I was watching TV with my mom, and my mom said jokingly that my grandmother could not sleep with me because the bed in my room belonged to my mother. The next day, after my grandmother slept with me, I repeated what my mom said to me the night before. After I told my grandmother that she could not sleep with me in my bed, my grandma felt hurt and got very angry. This created a huge argument between my mother and my grandmother. They were yelling, and my mother was crying while she was arguing with my grandma. Then my mother knelt down beside my grandmother and held her hand to ask for forgiveness. My grandmother, however, was still mad at her, and she strongly said, "You don't have to kneel to me." In my culture, when you kneel down to someone it means that they are already dead. My grandmother understood this as my mother feeling like she wanted my grandmother dead, but this was not true. My mother just wanted to ask for forgiveness. During this time I was so scared because I felt like I was responsible for disrespecting both of them. After, I felt like it was wrong to have repeated what my mother said to my grandmother. If I had never told my grandmother that my mom did not want her to sleep in the bed with me, none of this would have happened. I felt that I disrespected my grandmother by making her feel hurt.

I also do some things to make my grandma happy, and she knows I love her. When I first came to the United States, I talked to my grandma on the phone and cried. I don't know why, but when I heard her voice, I just wanted to cry. She knew that she was going to cry with me. She didn't want me to know that, so she tried to talk to me in an ordinary way, but I heard her voice had changed.

In China, it is traditional for young people to love to be with their grandmas when they have the chance. I have little understanding of why the Chinese kids born here don't like their grandparents so much. I think maybe it is because they don't speak the same language. The grandparents don't speak English because they are immigrants, so the grandchildren don't talk too much with them. The grandparents care about their grand-children, but the language barrier stands in the way. The Chinese kids who were born here sometimes don't know how to treat their grandparents.

I feel relationships are different here than in China. For example, I have a Chinese friend who was born in the United States. I asked her how her relationship was with her grandparents, and she said not very good because she didn't talk to them a lot because her Chinese was so bad. She did not speak Chinese in her daily life. Sometimes I see the grandparents in this country taking care of children who are six to ten years of age. In China, the grandparent and the grandchild shop together, and they do things together like friends. Because I haven't seen grandparents shop-ping with their grandchildren, it doesn't mean grandchildren don't re-spect their grandparents. Maybe they just don't know how to have a good relationship with them. I think they should spend more time talking to their grandparents because I know if you talk to them, they'll be so happy. A friend relationship with the grandparents will make the grandchildren happy too.

When I first came to this country, my grandma told me I should find a job and get more experience. My friend told me there was a job work-ing with senior citizens at a place called Youth Cares Intergenerational. I didn't know whether or not to apply for this job. I thought to myself that I have a good relationship with my grandma and my grandma taught me I have to be responsible. This would be the first time I would have to be responsible at a job.

I got hired working with the seniors, and when I first walked into the senior room, I felt so shy and afraid. I had not met many senior citizens, and I saw them sitting there and looking at me. At that moment, I wanted to leave because I didn't know how to talk to them and have a good rela-tionship with them. But when I started becoming shy, an old man walked close to me. We call him Mr. Kao. He talked to me so nicely, and he told me something about how to get along with the senior citizens. Even though he's an old man he reminds me of my grandma, because my grandma always talks to me nicely. He told me so many details about how to talk to seniors, like understanding what they need and trying to make them happy. He told me he understood how I was feeling at that time because he knows many young people go there like me, and they feel shy and nervous. The next time I went there, I talked to the seniors and tried to understand what they needed. I tried and tried to spend more time getting to know them. Now, I never feel nervous and shy when I stand in front of them because they know me. Mr. Kao told me I'm doing very well, and I thank him so much because he taught me many things. Now, when I go in the room, we are just like a family. When Mr. Kao tells a joke, they smile and I smile. I told my grandma about it, and she said, "Now you have many grandparents."

Even though I have many grandparents here, I still miss my grandma. I wish I could go back to China soon to see my grandma.

My grandma is truly my friend. I go shopping with her, I watch TV with her, I cook with her, and, when I feel like I am struggling, I talk to her as if she is my best friend. She really cares about me and wants to make sure that I am doing all right. She is so special because she loves me unconditionally. To her, it doesn't matter if I am a boy or a girl. She would still loves me the same. That is why my story is so important. I want people to understand how to respect their grandparents, or any elders that care, because these people are so important to us. Sometimes we take these people for granted, just as I did with my grandmother. I didn't realize how much she meant to me until I moved away from her. Everything became more difficult without her by my side. So now I ask you to pay attention to people in your life who matter to you. Make sure you respect them, form a good relationship with them, and never take them for granted.

EN ESE MOMENTO/
IN THAT MOMENT

Ruth Velasquez

Ever since I was ten years old, I always felt a fear that I couldn't control. My fear was that something would happen, and I would never be able to see my parents or anyone in my family ever again. I had this fear because of something I saw happen to my friend's family. This fear stuck with me, every moment of every day. My real problem was my family and trying to finish my studies.

When I was growing up, I dreamt about going to college, and I wanted to make this dream a reality. My fear was strong because I always thought my parents might change their minds and not let me pursue my dream, which I knew in my heart could come true. It was what I was expecting because of what I saw in my friend's situation. Her father was a violent drunk and the epitome of evil for her family. I was afraid that my life would end up just like my friend's, with me dropping out of school and not having the chance to go to college. But my dad is not that kind of person. I said to myself, "Trust yourself and think positively. The fear is not impossible to control."

In the beginning, I thought that I wouldn't be able to control my fear, but I just took a deep breath and told myself that my parents are unique in this world and that they would support me so that my dreams can come true. I took the right road by coming to the United States, and now I am trying to follow my dreams and support myself. Through this experience with my friend, I am learning more about life and how important it is to trust yourself, *en ese momento.*

Now my goals are giving me a new direction in life. Making a life choice is difficult because we never know where our decision will take us, and obstacles tend to arise. Once I get over one obstacle, another one gets in my way. When I decided to come to the United States, I knew it was the right road, but I didn't think about all the dilemmas I would have to deal with.

I say all of this because a few months ago, I thought about leaving my uncle's house to live by myself. I did this when he was telling me what to do with my life. I believed that I would be able to live a better life on my own because I did not like someone discouraging me from my goal of going to college. He just did it because he wants me to do everything right and not make mistakes in life that one day I will regret. I didn't pay attention to him. Instead I just got mad and said, "You are not my father to talk to me in that way." I wanted to leave his house and go away to live with friends or see where I could live well and without restrictions. My uncle was really angry with me. He said, "You don't appreciate anything I am doing for you. It is to make your dreams true." Even though he told me all that, I didn't care; I just wanted go somewhere else.

My uncle and I have not had a good relationship since I got to the United States. In the beginning, my uncle and I had all these disagreements. He didn't understand me or even try to. His opinion was that I didn't respect him enough to obey his rules or hear his advice. However, if I didn't follow his rules or advice, it was because I felt there was no good reason to. I was doing everything he said, but he didn't see it that way because he thought that I didn't take things seriously. For example, he said, "Perhaps you decided to come to the United State just for an adventure and not to be useful." He said that because my first grades at school were really low, but I was confused because he knew that I came to the United States without knowing any English.

Then he said in an angry voice, "I offered to bring you to this country to make your dreams come true, so you could reach all your goals in life, not just to visit different places. But now I am seeing that you are not really interested in it because your grades are not good enough make me see that you care about it." Then I told him that it was not my fault that I didn't know English and didn't really understand what the homework was about. The tests were not easy for me to do because I didn't understand what the questions were asking, but I told him that I would do my best to get the grades up. He just said, "Oh, yeah right." I could tell by his voice and his face that he really meant to say, "I don't believe you." When he said that, I felt angry and really mad at him. I started acting rebellious towards everybody, even my parents. I felt that my parents were part of my problems and that it was their fault because they let me come to the United States so young. But they didn't force me to come to the United States. Ultimately, it was my own decision.

I came to the United States when I was fifteen years old and I wasn't completely sure if I really wanted to come in the first place. I made my decision in approximately three weeks. I made my decision because my uncle talked to me about better opportunities that I could have in this country. I moved to the United States from Honduras where my family, friends, and my hometown were. That is where I spent my childhood with all the kids that grew up like me, playing soccer in the streets, going to after-school programs, and just hanging out at each others' houses.

Another thing I left behind was my school. I was studying in a private high school that I really liked, but I decided to leave it. My parents were not in agreement with me leaving it and they were mad at me because they thought I had no reason to come here. They didn't see that I would have a lot of opportunities.

After I arrived in the United States, I regretted not following my parents' advice. It was not easy living far from my parents. When I got to my uncle's house, I felt strange because I didn't know him at all. My uncle was taken to Belize by my grandfather when he was younger and never saw much of the family. However, he made trips to Honduras, so I was able to see him then, even though he did not come down very often. From the few times I saw him, I knew that my uncle was a nice and friendly man, and that's why I decided to come to the United States and accepted his help to get into this country.

I was very excited and happy about moving to the United States because I knew that if I did well, I would go far and triumph in life. My first months in school were difficult because I didn't understand anything in English, and most of the students didn't understand me. Even the teachers didn't understand me. Everyone around me talked in English, so I felt alone and lost because I didn't know what anyone was talking about. I told myself it was a lack of respect on their part because they knew that I didn't speak English, and they didn't try to understand me. I did everything I could to learn fast and get good grades so that I could do well and succeed when I got older.

It was hard learning English at first, but I applied myself and worked hard by watching movies, cartoons, and reading books in English. I started working hard to get my grades up and gradually, I started to learn how to write, read and understand English. I did that to make my uncle see that I cared about my studies. After five or six months, I could write, read, and understand a little more of what my teachers talked about in the classroom.

Besides all this, I learned how to help other students with homework that they didn't understand. I tried to help students who also didn't speak English. I started doing all my homework and brought up my grades. I put all my efforts into school and focused in class so I could do well in the quizzes. I didn't want to disappoint my uncle with my studies or my attitude. I did my best to make him feel proud and make myself proud too.

Since I started studying in a different language, I learned that it is not easy to do everything right. You have to struggle with the assignments and homework. My experience on the first days at school in this country made me understand everybody else better and taught me to help other students feel comfortable and equal.

When new students came to class, I tried to help them because I knew that it was not easy being new and unable to speak English. In class, I would translate what the teacher was saying in order to make the new students feel comfortable, and I would even help them with their homework after school. The new students and I would work in groups. Even if they didn't speak Spanish, I still tried to help them learn English. All of this helped me to improve my studies and get good grades. I wanted my uncle to be proud of me because he brought me into his home and to see that I really cared about my education and the opportunities it will allow me to have.

Unfortunately, my uncle didn't see it that way. I felt that he didn't want me to be in school. I told myself that he didn't care about me. He basically said, "You are in school all day, but now you're going to stop school and start working. It is time to think about how you're going to be responsible and independent. It is time for you to start paying rent. I know that you are in school, but it is not a problem because you just can drop out of school and be done. Then you can start working to get everything you need to keep going. Furthermore, I do not believe that your studies are important enough to not be able to leave them."

What made everything even worse was the fact that my uncle not only wanted me to quit my studies, but he also wanted me to quit the soccer team, which was my hobby. He told me that I had to quit because my grades were bad and that I needed to focus on working and paying rent. Unfortunately, I quit the soccer team. I was so upset that I had to quit during the playoffs, especially as we were getting closer and closer to the championship round. I didn't understand because my uncle initially told me that he wanted me to be involved in after-school activities and programs. I wondered why he told me be more involved in school, but then changed his mind and told me to quit. Quitting the team was difficult, but my uncle did not give me a choice. After quitting the soccer team, I felt sad because I had to give up something I truly loved, but I also felt equally angry that my uncle would make such a decision for me.

In reality he is not that kind of person. I know he wants me to study and stay in school. When he brought me to the United States, he told my parents not to worry because he was going to help me. Well, I have his support, but sometimes I feel that he doesn't care any more about me. That's why I disrespect his advice and break his rules.

It was not his intention to ask me for rent, but he did it because my attitude made him think that I should work and not go to school. He thought this because my grades were bad and I always said, "I can't do it." Finally he decided: She doesn't want to improve so she is not going to school anymore. He didn't say it, but I saw it in his face.

After I saw that, I just turned around and walked to my room. When I got to my room, I laid down in my bed, and my father's words came to my mind: "Where there's a will, there's a way; the impossible can be possible if you see it in the positive way." *En ese momento*, I decided that I was not going to live by myself. I realized that living on my own would bring about more dilemmas, but I also told myself that I would not give up on my dream of going to college. I would not drop out of school like my uncle wanted but would continue with my studies. With my father's words echoing in my mind, I got up and told my uncle that I was going to take things more seriously, especially my studies, without worrying that English was difficult. My dad's words helped me to continue and to change my character with my uncle. I promised myself to be a different girl, one who was going to make people feel proud and happy.

I went to my uncle's room to speak with him about all the things that I did wrong, for being a rebellious girl and disrespecting him when he gave me advice about my life. I felt bad because whenever he was mad at me I always answered him with, "Who are you to tell me what to do? You are not my father." I understand now that my uncle had his reasons because I was under his responsibility, so he had to make sure that everything was going right.

After I talked with my uncle, I recognized what was important to me. Not only did I want to keep studying in school and get good grades, but I wanted to be more involved with people at school. I didn't want to just think about myself. I wanted to start thinking about others and not only be a better friend to those in my life, but to make new friends, too.

I decided to try out again for the soccer team that my uncle had made me quit the year before. Since I made the team, I had the wonderful opportunity of going to a summer soccer camp. The camp taught me many useful techniques that helped improve my soccer skills. Had I not taken a stand against my uncle, I would not have had this opportunity to do what I love. Now I am a starting forward and mid-fielder for my soccer team even though I took that one year off. Not only am I a better soccer player, I have also become a better friend to all of my teammates. Being on a team has shown me that we cannot always do things on our own but need the support of others as well. Recognizing this, I have made it a point to think about those around me and lend a helping hand whenever it is needed.

Now that I have gotten through these struggles, I want to be a benevolent person to everyone. I don't want to be an instigator or act like a kid. These lessons really stuck with me because my story makes me understand how valorous it is to show others respect. Respect makes your life and others' lives easier because it avoids problems and helps build relationships with everybody who is of a different race, color, or personality. I hope that now I can be an honest person with everyone. I will struggle to succeed and not let myself down again.

THE REAL LIFE OF IMMIGRANTS

Karla Poot-Polanco

Illegal immigration of poor people to developed countries has become a serious problem in the world. The quality of life in the home countries of immigrants and in their new countries is very different. They can't find jobs in their native countries which is the reason they go to new countries. Once in the new country, it is difficult for them to return to their home country.

Countless people die when they try to cross the borders, and the lucky ones become illegal immigrants in America. Often, they never even get to return to their families.

There is a noticeable distinction between the rich and poor, especially in a nation where the economy is an issue. In countries where a majority of people are poor, more people tend to risk their lives for a better future. The poor decide to go to another country to give their families a better life.

They are going to cross the borders again and again because they think first about their families, not about themselves. They do not care if they die when trying to cross the borders. They only care about their families. Should the developed countries feel responsible after they send the illegal immigrants back to their own countries, causing major risk to those immigrants' lives since they will keep trying to cross the border again? What is the fundamental solution for the illegal immigration of the poor people?

The solution is to have work available in their home countries. If immigrants have work in their countries, they wouldn't need to cross borders to go to another place. They can stay with their families, and they can give them something that they never had in their lives. Sometimes this is the reason why people decide to go to other countries.

They are only illegal immigrants from the perspective of the developed nation, where the people don't need to go to other places because they have work in their own countries. However, illegal immigrants are escaping from the endless poverty in their own nations. The developed nation should have a just attitude to help the weaknesses in other lands, to help illegal immigrants return to their countries with joy and hope, not with sorrow and pain. That will be the true way to solve the problem of illegal immigration. Instead, the United States forces illegal immigrants to return to their own country. Developed nations need to understand the inefficiency of the education, work, housing, and social welfare system, and the lack of opportunities that the illegal immigrants face. Just as the healthy help the sick and the strong protect the weak, the rich should help the poor. Helping immigrants even though they are illegal is true globalization. Some might have dreams of being rich, however the majority only expects to find any type of work and does not hesitate to take three jobs to earn a living. Immigrants work as hard or harder than the people who were born in developed countries, because they know what they want for their lives. They have to work hard, not just for themselves and for joy, but also for their families.

Immigrants have dignity. They want to protect their homes and families. It's how they show the world what they can do. They always try to help one another if they can. They feel like wealthy people. Some of the rich people try to help because they know how they feel.

Immigrants have humility. Humility is when someone does not think that he or she is better or more important than others. They don't need to be something that they aren't. They are just themselves. They try to do their best for their families. People around the world migrate to achieve their dreams because they believe in the possibilities of a better life in a new place.

Immigrants have dreams. They want to make their dreams come true. Every person in the world has a dream. Immigrants have to do different things if they want their dreams to come true. One of the dreams of immigrants is to work, earn money, and return to their countries to be with their families again. People around the world cross borders to start their dreams because they believe in the possibility of a better life in a new place. Even though immigrants cannot ensure their future well-being in the new land, they are not only willing to risk their lives on a dangerous journey, but also are willing to keep attempting the dangerous journey to cross borders into developed nations.

These are some examples of what immigrants do when they come to this country. In the United States, they demonstrate that they are able to get what they want, to help each other in this country, and to do their best to get an education. Immigrants don't have the same opportunities in school; that's why they need to work harder. Parents work to help their children. They feel proud about their children. Kids should accomplish what their parents didn't in their countries. Immigration means becoming someone, showing that anything is possible if you want it. Immigrants realize that education is the key that opens many doors.

Some immigrants don't have their own place to live. They live in small apartments that they share with other people. They take any job they can get, even in the fields, because they just want to work. Field jobs are very dangerous; people can die doing them. Some immigrants work cleaning houses. Some immigrants make their dreams come true with help or without it. They do their best for their families and for themselves. When they move to the new country they feel worried because they don't know if they will be able to see their families again, and they do not know what the new country has in store for their future. They don't know if they will ever go back to their county, or if they will see their families again, or if they will be the same people who left their country, or if their lives are going to change forever.

Like other immigrants, my friend Andrea came here with her mother to lead a better life. There was hardly any work in Mexico, and she hoped that once she was here she would be able to find work. She told me about her dangerous journey to the United States. Her father was already here, but he was in the United States illegally and had no way to bring them together. She and her mother had to pay a coyote, a person who illegally brings others to the States.

Once she was in the United States she had trouble finding a job, but she continued to search for one so that she could afford to have the rest of her family, especially her grandmother, join her in the United States. She worried that she would never see her grandmother again because of her age. She had difficulty finding a job, and a year passed before she got one. Once she had a job and began to save money, her grandmother passed away.

Life in the United States was difficult, and eventually she and her mother returned to Mexico. They had saved up a little bit of money and used this money to open a little market. By coming to the United States, Andrea was able to save enough money to return to her country to make a living. If her country had a program to help the poor, Andrea would not have had to risk her life to get enough money to survive.

HELPFUL

Van Tran

San Francisco is a big city. It is large, modern, developed, noisy, and busy. Within the city, a person can see big buildings and many cars in the streets. Almost all San Francisco residents drive their cars to work or take the bus, MUNI, or BART. You see people on the streets with different skin colors talking in different languages. There are African Americans, Mexicans, Chinese, Filipinos, Vietnamese, and many others. This mix of people represents different cultures, customs, and habits. With so many people from other countries coming to the city, San Francisco is a lot more diverse than my town in Vietnam.

The town where I came from had only a few cars. The people travelled mostly by motorbikes and bicycles. People walked on the streets to relax and have fun with friends. In my town, most of the people were Vietnamese and spoke the same Vietnamese language. San Francisco is very different.

When I came to San Francisco on May 9, 2007, everything was new to me. I was afraid because the people were taller and bigger than in my country. I was worried because I did not know enough English. That was a big problem for me, but I felt excited that I could meet different kinds of people and learn about different cultures.

That summer, on a cold and brisk Saturday afternoon, I was waiting to cross the street. I was standing on the corner of Mason and Eddy Street downtown near the shopping mall. A lot of people were there to shop, play, and hang out with their friends. I heard a loud siren. A fire truck with flashing lights was trying to get down the street. There were lots of cars in the street blocking the fire truck.

An old woman was standing next to me. She also wanted to cross the street like me. She must have been at least eighty years old. She was small and had a hunchback, which was bigger than her because she was so small. She was pushing a cart holding a black trash bag full of old water bottles, soda cans, and glass bottles. There were also lots of old newspapers in the cart, which made it very heavy. The weight of the cart made it difficult for the old woman to push it across the street. It was taking her a long time, and the green light only lasted thirteen seconds. There were lots of cars in the street going very fast. It was dangerous for the old woman to cross the street because she was moving so slowly.

I wanted to help her cross the street. However, I thought about something my uncle had told me the night before during dinner: "Do not talk to or help old people you do not know on the street if they don't need your help. Maybe you will have problems later." That meant that some people who do not have a home, money, or a job might sue you. They might say, "Why did you hit me?" even if you did not hit them, or, "Why did you touch me?" even if you did not touch them. My uncle said that in the United States, no one has a right to touch someone else without permission. This is an easy way to get money. My uncle was worried that I might get into this kind of trouble. I was new here and did not understand. In my town in Vietnam, every person was kind to others. I did not have to think about helping someone. I just did it.

But in San Francisco it is different. When I remembered what my uncle said to me, I did not know what to do. I saw the old woman having a hard time, and I was not worried about what my uncle said. I went to her and said, "May I help you?" and smiled. She smiled, too, and said, "You are so nice." With one hand I held her hand to guide her. With the other hand I pushed the heavy laundry cart across the street. It was a good thing that I helped her because the light turned red right when we reached the other side of the street. She smiled and said, "Thank you." That feeling was good. I said "bye" to her and continued my walk. In my mind I was thinking about my uncle worrying about me. I knew he was a good guy, and I wanted him to know helping people is not bad. When you do good things to help other people, you shouldn't have to worry about getting into trouble. We should all help each other and make the world a better place.

Helping the old lady made me feel good, but the feeling did not last.

On the first day I came to Mission High School, I saw so many people from different countries talking in different languages. I was scared and worried about my limited English. I could not find one person who could speak Vietnamese. On that day, my first class was history. I met my history teacher, Ms. Rodriguez, and she was very nice. She introduced herself to me and told me to sit on the chair to wait for the bell to ring. The class-room was big, clean, organized, and full of books. The desks were arranged in one big circle. In my country, the classrooms were small and barren. We did not have many books or supplies. The desks were arranged in neat rows, not one big circle.

I looked around the classroom. People were talking together and laughing. Some were speaking English. They were so good and talked so fast and fluently. I tried to listen to them when they talked but felt sad because I did not understand what they were talking about.

I saw two girls and one boy who looked Vietnamese. I hoped and wished that they would be Vietnamese so that I could become friends with them. I wanted someone to talk to in history class. When class started, all of the students in class needed to introduce themselves. Some people were from Mexico, some people were from China, some people were from Brazil, some people were from other countries. The Latino people could speak the same language, Spanish. No one was from Vietnam. It was only me. The three people who I thought were Vietnamese turned out to be Filipino. I was disappointed because no one spoke Vietnamese.

I sat alone and tried to listen to the history teacher and the other students. However, I only understood about one third of what they said. It was hard for me because English was not my main language. I felt sad and wanted to cry. I blamed myself. Why had I not learned more English and practiced it in my country? If I had learned more English back then, I would have been able to understand when people talked. I could also talk with them, not only listen to them.

After that class, I made friends with the Filipino girls and boy because we had another class together. Their English was good. They could speak fluently. They were considerate with me. They spoke English very slowly or made the action to let me know what they meant. However, I could not understand everything, because my English was limited. They said, "Why don't you respond when we talk?" I could only answer them with simple English words. I said, "My English is not good and you would not understand what I am saying." They smiled and said, "It does not matter, we are friends."

I felt shy and worried when I pronounced English wrong. They could not know, and some words I did not know. That's why I needed to find more words in the dictionary, but that would take time. When I hung out with my new friends, I listened more than talked. The Filipino kids were very kind. They knew my problems with English. They helped me with new vocabulary words so that I could understand them. They helped to edit my essay before I gave it to the teacher. They made me feel like I was their real friend. The friendship was marvelous. I wanted to make my friends happy and I wished other people would make them happy, too. Naturally, I learned more English from them when they talked with me. They were my second teachers at school.

Then, last September, I started going to the Vietnamese Youth Development Center (VYDC), a community organization that helps immigrants like me. (I learned about it from my sister's friend.) I have been going to the center for about a year now, and the people there help me a lot. I am very thankful to all the people who work at VYDC. I am able to speak my own language there and have other people understand. Half of the workers are Vietnamese. I have met a lot of new people at VYDC because I can speak Vietnamese with them. It feels good. It is the same feeling you get when you have not seen your friends for a long time and get to see them again.

VYDC also has many activities for immigrants like me. They have tutoring to help people who do not know English. They can translate to let you know what a word means in Vietnamese or help you do homework. I am lucky.

Before, when I went to school, I had a lot more homework to do. The teacher gave us homework and we needed to finish it at home, then bring it to class if you wanted credit for that period. I felt terrible because my homework was all in English. I read it for a long time but did not understand. I would go to the Vietnamese Youth Development Center and ask them to help me with my homework. I went there every day after school when I had homework. They helped me translate the words I did not understand. They told me to memorize new vocabulary that would help me understand the homework. They helped me fix my essays when the grammar was not correct, and they would correct it with me. They taught me how to pronounce hard words. We went to some places in San Francisco that were interesting, such as Water World, biking, camping in the mountains, and so on. I learned a lot of things when I went with them and had fun. I wanted to help the person who had already helped me. Or, I would help someone who needed me to help. People who help others have close relationships and will make the world become a better place. They make me want to help others. People who help other people have a wonderful life.

In the summer, I also worked at the Boys and Girls Club in the Tenderloin. That was my first job since I had come to San Francisco. After school I went to work. The Boys and Girls Club was interesting: all the kids were different ages, almost all were born here, and everyone spoke English fluently. It was hard for me because I needed to talk and play with them, but my English was not good. I told my supervisor that, and he said,

"You need to learn English. The best way I improved my English was when I talked with all the kids." He was from Cambodia. I tried it, but sometimes when I talked it was so hard to pronounce some English words. My job at the Boys and Girls Club was cleaning things, reading books with the kids, and playing with them. If they wanted to buy something outside or go to the Learning Center, my job was to protect them on the street (because the Learning Center and Main Club are one, but in different places—one block away). I was happy working there. Every person there was kind and funny. They helped me with everything I did not know. It was the first job to give me experience because I had never worked before.

In the year and a half that I have lived in San Francisco, I have learned that helping people is a wonderful thing. I realize that I should try and help people instead of worrying about getting sued. A lot of people have helped me since I came here. My Filipino friends helped me feel welcome. VYDC helped me with my homework and gave me a place to go after school to meet people like me. And the people at the Boys and Girls Club helped me learn how to work with children. I am very thankful to all of the people who have helped me. I want to help other people who need my help like the old woman did.

DOING SOMETHING YOU SHOULDN'T DO IN THE FIRST PLACE

Don Pacia

There is a culture of disrespect among youth because of the way that youth try to get respect—by making other people afraid of them. I have been doing something for years, knowing it was disrespectful. It is something that I can't get out of my mind, something that is wrong. I don't really know why I did it, but eventually I realized that it was something that I shouldn't be doing.

Every day I hear my alarm buzzing so loud, I know that I should get up. I am still tired from doing my homework the night before, so I get up slowly, feeling my back ache. I still want to go back and lie down, but I know that if I waste some more time I will miss the J-train, which I usually take at 7 AM from Balboa Park to school. Every morning it is so cold that people tend to stand together in one place to make themselves comfortable and warm. I catch the train at the first stop, therefore the train is empty.

As the train gradually gets closer to town, more passengers board it. Riding on the J-train is the same every morning. Most of the time I smell the nice aroma of coffee from people who are drinking it on their way to work. I hear students screaming and playing with each other, babies crying because they want to be carried by their moms, some people shouting from the back because they want the door to open or the driver didn't stop at their stop, and loud music blaring from iPods.

Every time I take a seat on the train, I go to the back of it and put my legs and feet on the next seat. I do it all the time because I saw some teenagers do it—which I thought was cool—even though I knew it wasn't right. Like many of us, when I want to relate to other people, I do what they do. If my friends wear saggy jeans, then I have to wear saggy jeans. If I don't do it, I could get left alone. On the train, some people who want to sit will stand instead of sitting in that seat with my feet on it. Young people won't sit on it unless I offer it to them because they're scared or shy or they don't speak English that well. Old people will say in a respectful way, "Excuse me, may I take a seat?" When an old person has said that to me, I have taken my feet down and moved.

As I was thinking, looking at people jogging, some walking their dogs, others eating their breakfast in a café, I saw a dad with two daughters. One girl was on his arm and the other was holding his hand. They were running, trying to catch up with the train. Good thing they were able to get in before the door closed because the next train might be a while. The dad was a white man who was maybe thirty-five years old and was wearing a suit for work. He was holding his daughters' lunch boxes and his briefcase. The two daughters were maybe around five and six years old and looked alike. They were arguing with their dad. The oldest one was mad because the younger one was being carried, and she wanted to be carried also because she was tired. The dad wanted to find a seat where all three of them could sit, but there weren't any more seats because the train was full of passengers. They decided to move to the back of the train.

As I saw them walking to the back, I felt something, as if I cared for him. He was having a hard time carrying the one kid and hurrying and carrying the lunch boxes. I had seen him every morning for about two months being brought to the train stop by a lady who I think was his wife because the kids had black hair like hers. I saw them standing in front of me, and I wanted to give them my seat because I knew that they needed it more than I did. When I offered it, I stood and said, "Would you want to sit?" He said in reply, "Sure," and as they sat he smiled at me, and then his older daughter said, "Thank you." That simple thanks placed a smile on my face and made me really proud of myself, knowing that what I did was right. I knew that not everybody could do the simple thing that I did—which can make a big difference. After that I stood thinking of the problems that dad may have faced. Maybe he didn't have enough time to spend with his daughters because of his work or maybe because he had trouble doing house chores on his own. Or maybe he went to sleep late because he had to help his kids do their homework and then do stuff for work and then wake up to prepare his daughters' breakfast and lunch and get them ready for school. As I got off the train, I watched them as it moved slowly away. At school I found myself still thinking about the good deed that I did that would stay with me all day. I wondered if my act stayed with the man through his day as well. I hope that it made his day less stressful or put him in a better mood. Or maybe it left a good impression on his daughters, or maybe they were wondering if they should do the same thing some day.

I am telling this story because it happens differently all the time. A teenager doesn't respect someone who is older than them and doesn't think that person needs something more than they do. Some people do have the integrity to do things that are best for themselves and for others, such as respecting their elders, but they just have to let it out. Most people can't do that because they are shy and still aren't outgoing or some are just raised like that and have never been taught manners by their parents.

When something disrespectful happens, sometimes I want to change it. It always sticks with me, because I regret putting my feet on that seat, and I wanted to do the right thing. Deciding whether to do the right thing wasn't easy for me; it took me a month to realize that I shouldn't have my feet up when someone needs it. Everyone knows that if a person does something wrong, it is never too late to change and do the right thing.

When I knew that what I did was wrong, I realized that we human beings should be kind to others in order to receive kindness from others. I think it works like that because when someone sees someone do something nice, they might want to do it too. A small thing can make a big difference. Other people sometimes choose to receive, which is most likely rude and unacceptable for others. But we can't force someone to do something they don't want to do. In time they realize that what they did was wrong, and then they learn from their mistakes. Realizing our mistakes isn't a simple thing to accomplish because sometimes we need someone to let us know whether what we're doing is right or wrong. If I was with someone who I noticed is not respectful or thoughtful, I would gladly talk to them about what they're doing wrong.

Friends are the ones that are always there for us; they are the first ones who let us realize our mistakes. There have been times that I have let them know that they should have done the right thing, and there have been times that they have let me know as well. Once when my friend and I were on our way home, a pregnant lady was standing beside me. I didn't notice her because I was listening to my iPod and I was staring out the window. When my friend saw that there was a pregnant lady standing beside me, she immediately tapped me and told me to offer that seat to that lady. Then I apologized to the pregnant lady for not noticing her. She smiled and said, "Thank you."

We should be kind to other people to receive kindness from them. It's not like if you found someone's important belonging, then you give it back to the rightful owner and expect them to reward you with money. If you did the right thing you should not expect something else from them. Some people don't want to give something to others unless something is given back to them, like if you found a missing pet or maybe you found a purse in some place and you wouldn't return it unless someone posted a missing sign with a reward. You should only be happy because you did what you think is right. Receiving kindness from someone doesn't really happen all the time, but it is still better to do something good for others even though you don't expect something back from them. Like what I did offering my seat to the dad with two daughters and the pregnant lady. I might someday be rewarded; maybe when I am the one who needs it, someone will offer their seat to me. Or maybe some day when I'm trying to cross the street with my cane on my right hand and the other hand on my back and in need of someone to walk with to the opposite side of the street, a kind, strong-hearted kid might see me and help me.

Last week, after I had been writing this essay for weeks, I was sitting on the train with my feet on the seat next to me. A guy popped out from nowhere and said, "May I please take a seat?" I placed my feet down and said, "Sure." I was surprised because I didn't expect him to ask me to move over since there were still a lot of vacant seats and there weren't that many people on the train. Still he decided to sit next to me. This happened because I wasn't that scary; I was decent, and he had the courage to ask me something that a simple person would not ask all the time.

A GOOD TEACHER
Kelvin Funes Gomez

I want to tell you a story about how thankful I am for all the things that Ms. Ramirez did when she was my teacher. I am not going to forget her easily even though she moved. Why? Because she was a good person and a good teacher. I am telling you my opinion and at the same time, a story that my friends and I will pass on to you. If somebody reads this, they will know that she is a good person and I hope that she continues teaching the way that she did when she taught at Mission High School.

I remember when we went to Yosemite Park and how Ms. Ramirez helped my friends and me. She was always showing us the way that we had to go. She and the Yosemite workers guided us. I think that if she wasn't there, maybe we would have gotten lost. Or maybe we could have found the way to go, but it would have been harder. With her there, the place was easier to find. For example, one day we went on a walk into the forest and later we went to a cave. The cave was tiny. We were ten students, and we all had to go in there. But to go into the cave we had to guide the students who were behind us. Leading was hard to do but when all the people were in the middle of the cave, the Yosemite workers turned on a candle and the cave looked wonderful. There was only one rock in the cave and behind that rock there was an abyss. But we were happy because we were in the middle of the cave and we stayed there for ten minutes talking about how cool the cave was.

When I broke up with my girlfriend (I was going out with another girl at the same time), Ms. Ramirez called me to go out of the room because she wanted to talk to me. She asked me what was happening and I told her the truth. Ms. Ramirez said that it was not good to play with the feelings of other people. I told her that she was right. I told her that I would try to talk with my girlfriend. I spoke with my girlfriend and I asked her if she could forgive me and she told me yes, because she really loved me and that she was going to forgive me, but that was going to be the last time. That was nice of Ms. Ramirez.

We miss Ms. Ramirez because she was a good teacher and because when somebody had a problem, she tried to help us. She did what she could. For example, one day I had a problem with my mom. Ms. Ramirez knew that I had a problem, but at that time she wasn't my teacher anymore. She saw me in the hallway and she told me that she wanted to talk to me. We started to talk and when I saw her face I thought that she was mad, and she asked me how I was doing in my classes and how my family was. I explained to her about my classes and then she asked me how I was doing at my home.

I was not living at my house, I was living in San Leandro with my uncles, and I told her about the problems with my family. I was mad at my mom but also sad for her, because I knew she was sad that I was not at home. But still I was really mad at my mom. She was always listening to my stepfather and doing what he told her to do.

He makes almost all of the problems that I have with my mom. For example, one of my friends asked me if I want to go to Las Vegas with him and his soccer team friends. They were going to have a game there. I talked to my mom and asked her to let me go and she said yes. But the next day in the afternoon, she came to my room and she told me that I was not going to Las Vegas anymore. She told me I have to go with my stepfather to the city to do a job, and he told her this because he didn't want me to go to Las Vegas.

Ms. Ramirez told me that I have to understand my mom, and I said I was going to try to talk to her about our problems. She told me that talking with my mom was the best thing I could do. The next day I saw Ms. Ramirez and told her that my uncles were going to talk with my mom like family. They were going try to fix the problem. A couple of days later, I went to talk with Ms. Ramirez and she was delighted because my mom and I had made up. I felt terrific. First my uncles talked with her and later I talked with my mom and she was glad because I was going back home, even if my relationship with her husband is not always good.

One time Ms. Ramirez told me that I was ready to go to regular classes. I told her, "OK, maybe I can try." She started talking to me and other students about how the regular classes work and what to expect. She gave us a lot of work to do and at the end, we had to go to the front of the class for five minutes to talk about a topic of our choice. I chose to talk about alcohol and drugs, because many people who don't know how to control drugs can lose many things: cars, a home, and, most importantly, family. I chose this topic because when my father was twenty years old he used a lot of drugs and alcohol. I talk about these things because they created a lot of problems for my family. My father wasted ten years of his life on those vices. My father doesn't drink anymore, but he can't do anything to fix the problems that he created when he was young. Now he is living in El Salvador with his new wife and his daughter.

Another thing about Ms. Ramirez: she was a freedom person. If she wanted to do something or say something, she would just do it without thinking twice. One day she shared a little part of her life. She told us that when she was little, (I don't remember what age, but that doesn't matter) she didn't feel anything for boys, but when she was with girls she was fine. She didn't want to talk about that with her mother and her father, because she thought that they were not going to accept her, because she liked girls and not boys. Eventually she told her mother first and her mother told her that she didn't have to be worried, that she was going to talk with her father and he would understand. When she told us this story, I felt really sad but also proud because she was telling us something about herself. I felt sad because she told us that her father would not understand. I felt proud of her also because when she was younger she was afraid to tell her father the truth about herself, but years later she got more courage, and she told the truth about herself.

Something that I really like about Ms. Ramirez is that she always helps people in need. For example, I like to do graffiti and I told her that my stepfather says only the gangs do graffiti. She told me that was not true, then she told me about Precita Eyes, an arts center for community murals in the Mission, and I went there. They told me I could take some free classes, and after two weeks we went to do a mural about immigration, which we finished in one day. The mural was really nice, so I told Ms. Ramirez about it and she was happy that I was working with professionals. I was also really happy that I was working with those people.

If Ms. Ramirez were here, I would talk with her about the problems that I have in my classes and ask her how she was doing. I think that she would help me, asking me why things happened and how they started, and I think she would be glad to help me. If you tell her a secret she is not going to tell it to anybody.

I know things have changed a lot, because she does not live here any more and many people miss her. I think that she already knows why people miss her. I think that they miss her because she was good with them and because she always was helping them with their homework and their problems, like she did with me.

If I could see Ms. Ramirez right now, this is what I would say to her: "Hey, Ms. Ramirez, it's been a long time since I've seen you." And I would give her a hug.

DO SOMETHING FOR YOURSELF

Genesis Miranda

This story is about me. I am a person who likes to help someone else without receiving anything in return. These kinds of actions run in my family. We are noble and we like helping people by doing such things as inviting the neighbors to our house, or when people pass by the house we give them food or clothing. We like doing this because we really like helping others and it makes us feel good. What I have learned from my family is that you give without receiving. That is the way my family works.

I came from Mexico, a city called San Luis Sonora. All the people in my country are very friendly. They reach out to others. People help even with the little things, like taking the groceries to your car. Being nice to people and getting to know new people every day made me feel good because not everybody has good influences. Being with people that treat me with respect has taught me how to be a better influence for myself and others.

In San Luis I enjoyed being with my family (my mom, dad, and brothers) because I always had good times with them, but what I liked the most was being with my grandma. I miss being with her because she has these big orange and mandarin trees; you can climb on them, and eat the fruit. I love her a lot and she cooks very delicious meals. Every time she cooks she has to invite somebody to the house, just like my mom does. My mom also taught me generosity. Whenever the neighbors needed help with childcare, my mom used to take care of their children. These actions taught me every day how important it is to share with others and to become a better individual.

In my family we always talked about the problems that we had, and everybody helped whoever had problems. One day I was outside playing with my cousins. I ran into the kitchen to get some water and saw my mom and dad talking. When they saw me going to the kitchen they stopped talking and just looked at me. I asked, "Why are you guys so quiet?" They told me that there was nothing wrong. My family doesn't usually keep secrets from me or stop me from hearing their conservations. They didn't tell me what, but that day I knew that something was about to happen. One week later my mom and dad wanted to talk to me, and usually we don't talk in private or about serious stuff. That day both things were happening and I was a little bit scared.

What my mom and dad wanted to talk about was what I saw them talking about before. They wanted me to come to San Francisco, live with my aunt and uncle, go to school here, and learn English. My family started saying that it was for my own benefit and that it would help me get a good career. They didn't want me to drop out of school in Mexico or not have a good education. When they told me that, many thoughts came to my mind. I started thinking that my family didn't love me anymore and that they wanted me to leave because they were annoyed with me. Then I thought that it was not like that, and my family wanted to help me and do something for me. They wanted me to come to San Francisco to have a better career and for me to have better health care. I started to think positively.

A few months later I started packing and getting ready to come to San Francisco. At the time, I was excited but scared. I didn't want to leave my family; it was so sad to leave everybody that I love so much.

When I came to San Francisco, I called my family as soon as I could and made sure that they were doing fine. I already missed them. Here I live with my uncle and aunt. I do get along with them but not as much as with my family. When I first came, I didn't know that much vocabulary in English. I could speak but not as well as I can now. My uncle was born in Oregon so he can speak English very well, but when I wanted to talk with him about something, I couldn't express myself. Since my aunt is from Mexico, she could understand me and I talked to her about everything.

The first months were very depressing, and I used to cry almost every night for my family. Then I realized that wasn't taking me anywhere. I stopped and thought that I should do something to stop thinking about my family. I started doing things that I liked, such as going to the mall or reading, which really helped me out. The more I knew the city, the more it felt like home. Then a few weeks later I started school. I was so scared because I didn't know how school works here in the United States, but I started doing well in school and my English was understandable.

A few months later I found out that I was going to Mexico to visit my family. I was so happy and couldn't wait for that to happen. When I went to Mexico, my mom and dad were really happy to see me. Since I flew to San Diego, I had to use my English. When my family heard me talking, they were so proud of my progress. Now they use me whenever they need to speak English.

When I went to San Luis, I had a good time with my family and friends because I went out to places San Francisco doesn't have. Over in San Luis I used to go out to the clubs with my friends, and here I can't do that because my uncle does not let me go out. While in San Luis I try to enjoy my family the most because then I have to come back and start all over with the usual thing. With my family I have many good times. We go out to eat, to swim, and to spend time with friends. I like visiting because it makes me feel good to have a family and friends that love me a lot and that I can share beautiful moments with, which will never be forgotten. They are very special people to me.

While growing up I used to spend most of the time with my grandma, sharing each other's company and having good times. What I learned from my grandma is that even if you only have a little, you have to share because you have to treat others the way you want to be treated. When my parents told me that I was moving I was so angry and depressed. I felt so mad that I thought they broke the trust that we had in the family. I realized later on that it was for my own benefit because this kind of opportunity happens once in your life. What this taught me was that they were trying to help me in the ways they taught me to treat others. What my family also taught me is to be self confident, trustful, and to share.

There are people that sometimes need somebody to trust or to talk to. Trying to help others makes me feel satisfied and confident. In my culture in México, they taught me not to always think about myself, and to help others. By helping somebody, you are doing something for yourself, too.

YES OBAMA CAN! CREATING CHANGE FROM STRUGGLE

Dante Calonsag

Our country is struggling right now, and it's time for change. We need an empathetic president, someone who will care more about the people and our country's needs. I know that Mr. Barack Obama would make a great president if he continues to be positive, keeps his promises, and wishes to do helpful things for our country. We need Barack Obama as our president because with his positive plans and ability, our country will finally stop the madness that is occurring.

Ever since George W. Bush became president, our country has completely fallen off track. People are getting laid off their jobs. Basically our economy is not as strong as it used to be. Losing one's job is disappointing and one of the worst feelings to experience. A lot of people I see in my neighborhood or community had very good jobs as I was growing up, but today I see some of them working at fast food markets and retail stores. Having a good-paying job and enjoying what you do is a very rare thing to encounter, but getting laid off your job, out of the blue, is not. I feel bad for those who have to start over and find a new job. There has to be a solution to this problem.

Another important struggle that we are dealing with is skyrocketing gas prices. I recently was at a gas station. My auntie spent twenty-five dollars on gas and only put the tank just past half. From that point, I knew that the gas prices were getting ridiculous. How long can people go on paying these high gas prices? A president can truly respect citizens' concerns by giving the people what they need. I hope we get a big change and find a solution to this problem because the bad economy affects people every day.

Even more important than gas prices or unemployment is the war in Iraq, because the tragedies of the war are affecting a lot of people, including me. I don't think that George Bush is trying to make a change. He is not doing his job. George Bush should act like he is president and help our country by solving our problems. He should also show that he cares more by sending most of our troops home and halting the war. I'm affected when every morning I wake up and walk by a newspaper stand, and I'm reminded that overnight a whole bunch of people died and some other troops were wounded. Seeing that a whole bunch of people around my age are risking their lives for my safety touches me because they're fighting every day, not solving major issues, and dying for minor issues. The war should have been handled very differently by getting our troops out of Iraq. Getting them out would show a lot of caring and compassion from the president by letting them come home to their families.

We need a president that will put heart and effort into our country, making very important decisions during a crisis, if not beforehand. For example, when Hurricane Katrina occurred, so many people struggled for a long time to get out of New Orleans. Bush should have already had plans about how to prepare for the hurricane. Also, not just during the hurricane but after, Bush should have had more places for people to stay besides the Superdome and sports arenas.

You see, President Bush knew about the hurricane's status and situation, but still he did not react in time to help. Bush had enough time to make plans and decisions to try and help the innocent people that were struggling to survive the hurricane. So when President Bush arrived in

Louisiana, he already realized that he was too late, and personally, I know he felt embarrassed and guilty. He said, "I take responsibility for government failures in dealing with Hurricane Katrina."

Bush could have reacted to the hurricane in a more precise and responsible way. If Bush's family members had been in this situation, he would have reacted to this problem ten times faster. He should have reacted faster regardless, since he is in charge of the country's decisions. In general, presidents in this situation should act more responsibly by keeping track of hurricanes to know what to do next when they hit.

Having George Bush as our president makes me ask questions like, "Is he telling the truth? Is he really capable of being our country's leader?" The answer to that would be no. Most of his thoughts and opinions seem to be fake and one big lie. It is very important for United States citizens to be able to trust in their leaders because as citizens we are the ones that experience the country's successes and struggles. We should be able to depend on our president to take care of our country. We expect our leaders to guide us through our problems with solutions, and to welcome new ideas. We do not need a person like Bush to make our country's decisions because we need a president who is going to keep his or her promises and ideas alive.

The upcoming presidential election will be one of the most important moments for our country ever. I look at our future scenario if John McCain were to become president; our country would not change in the ways that this country needs to. It would seem like George Bush is still president because they're both supporting the war by continuing to have our troops fighting in Iraq. However, I think if Barack Obama is president, there will be more opportunities for people to get or keep their jobs, programs for education and for finding more alternatives to oil. He will focus on lowering gas prices, bringing our troops home to end the war, and, most importantly, making a huge change for our country.

Barack believes in early childhood education, and he proposed ten billion dollars a year to increase the number of children eligible for Early Head Start programs. Also, he proposes one billion dollars in funding to create mentoring programs. Starting an Early Head Start education program is a very good idea. For one, a lot of students, including me, have their individual struggles in education, and it would be better to have more high-quality educational programs to help us understand things better in the future. For a lot of people having financial problems with tuition and fees, Barack Obama is willing to expand the Pell Grant and lower interest rates on existing federal student loan programs. Once a lot of people, like students, begin to commit to educational opportunities, we can begin to grow as a country and live up to our high capabilities, becoming very intelligent educators and learners ourselves.

The issue of education is affecting a lot of students and educators all over the country. There are not enough education programs for people who are having financial problems and who have personal issues with their education. Obama's plan for education reflects the Golden Rule by coming up with ideas or solutions to problems. I can say that sometimes I have some issues with my education because of the lack of educational programs, so that's why it's affecting me.

Barack Obama has powerful words that will be followed up by his actions, but what makes me believe that he is true to his word is the expression and tone of his voice. I can visualize the changes and plans that he has for us just by how he expresses his views. Barack Obama inspires me because he is unafraid to speak hard truths when necessary. Obama's expression captures my attention because I can relate to the issues that he is discussing. The energy and dignity that he shows make me believe in the truthfulness of Barack Obama.

The president must care for and respect everyone because if the president does not have respect for one, he doesn't have respect for his entire country. Mutual respect is very important in politician-citizen relationships because the way a president treats an individual should be an example for how the citizens should treat each other. The president's ideas, decisions, and actions reflect upon our country and its citizens regardless of whether they are good or bad. Hopefully we will not have to live with these problems for long. Big changes like lowering gas prices, starting new education programs, and bringing the troops home will affect everyone positively and will take a lot of pressure off of people. Obama's plan is wonderful, and it is a relief to know that he plans to bring our troops home in sixteen months, which will finally bring the war to an end. All of these positive changes will soon occur with an empathetic president like Barack Obama.

MY MOTHER'S TEARS
Maynor Escalante

It is at the heart of my moral code, and it is how I understand the Golden Rule—not simply as a call to sympathy or charity, but as something more demanding, a call to stand in somebody else's shoes and see through their eyes.
—*Barack Obama,* The Audacity of Hope

When I was a young boy living in Honduras, my father was gone from my life. In addition to his physical absence, he was also emotionally absent. Long before I knew what it meant to be a father, I lived through the effects of my father's mistakes with my family. Although I understand that he is only human, one day I aspire to be a better father and husband to my family than my father was to me and my family.

When I was a little kid, I looked up to and admired my father. I felt like he was a good father despite our poor circumstances. In my eyes, he possessed all the characteristics I was brought up to believe that a strong man should possess. He was tall, proud, a good provider, and a strong "macho" man. He was the head of our household, and everyone within my family was expected to follow and respect his rules. What I didn't know back then is that it takes more be a father. A father must have an emotional connection and learn to lead his family with respect, which was missing in my family.

Early in life, I learned that a big part of being a strong man was to buy into the belief that women and children come second in priority to men. It was the natural rule of Honduras, where men held the ultimate power. I also learned that being a strong "macho" man came at a price; it meant that a strong man could seldom show emotion because if they did, they would be seen as weak. I think my father may have been afraid to be vulnerable. Perhaps he was scared that we would see him as weak. However, what he didn't realize is that the best gift he could have given me was a father-and-son relationship.

During my childhood, I saw that my father didn't always treat my mother with respect. I love and admire my father to the point that I would exchange my life for his if he was ever in danger, but I don't want to repeat my father's mistakes. Barack Obama once said that every man is out to impress his father or make up for his mistakes. In my life, I have found this to be true because I hope to become a better person than my father ever was.

When I was thirteen, I began to notice the flaws of my father. The man I once held great respect and admiration for became more human through his flaws, and I knew there was something wrong within my family. I noticed that there was an abusive circle within my family. The way I saw my mother also changed; I noticed that my mother suffered emotionally and physically in my family. The circle of abuse was verbal, mental, and physical. Every time some form of abuse happened within my family, I felt like it was a blow to my mind, body, and spirit. I wanted to take ownership of every pain that I witnessed my mother endure. I felt her pain, her scars, her tears, her heartbreak, her separation, and her protection for us as a mother. I felt like her pain was my responsibility. As her son, I held the responsibility to protect her. In my eyes, she was a delicate rose, and it hurt my heart to see her helpless and in so much pain.

One night when I was eleven, my father came home on one of his worst days. He was out playing pool with his friends and came home drunk. I was watching television in my bedroom when I heard him come through the front door. I heard his hard footsteps walk towards his bedroom. I turned down the volume and heard my father yelling at my mother, accusing her of cheating on him. I couldn't hear his exact words, but I heard the anger in his voice. Since he had been drinking, he wasn't in the right frame of mind. I remember feeling scared about what he would do. As soon as I heard him stop yelling and leave his room, I ran into my parents' room to see if my mother was OK. My father had left towards the back of the house.

When I walked into her room, my mother was sitting on the bed looking at the floor in silence. She had tears falling down her face as I sat down next to her on the bed and tried to comfort her with my presence, and we both sat on the bed in silence.

All of a sudden, I heard a loud noise that came from the back of the house. I quickly got up and left my mother's room and ran towards the back of the house. I immediately locked the back door, because I knew my father was outside in the back of the house.

After I locked the back door, I ran into the kitchen. The kitchen had a window that allowed me to see the outdoor bathroom where the noise came from. The bathroom door was open, and I saw that my father had smashed the bathtub. I didn't see him actually break it, but I heard the bathtub break from my parent's room, and when I saw a big rock by the broken bathtub, I knew my father had broken it in anger. The tub had broken into what looked like a million pieces. Looking at the broken pieces, I felt scared inside. I felt like it was my duty as a son to step up and protect my family, but in many ways I was also helpless against my father.

I ran back into my parents' room to tell my mother what I had seen. My mother was still sitting on the bed with tears rolling down her face. I told her what my father did to the bathroom, and she looked worried. She must have come to her breaking point, and figured we all had to leave for our well-being. She told me that we had to leave the house and call the police.

Since my older sister was sleeping in her room the whole time, my mother and I went to her room and woke her up. She was scared and confused and asked us why we were in her room. We explained to her what was going on with my father and we told her that we needed to leave the house because my father was angry.

As we were walking out of the house, we heard a loud noise coming from the back of the house. The noise sounded like my father was pounding on the back door with his fist.

As we were walking down the stairs, I heard another loud noise. It sounded like my father threw another big rock at the back door in an attempt to break into the house. Although we wanted to see what my father was doing, we kept walking down the stairs to the street. We walked to the police station to file a police report. We also explained to my sister what happened and why we were walking to the police station.

When we got to the police station, they wrote down what my mother told them. Four policemen came back with us to the house to see if my father was still there.

When we walked back into the house, my father was sitting on the sofa in the living room. The police arrested him that day. They took him into custody, and my father spent the night in jail. I felt guilty that we had to call the police on my father, but he brought it upon himself.

After that day, my father never came back home again. He decided to live at his mother's house in a town called Talanga, which was two to three hours away. I never heard from him again. Four months later, my mother, my sister, and I moved to the United States and began a new chapter in our lives without him. I have been without a father for three years now. Sometimes I lie in bed and think about how much damage my father did to my family. I also think about how my life would be if he had made different choices.

What if he had chosen not to drink that night? Would he have acted differently towards my family? Would we still be together as a family? I suppose I will never really know the answers to these questions, because he chose not to live with us. Sometimes I think if we had stayed in Honduras, things would have remained the same, because when we lived there, he wasn't around anyway.

The most important person in my life was my grandfather. He died about a year ago, and I miss him still to this day. He was the only male figure in my life. He taught me things my own father did not. My grandfather taught me how to be a man and how to live by the Golden Rule. He led by example and taught me to treat all people as equals and to always put myself in their shoes. My grandfather also taught me that I have to forgive my father for everything he did to my family. He helped me understand that forgiveness is part of the Golden Rule.

Looking back at my childhood, I realize that hurting my mother and my family was not my father's intention but more a result of the problems he faced in his own life. My father's alcoholism was an emotional refuge for him, because he was overwhelmed by his own life obstacles. A major part of his mistake was that he took his frustrations out on my family, instead of trying to understand his own feelings.

I also understand my mother's side of the story. I understand why she chose to stay and put up with the abuse. My mother tried to keep the family together because she didn't want to leave her children without a father.

A little while after that night, my mother finally mustered up the courage to walk away from my father. She realized that her children deserved better. She understood that our lives would be better without abuse, and sometimes not having an abusive father is better than keeping him in our lives.

Over the years, my mother grew to be an irreplaceable and fundamental rock in my life. I see the sacrifices she made in her own life for the benefit of ours; my sister and I always came first.

Despite the challenges my family faced in coming to the United States, my family is happier in this country. We are happy to finally have peace in our lives. My father chose to stay in Honduras, and he still lives there to this day. I don't know if he ever realized what his alcoholism did to our family, but I do know that I do not want to be like him one day. When

I look at my mother today, I am more comfortable with her happiness. She has since remarried and received an apology from my father.

Barack Obama's life is connected to my life. His father died, and my father does not live with me. He lived with his grandmother, and I grew up with my grandfather. My grandfather taught me to respect all kinds of people, no matter what their race. His life inspires me to take advantage of more opportunities. He inspires me to believe in myself and to be capable of achieving success despite the bad things that happened in my life. He inspires me to realize that people make mistakes, because no one is perfect, but they don't have to be defined by their mistakes.

TRAPPED INSIDE MY CAGE
Eryn-Rose Manzano

I want to fly high and be free as a bird, but I'm trapped in a cage with nowhere to go, slowly dying of hunger and thirst. There are things that weaken me day by day and stop me from believing in what I can do. I feel like a prisoner inside of myself, my own image. Some people blame me for who I am and not for what I do. Some people don't trust me. They assume that I'm guilty of some crime. I am one of those who is treated unjustly and not given a chance to talk and defend herself. Why is it all about them? Why is it always about what they think?

My thoughts of what I want to do are all confined inside of me. I was held back for a reason that I don't understand. I want to show the world who I really am and that I believe there is still an answer for everything, but all the hatred and doubt makes me tired. Being locked up for so long within myself stops me from thinking that there is a chance of getting out.

Maybe there is a way, but I can't figure it out because my heart is filled up with so much anguish and I am losing hope. At times, I almost unlock the door but, because I am really excited to be free, I forget that there is still a padlock on *me*. I am losing faith that I can escape this cage of suffering. A lot of times I try to get out of it, but I don't have the key. Then, I wonder, where is the key? Where is it?

They say America is the land of opportunities, and that America can give you a great life, regardless of your past experiences. We've all heard of the immigrants who come here wanting to see the streets that are paved with gold. Many immigrants leave their families and friends for the opportunity to make a new life and prosper. Sometimes people move here for a simple reason: to follow their family members and friends and live life as they did before. Everything people are looking for is found in this country. It is the promise of a fresh start. They can make more money and are given opportunities that help ease their families' lives. They can give their families a better future and experience the opportunities this country holds for them.

However, these good things don't always happen. The happiness and the relationships between family members are at risk. Unfortunately, that happened to me.

When I was growing up in the Philippines, I led a life that didn't need a lot of effort. We had a maid who did everything for us. Everybody in the house depended on the maid—she cooked, did the laundry, made the beds, dropped us at school, and cleaned the house. Also, I admit that I wasn't a good role model for my siblings. I always came home late because I hung out with my friends, and I didn't do that well in school—my grades were mostly Bs. However, even though my achievements weren't perfect, I was content with what I had and didn't seek anything more. There was never a time when I felt I was alone or tired, because my friends were always there for me. They knew everything about me. They eased the pain I had inside when there was something wrong. I can still remember the times when I went to school crying because something bad had happened at home. My friends showed a lot of concern for me, asked a lot of questions, and tried to crack jokes to make me feel better. Because of this, I always felt safe and supported. I always saw the bright side of life, even when I was down. I was the girl who everybody thought was perfect in terms of happiness and being content. There was never a day when I put a frown on my face, even if something was wrong in my life. I never questioned my character or my integrity since I knew how to get the most out of life. I was like a bird flying and soaring high with the happiness it carried.

Then something big happened. I found out that we were to leave the Philippines in a month, and I wasn't ready. But since I was the type that saw the bright side of life, I was happy. My dad had been living in the United States for a long time, working so that we could eventually join him. He thought that living here would be the best thing for us because we could be independent and learn things that were not taught at Filipino schools. I felt excited but I realized that life wouldn't be the same.

We moved here about a year ago, and my life slowly began to change. It changed in some ways that I didn't notice—I didn't get to be the princess I used to be. I learned to wash the dishes, make my bed, clean the kitchen, do the laundry, and even cook for and babysit my siblings. At first, I was not ready for the changes. I felt mad. Sometimes I thought that being the eldest meant that I had to take on all of the responsibility. But as time passed I got used to it, and became more dependable. My mom told me, "You can't survive living here when you don't know how to be independent and how to deal with life. Your dad worked hard so that we could have the good life we always wanted, so don't waste it." That statement made me realize that there is not always someone who can do things for you. There will be a time when you'll need to do things alone and be independent.

I was the only one who could make things better and who could help our family to do better. I did succeed in some things: I became a straight-A student, I did well at my job, and I got used to the chores I had at home. But when I thought of it, there was something missing, the "something" that makes life complete and happy. I thought by doing the things my parents wanted me to do I could feel the security and happiness I had before, but I was wrong. Even with the success I already had, I forgot to be happy. I forgot to make friends and I forgot to be me. I was too busy with the responsibilities in my life to think of the things that could fulfill me. I was focused on things that I shouldn't have been worried about. The change in my life was stopping me from getting what I really wanted. The success I had in school and with my family didn't equal the happiness I had before. My achievements made my family feel great, but the happiness I had before was gone.

I was trapped inside this cage of pain, going through the same routine every day. I didn't get to spend time with my friends because my dad didn't let me go outside on the weekend. I only saw them during school hours. I had the feeling that I was getting used to my life here. There have been a lot of transformations within me since I came here; I changed without even knowing it. After a period of time, I wasn't the girl everybody used to know—I went from being happy to being sad, and from being loud and outspoken to being quiet and shy. These changes in my character took away my confidence.

The way that I treated other people also changed. I became selfish, and didn't mind how other people felt about the harsh words I said to them. I was moody and people began to ask me what was wrong. I kept on telling them that I was fine, because I didn't think that there was something wrong with me. I just ignored them and didn't pay attention, because I knew I was good and didn't need to worry about anything. My behavior caused people to turn their backs on me, one by one. Even my family didn't want to hear about what was happening to me. They didn't believe what I said; it was like they took me for granted.

One day, I realized that I should not be treating them this way. I became so miserable that I made my friends and family leave me. I remembered the saying "The more you look for somebody else to fulfill your happiness, the more people you lose." I was looking for the things I lacked and didn't see that I already had them. I wasn't content with what I had. I was so focused that I ignored people and bumped them if they were in my way. In spite of all the concern they showed me, I still chose to be mad at them. Instead of giving them the same concern and love they had for me, I did the opposite. I've caused so much pain to others. I treated them unfairly, and now that they are gone, I realize I shouldn't have done that.

We don't make the right decisions all the time. Sometimes when we think we're doing the right thing, we are actually choosing a path that makes us feel bad. There was a person in my life that made me realize this. Her face is still fresh in my mind, as well as all she told me and the way she held my hand before she left.

It was just a regular Saturday afternoon. I was already on my way home. On the 14-Mission bus, I saw this old lady standing with grocery bags. I wanted to help her carry her bags, but I was ready to get off the bus. It was already 5:30 PM and I was hurrying to get home. Then I saw a car in the crosswalk. *Shoot! Damn this car, it's in my way*, I thought. I was only a block away from home. I had crossed the street and was about to pass another pedestrian when I heard a loud *boom*. I looked back to see what happened and saw the old lady with the bags from the bus. She got hit by the car in the crosswalk and was lying on the road with her bags around her.

The cars started to honk to try to make the old lady move out of their way. I didn't know whether to help her or just run toward my home and pretend that nothing had happened. Then I thought, *What if I was the one in her position? Would anybody help me?* I quickly ran over, got two of her bags, and helped her walk to the side to keep the street clear. While I was standing beside her, I was memorizing the plate number of the car in case he took off. The driver pulled over and ran towards us. He asked the lady if he could just drop her off somewhere and give her money, but she just kept on saying, "It's your fault. I was crossing the street and then there you were in the crosswalk."

People around her told her to not let the man take her away and give her money. The old lady was really hurt. She was crying really hard and we could barely understand what she was saying. A man who was help-ing her asked if someone knew what language she was speaking and if they could translate it for him. I had the feeling that she was a Filipino. "Are you a Filipino?" I asked her. "Yes," she answered, with a shaky voice. She started to speak to me in Tagalog and described to me what she felt. I could tell that she was really hurt. I heard someone call 911 and describe the accident to the operator. Before the police came, she rolled up her pants and showed me her bruises and wounds. She was bleeding and she kept on telling me that she couldn't breathe well. She was afraid that she could have an attack.

I asked her who I could call, so that her family would know that she had been in an accident, but she told me that she was living by herself and that she didn't have anybody with her at her house. I was worried about her since the ambulance was coming and she didn't have somebody to go to the hospital with. After a minute or two, I heard sirens all over the place. Police came in first and they started to ask questions. There was a couple who helped the old lady and stayed there at the same time I was there. The police started to ask them questions. Then the ambulance came. They asked me if I was a relative and could come with her, but I wasn't. "I don't want to go to the hospital," she kept on telling me. I told her that she needed to because of her wounds and bruises. The old lady asked me to tell them what she had told me—that she couldn't breathe and that she felt that she'd have an attack.

When they laid the old lady on the stretcher, she held my hand so hard. It felt so cold and I could tell that she was scared. While she had my hands, she didn't want to let go. She kept on telling me that I should stay, and that I was the only family she has here. I was touched. I could feel the tears in my eyes, but kept on holding them back. They took her inside the ambulance and she was still yelling that I needed to go with her, but I couldn't. I was cold, but I was sweating. I was scared for her—she was all alone in this country and had no one to turn to.

Even when I know that something wrong is going on inside of me, this feeling shouldn't affect how I treat other people. I experience hardships in life, but they don't need to change everything in me, including how I see the people around me. There is no reason to be mad at someone for my problems because I am the one responsible for the decisions I make.

If I only do the things other people want me to do, instead of the things I want to do, I could end up crying, looking back on the choices that made me miserable. When my dad told me that doing well in school would make my life better, I chose to do what he told me. However, after making this choice, I realized that my life isn't only about what others want me to do; it is also about what I want and how I can make my life better. Maybe others don't want me to make mistakes that I can never undo. But I believe that mistakes teach you lessons that help you figure out how to make your life better.

I figured out that if life is a game, why not play it? For a long time, I blamed others for my actions, not realizing that I was the one making the moves. Players come and go but they aren't responsible for the moves *you* make.

While playing the game of life, I realized that the key I was looking for could be found anywhere. While life can be so cruel and unfair, it took time for me to realize where to find the key, the key that could unlock the sorrow in me and make me free. The key I want can only be found within me. The answer doesn't depend on the people around you; it's your own thoughts that can help you get through the challenges you face.

WHAT I HOPE
Cristian Gomez

Dear President Bush,

  During your last term in office, there were two events that impacted me personally. The first was the 9/11 terrorist attack. The second life-changing event was Hurricane Katrina. Both historical events showed that you were not doing well as a president. Although you say your strength is military power, I have never felt so insecure about my well-being in the United States.

  After 9/11, how would you have felt if you were in the same situation as the people who died in the terrorist attack? Imagine being one of those people who stood there—helpless—looking at the burning buildings, watching their families dying with no way to escape. How would you feel knowing that a member of your family was in a building attacked by terrorists? How could you and your administration just wait until an idea popped into your head about what to do? I understand that this event was out of the norm and unforeseen, but your reaction to the situation was not noble. I felt your reaction was not in the best interest of the country you serve. I would have felt better if you had kept talking to the people in an effort to encourage them not to freak out. You should have made people feel safe and told them to wait until it was all over. Instead, I felt that you did nothing to make the public feel secure. That was the defining moment for me that influenced my opinion about you. That was the first moment people got to see what kind of president they had entrusted with their lives. I wish you would have done more for the people in the rubble who were still fighting for their lives.

I know you are a really good person, but you don't show it most of the time. I feel that although you may care on the inside about our livelihood, you are aloof on the outside. I think you have trouble solving problems. I also think you are nervous or afraid of everyone blaming you if you do something wrong.

I felt so bad for the families of the 2,819 people that died. 1,609 people lost their partners or spouses in the attack, and about 3,051 children lost their parents. How would you feel if that kid was yours? How would you feel if one of those people was your wife? I felt so frustrated seeing all those people die. I wondered what the president was doing. What was he thinking? What was he doing about it? I actually felt bad for all the people who voted for him as president. They looked to him for help but were let down. I felt insecure knowing that my family, living in the United States, was not safe. I was worried about what would happen if the attack was on San Francisco, where my family lives. I was scared knowing that my mother could be living in danger.

I remember that day like it was yesterday. I was nine years old and living in El Salvador. I was watching *Spiderman*, my favorite TV show, and eating my favorite Kellogg's cereal when, from nowhere, the news broke in.

"And now for the international news ... the United States has been attacked by terrorists. Just minutes ago, two airplanes crashed into one of the most important buildings in the United States, making the towers fall and killing thousands of people. Our hearts are with them." I was kind of confused and angry because I wanted to see my cartoons, but then I noticed everyone was serious and scared about what was happening. I remember my eyes being glued to the TV, and when they showed the images of the airplanes crashing into the towers, I was even more interested. I had family living in the United States. I was afraid that something could happen to my mother, cousins, and my aunt. I was thinking of what my mother was doing at that moment. I was wondering if she was OK and afraid of what may have happened to her.

After that it was like a normal day. I ate breakfast, got ready to go to school, and waited for my grandmother to take me to school. While I waited I talked with my friends and played outside. But the images from the TV were still on my mind. I couldn't forget all of that fire coming from the towers and the people actually jumping from the windows. I was really stuck on that.

People were talking about it at school.

"Did you see in the news what just happened?" a teacher asked.

Another said, "Yeah, I saw it. It really shocked me to see those people jumping out of the windows." I didn't understand why it was a big deal to her. Did she have family there? Why were all of these people talking about it? I was too young to know what had just happened. In school my friends talked about it without any interest in the reason behind it; they just were talking about how cool it was to see the airplane destroyed.

"It was like a movie!" they would say without any feeling. But the older people were more serious about it. They knew it was not a movie. They knew it was real, and they were shocked to see all those people dying. I was worried because I didn't know anything about my mother yet. Was she safe?

I still can't help but wonder what would have happened if all the money lost after the attack had been spent beforehand on more security. Would it still have happened?

Then there was Hurricane Katrina. I want to know why you didn't help those people who were on their rooftops waiting for help. Why you left those people there for days. How would you feel staying on a roof for days, waiting for some help, knowing that you can't go anywhere? I felt really sorry for all of those who died waiting for help to come. Is that how a president should act?

When I saw Katrina, I was living here in the United States. It was even scarier than 9/11. I kept thinking, *What if that happened here?* I was really scared because I felt like my life was in danger. I was afraid of living in a country where there is always something bad that could happen to me, or my family and friends. I thought, *What is the president going to do about this now?*

I remember that day like it was yesterday. I was doing the same things as always. I was just about to leave for school. I brushed my teeth, I did my hair, got my stuff ready, and texted to my friends to see where they were. I told them what had just happened on the news. There was a guy talking about a hurricane. He said, "Hurricane Katrina had become category five before it hit land overnight. Most of the damage was in New Orleans. It is a complete tragedy." It killed so many people and destroyed thousands of dollars worth of property. Millions of dollars were lost because of the hurricane. I was so shocked to see the city full of water. You couldn't see anything. Instead of cars, there were boats going up and down the streets. The cars were on top of roofs or on top of trees. All you could see of the city were the roofs of houses and the tops of trees. Just think of all of those who died trying to hide and run away from the hurricane. I felt really bad for all of those families who were alone, for all those kids who don't have families anymore. What will their lives be like now? I would feel like dying if my family were gone. I was really scared that day because if it could happen in New Orleans, why couldn't we have a worse natural disaster in San Francisco? The whole city could disappear, along with the people living here. Millions could die, including my family. What would I do after that?

I just keep thinking of the people after the hurricane—all of those people who survived, who were waiting on the rooftops, trees, and grabbing anything they could find to hold, waiting for help to come, wishing every single second someone would bring them shelter, food, or something to take them away from that nightmare. How long did they have to wait? Days, weeks, months? They were waiting for someone to bring them help and take them away from the place where they lived for such a long time, from the place where they constructed their lives, from their families. Thinking about how they stayed there alone is really hard. Just think for a second and put yourself in the place of those people.

Mr. President, what I hope you learn from these two tragedies is that you should not leave the people on their own when some disaster comes and destroys everything. Help them. We are human beings. We are all the same. Why let anyone die? I just want you to learn that you should help anyone who needs help from now on, to take those two experiences as examples of the mistakes you have made, and to correct them in the future. I'm just asking you to give protection to those who you promise to protect, to give them a reason to trust you, Mr. President. Is that too much to ask for, Mr. President? Is it too much to ask you to help people who are in real danger, who have families waiting for them? I don't think so.

MAKING MY MOTHER PROUD

Jian Pei Ruan

This is the story of my first time helping other people.

This story is in my hometown, Guangdong, China. I was born in Guangdong. It is a small city as close to Hong Kong as San Francisco is to Oakland. Everybody in my hometown is very into playing volleyball. Everyone begins to study volleyball in primary school. So I really like to play volleyball too. China has many languages. My hometown has three that everybody knows. They are Cantonese, Mandarin, and Tai Shan. The other big thing is tourism. The tourists come from other cities in China. Many of the people that come from other cities to Guangdong do not know Cantonese. The sand in my hometown is black sand. Because sand is usually yellow, many people come to see the black sand and they want to take it home as a souvenir. This is what my hometown is like.

I was twelve years old. It was during the one-month holiday from school for the New Year. The New Year is a very big holiday for the Chinese. On New Year's Day, my mother and father gave me red paper envelopes containing money as a gift so I could buy new shoes and clothing because the New Year is a new beginning. I like the holiday! I was excited.

I did not have go to school. I could stay home and play video games with all my friends.

At night people went out. It had the New Year holiday feeling and many people were in the street. Many people were cooking BBQ and selling chicken and corn on wooden sticks. They were cooking with kerosene grills on push carts. The chicken made sounds on the fire—*tsjaaaaah, tsjaaaaah, tsjaaaaah*—and I could see chicken and corn change from yellow to black. The smell made me hungry. There was also fried food served with buns, dry fish, vegetables, and other meats. I bought the chicken. It tasted very good. I felt happy. And to drink there was *boba* tea, milk tea, and green tea. The sweets were different ice creams. I like green tea flavor.

Many people were in the street playing. Men were gambling in the street, betting on a game played with a basketball. The game looks like basketball, so I call it street basketball. You pay money to stand behind a yellow line and throw the ball. You get three throws. If you make one basket, you get two more throws. If you get three baskets in a row you win a really cheap watch. I played this game many times and I lost many times. I won maybe two times.

They were also throwing darts—*peeeeewwh*—at balloons. You get three chances. If you pop the balloon the game is free and you get to play again. I like to play the dart and balloon game. It is very easy. I win any time I play.

On the first night of the New Year in Guangdong you might see men fighting in a rope square: King of The Fighters. People bet on the fighters. A man takes the money in a cardboard box. The fighters look like they use *chi gong*. Many have no shirt or shoes and they look like fighters in a video game, like Jackie Chan. There is a big crowd around them. They shout, "Haah!" Just like that. "Haah!" Six players can compete at one time, but they fight just two at a time. If you lose twice, you cannot keep playing. If you win twice, then you fight one of the other players of the original six. This keeps going until there are only two players left. After they fight there is just one, the King of the Fighters! The man with the box of money pays the people with winning bets.

Here in San Francisco, the Chinese New Year holiday is only seven days long instead of one month long. And here we do not have street games. So instead of spending a long holiday at the street fair, I stay home and play video games.

The holiday in China lasts many days. We go swimming in a public pool every day. One day my best friend and I went for a swim. That day was so hot.

We were in the street. Suddenly, a kid yelled, "Help me! Help me! Help me!" We went to see what was happening. A kid was almost drowning in the Pearl River. The river is very big. The width across is the same as from 17TH Street to 18TH Street here, in the Mission. The river water is black and warm and is full of garbage. People throw anything in there: unwanted food, plastic bags, old clothes, broken TVs and many things you cannot see because the water is dark with the black sand and dirt. Because that day was so hot the water smelled bad. When the temperature is high the floating garbage stinks very bad.

I knew the kid yelling in the river. He was from my village and my brother's best friend. My brother was six and the kid was five. I had seen them together. I remember him as small, very skinny, and weak. I asked myself, what was he doing here? I wanted to know if my brother was with him.

But even though there were many people in the street, no one wanted to help the kid. My friend said, "Jian Pei, let's go help that kid."

I knew how to swim very well. First, I took off my shoes. If I didn't take them off the water would get in. I started swimming very slow. Because the kid was very scared, I then swam very fast to him.

I wasn't afraid I might drown because I knew how I could help the kid. Everyone should know how to help. I did not take him by the hand because if I did he would grab onto me. He was already full of animal nature by that time; he was full of the fear of death, and he would try to hold on to me too strong and I would not be able to swim. I might drown too. I learned this from a swimming class in school. They taught us this because there were many children drowning in Guangdong.

As I was taught, I used my hand to take the kid by his hair and started to swim to the edge of the river. He was not heavy because the water cut most of his body weight. At the river bank, I dragged him out and dragged him to the grass. I knew he was alive because he was crying.

Some villagers went to get to his mother. When they brought her to him, she was crying and screaming. She told him not to play by the river. She was afraid he would drown. The fragile kid said, "Sorry, Ma."

"Now we'll see if you ever come to the river bank to play," she said.

"I won't come here to play next time," he said.

Some people watching laughed, because the boy was usually very bold. Every day he went out to fight and pilfer.

The boy told me, "Thank you."

The next time I saw the boy, we said hello but we did not talk about the river and what had happened. I felt he had changed; he was more of a good boy. He was not going out to fight and pilfer. Every day he went home right after school and did his homework, and did not play volleyball. He wanted to have a bike, and his mother told him he needed to get eighty points on the test to graduate from primary school and then she would buy him the bike. Now, every day he was at home reviewing for the test. He wanted to ride the bike to high school because the school did not have a school bus. So his effort to study was very strong now.

I felt very good because I had never before thought I would save anyone from drowning. My mother was happy too because I helped the boy. I saved his life! I had helped someone else. I was so happy. I was so proud.

HOPE FOR
A BETTER FUTURE

Ravon Anderson

Dear Barack Obama,

I am writing to share my opinions on what it means to have integrity. Integrity means that you care, that you have compassion, leadership, and understanding. I believe the president should have integrity because he should be able to handle what's happening with the people. This letter states facts and opinions about what goes on around me and the people in my life.

Communication is one of the major aspects in having integrity, because communication shows that you are able to understand other people and to see what they're going through. If you don't talk to people and just stereotype them and put them into a group, you will never get to know them on a personal level. Having integrity is being able to go out and talk to people, see what's happening to them, and see how they're doing. I always tell my friends that it's better to at least talk to a close friend to get out what's bothering them. They always come to me to tell me that it really helps them. They really do take it to heart that there is somebody who cares.

I remember a time that I showed integrity with my friend. She texted me on my phone and told me she needed help. She asked if I could come stay the night at her house. When I got there, we watched television and went down to Walgreens to get playing cards. After we got back, we played a couple of rounds of Speed and a game of Crazy Eights. Later on we went to her room to watch *The Kings of Comedy*, but then we started talking about her boyfriend, which confused me because I didn't know why she was crying about him. She asked me how I felt about him as a person and how he acted. I told her that I had a weird feeling about him, and that's why I didn't like being around him. I felt that he was a liar and didn't care about anybody but himself. She said that everybody was telling her that this was going to happen, but she didn't want to listen. I told her that I saw this coming but didn't tell her because she would find out sooner or later. Time seemed to fly by while we were talking. She told me thanks for coming over and helping her. We stayed up for awhile longer and then passed out. Later, they broke up with each other and stopped talking, but I felt glad that I was able to help her when she needed it.

Without communication in a community, people would never be able to get along. For example, in our communities there are a lot of kids outside that are supposed to be at school, but their parents don't care if they go or not. The kids that are trying to go to school have to deal with fights and people not getting along with each other. That makes students think of dropping out or cutting school. I often see violence in front of my house, at school, and downtown. I believe there is violence because some people never really learned to communicate with people. They may have gotten the wrong ideas from the examples that they had around them, such as their moms, dads, and other members of their families.

Sometimes people learn to be violent from their fathers because they're always seeing their fathers beat on their mothers. So, what they do is go out and beat up on other people, and they end up in jail. I believe that parents and teachers could get rid of violence by talking to the teens themselves to see why they are committing violence towards other people, because every person has his own story and problems. Teens have to deal with so much at home. Some try to help their mothers, but end up getting hurt in the process. So they go out and hurt other people—they are hurt and confused themselves. Kids just need somebody to show them ways of getting out anger other than hurting people. Not learning how to communicate anger is causing a lot of violence in our communities today.

Sometimes you feel you can't go anywhere without someone trying to kill you or wanting to fight with you because you're from somewhere else. You could get killed just by sitting in a car with the wrong person. It seems you can't even walk home when it's dark without someone trying to hurt you. That's what gets to me. I don't know what could happen to me when I'm walking around in the wrong neighborhood. You can't even go see a friend without a person trying to come up and start some drama with you because you don't live where they live. There is so much that a young teen has to deal with every single day going back and forth to school. People are just fighting each other for no reason at all. Also, there are people trying to sell speed, crack, hop, etc. We need to tell kids not to be followers. They should be their own person and not let people or friends decide what they are going to do.

My mom is always worrying about me and my brother, Travon, walking up the hill late at night. She feels that something bad will happen. She is worried that a person will mistake me for someone that I'm not and end up killing me. My family always has to deal with the death of friends they have grown to know and love. With all of this violence getting closer and closer to home, my mom and sisters just want to get up and move to a different city. The violence is getting too close to our family for them to handle. They have to deal with close family members getting killed, so they want to leave the city and never come back to it. My family would hate for me or Travon to get killed like that in the hellhole that we call home. But anywhere that we move to is going to have violence. It is dangerous for people to walk outside because there is the chance of getting killed by a bullet, a drunk driver trying to get home, or a person speeding down the street racing someone. If people were less violent, then fewer people would get killed and more would be alive today. If somebody at least talks to teens, it would be for the better.

Because of all the people getting killed and all the violence over the last several years, I've changed so much. I am a better person today. This violence makes me want to proceed forward and not make the same mistakes I have seen around me. I know in my mind that I made the right choice by not taking the violent road. Those who are violent might think that since they don't get the love that they want from their parents, they can just go out and join a gang or be on the corner selling drugs or their bodies. These kids are young, and they could be anything that they want to be if they could take that old drama of violence and put it all into the past. All they have to do is turn those negative things going on around them into positive actions, instead of thinking they can just run away from all of their problems. If you can't leave the negative things behind, you are showing that you can't face your fears and that you're going to fail in whatever you do. If you can't face your past, you can never face your future.

Young people have to think about whether or not they're going to finish high school and be able to have a degree. They could get a scholarship to go to college to follow their dreams. There are people who are trained to be able to talk to students about the problems that are bothering them. Being a person of integrity, you, Barack Obama, can create programs for teens committing violence on the streets, giving them the opportunity to change the direction of their lives in a more positive way.

Another way that you could show integrity is by coming into the community to see what the people need. Some people have problems with their health and can't go up and down stairs. Some people have a hard time paying the bills, and you could come by and make a better program that could help them. Then they won't feel like they're alone and have nobody to depend on for help when they really need it.

Health care is a major problem in today's society. People can't afford the medication that they need. They have to find a way to pay for the medication, so they try to get money from their family. But sometimes their own family doesn't even care about what happens to them. People who have no way to get the prescriptions that they need can end up going into debt. Mr. Obama, you could show that you have integrity by giving us the health care that we need.

Do you know what people go through every single day, having to deal with high bills and seeing all these parents that don't know what their children are doing? There are so many people that can't even afford to buy food because their rent is so high that they can't even pay that. I believe that you could help to find a way for the people to have affordable housing to live in and food on the table to feed their children. This will really help the people, and they would thank you for it. They would know that there are people that do care about what other people are going through.

I wonder what the word integrity means to you. Do you show integrity to people that you work with or meet? I have met so many wonderful people that have integrity and show it with others that they don't even know. Some people have so many definitions for the word integrity. Some people may not understand what the word means, but they do know that it comes from their heart. I see people every single day helping people out by giving them food, clothes, money, etc. This makes the person that is receiving help so happy to know that there are kind people out there that could help.

For example, my teacher, Ms. McKamey, has a lot of integrity, character, and grace. She cares for her students and she learns to love them. She starts to think of them as sons and daughters that she never had. Her character is welcoming, and she shows respect during and after class. If a student has a question, Ms. McKamey tries her best to answer it. She is graceful with everything that she does, and she makes sure that her students are very well prepared for anything that is coming up at school or with life.

Another person that has integrity is Ms. Kern, a wonderful teacher who I have known since freshman year of high school. She always told me that if I missed something, I shouldn't be afraid to go and ask the teacher what I am falling behind on. She would also try her best to do something for any of her students if they asked her. I remember my freshman year when she took her whole advisory group to the ice skating rink at the Embarcadero. We had so much fun while we were there, and after that she took us to go have burritos. That memory will always stay in my head no matter how old I get.

These two teachers are great examples of people who do not compromise their integrity for anyone. From Ms. McKamey and Ms. Kern I learned what it means to show your integrity to other people no matter what their background or where they come from. I have so much respect for these two wonderful people that care about their students. They always want the best for their students and would like to see them graduate from high school. They would like to see them alive and free, not dead or in jail, because they know these young, educated students are smarter than that. From my teachers, my friends and I have grown to learn how to have integrity with one another.

My friends that I have come to know and love from middle school are like brothers and sisters to me. I have grown to trust them and really talk about things. My close friends, Angelique and Jonathan B., will always be there when I need them. I've also grown to know and care for friends like Carlina, Dorrian, Daarina, and other people that I met in high school. These people care about their friends and I would hate to lose them. They would do anything for me if I just asked them, and I would do the same for them. I remember this one time that my two friends helped me pay to go to camp. I asked them to let me pay them back for it, but they told me not to worry about it because I already helped them out with so much.

Sometimes, the bravest people let fear mix with integrity when it comes to helping. When you have integrity and fear together, they won't mix at all. Fear can inhibit someone from taking action. For example, if you see a man or a woman getting hurt for no reason at all, you want to try to help. But sometimes fear kicks in, and the person ends up getting hurt. You feel bad about what happened because you could have helped with that problem. You think, *If I did this, then that person would still be alive*, or, *What if I just got in the middle of them? Then maybe they wouldn't be hurt*. It keeps playing over and over in your head that you could have helped.

But then you think, *What could have happened to me if I had helped that person? I could have been killed or hurt.* There is so much that you could do to help, but fear sometimes gets in the way of integrity.

With this letter, I am expressing how I feel about the word integrity, and I am trying to communicate how you could help. Mr. Obama, would you be compassionate about how the people are doing, and show that they did make the right decision by voting for you? I know that you don't want to be like President Bush by leaving people on rooftops for weeks before helping. He didn't come to help until days after Katrina, knowing that these people needed help right away. People from different cities came to help them before President Bush did. I know that you never want to leave people cold, hungry, without shelter, and in dangerous and harsh conditions like what happened in New Orleans. If you have compassion and care, and if you try to communicate with the people who voted for you, you will help us turn the negative things around us into positive actions.

Thank you, Mr. Obama, for listening to what I have to say. I am looking forward to a brighter future built on change and hope.

WHEN WILL THE CHANGE COME?

Kaya S. Lewis

Waking up at 5:30 in the morning is a disaster. Most days, while I'm still in bed, I can hear my mom in the kitchen. I think to myself, *Why is she on the phone and the computer so early?* I am forced by my mother's talking to wake up. While I lay there, I ask myself, *What kind of job will have you up at 5 AM?* But I know it's because she has to take care of us. I realize that she can't take care of everything alone so I get up to go take a shower. While my fifteen-year-old brother and ten-year-old sister are still sleeping, I get dressed and wake them up so they can get ready for school. My mom stays on the phone the whole time, talking to people from work where she is a receptionist. As soon as we are ready to leave, my mom always realizes that she misplaced the keys to my grandmother's house. Usually we have to wait for at least twenty minutes until she finds them.

After we find them, we walk down four long blocks to get to the street-car stop and then wait there for about fifteen to twenty minutes. While we are there we always tend to talk about the things that happened the day before, since every time we come home we do homework and go to bed. My mom doesn't get home from work until around 8 PM so we really don't get the time to see her. Once the streetcar pulls up, we sit right by the door because the car gets so crowded and there's no way to get out. It takes about forty-five minutes to get to school, and the ride is hot and boring. It gets so hot that you can't even move around without someone's breath in your face. When we finally get to our stop we rush everyone off the bus just so we won't miss our chance to get off. Once we get off the bus we go our own way. My mom drops my little sister off at Rosa Parks Elementary School, and my brother and I walk the opposite way so that we can go on to Mission High School.

When I arrive at school, I see all my friends in the lobby and start talking and laughing about the day before. Then the bell rings. We start walking to class and most of us have the same class so we stay together. As soon as I get to class, I immediately put my head down on the desk because I wonder why I need to come to these classes. I'm not going to ever need chemistry. I might need math once in a while. I don't understand the subjects. I lay there until my teacher sends me out to the office for not participating. Then I go to Mr. Zelaya, who is the dean and also a very close friend of my mom's. He basically watched me grow up. He tells me, "I'm tired of seeing you in here. The next time you come down here you're going home. What do you come to school for if you're not going to be in class? It doesn't make any sense." I walk out of his office not really caring about anything he just said. After I leave his office, I go to the office of Ms. Jordan, the attendance clerk. She says, "Girl, what are you doing down here? You're a mess. You need to go back to class and chill out." I leave her and walk back into the hallway and ask Iz, the school security guard and a very cool woman, where GiGi, the school's mentor, is. She says, "She isn't here yet, text her." I walk up the stairs and go back to my class. As soon as I get to the door the bell rings, so I leave.

When I get to my other class, I wait to find out what the Do Now is. The Do Now is a preparation for what our lesson will be for the day. Until then I sit and look around or send text messages. This is the only time it doesn't look obvious that I'm using my phone. Once the bell rings and my teacher comes in, he gives us the Do Now. I get started. For the rest of the day I am on task, until advisory comes. Advisory is my last, and also most boring, class. We don't do anything there but sit and talk. I actually don't understand why we need an advisory class. What is it benefiting? All it is to me is an extra waste of time! Once school is over I go to my granny's house. I wait for my little sister to get out of her program and go pick her up. Then we are on our way home. It's the same routine in the evening as it was in the morning, except my mom's not there, and the people on the streetcar are on their way home from work so it is even more packed.

We sometimes have to get off on our way home and go to Safeway just so we can get something for dinner for the next night. Once we leave the store, we walk home or wait for another bus, depending on how many bags we have. As soon as we get home, we open the curtains in the kitchen and the living room and let the little sun that is left shine in. I turn on the radio and fix my little sister and brother something to snack on, and we wait for our mother to come home. By the time my mom gets home, we are tired and ready to go to bed. My mom walks in with a phone in one hand, talking on it, and her pager in the other, letting her know that she has a call at the office that she forgot to check. Then we all just go into our rooms and go to sleep for the night. I hate seeing my mom work a lot and come in day after day on the phone because of some stupid job. If it was up to me, I would want her to work at home. At least I'd know she'd be there when we got home. The way it is now, we repeat the same thing every single morning and day after day. Sometimes I get so tired that I don't even get up and go to school, and then the school calls home asking why I was absent or why I was late. Did it ever occur to anybody that I was getting stressed out? Do people not think kids can get stressed out, too? I get tired of getting up every morning, getting dressed, getting my sister dressed, picking her up after school, going back home to get groceries for the night. I'm tired of doing a lot of things but no one would ever know because I bury it so deep that sometimes I even trick myself into believing that I'm OK. I live with it because I know that I'm prepared for whatever happens in the future.

Having a supportive family is a big deal to me. My mom supports me in whatever I do. She always says, "You can do whatever you please to do, just make sure those grades are in the right place. You're not going to be able to do nothing tomorrow if you're not making the right choices now." So that's why I come to school, so that when I graduate from high school and go on to college, I will get the job that I always dreamed of. Why just dream if you can make it reality? All things are possible if you set your mind to it. See, most people don't understand what it's like growing up in what I call the "hard-knock life." People think they know what it's like to not have anything; they think they know but they don't. I hate it when people say they understand. You don't understand. You don't understand what it's like to sit in the dark for two to three days. You don't understand what it's like for your mother to be the only one raising you with no father figure around. You don't understand what it's like to see your mom go into the grocery store and come out with nothing, but then when we walk into the house pull everything from under her shirt because the food stamps weren't put on the card yet. It's hard, but I know I can't do anything because I'm still a kid myself. I try my best to help out. When I have a little bit of money, I save it, so that if we run out of tissue I know that we have enough to get that.

I see a lot of people dying now, all over respect. When you're respected you have *power*. I make sure that what I have my little brother has, no matter how big or small it is, because I don't want him to get caught up in the streets just because he thinks a person needs to respect him like some of these other boys do. I can't lose him to the streets. The streets right now are like the black hole, just sucking in innocent people just because they don't fit in. When I look back, I think of all the things my mother has been through. She lost her baby, my little sister, to SIDS. After that she went through a little breakdown but pulled back and got better. Then she split with my dad because he was an alcoholic and liked to start trouble.

As my older brother got older and wiser, he knew we didn't have much money so he started doing for himself no matter what the consequences were. He was what they call nowadays a "beast." He began to hang outside, not much but just enough to drag him into some BS. My brother used to be a star football player for the PAL league. Everybody knew him. Slowly, he withdrew from sports and got sidetracked. All the money he was making sidetracked him. My brother got shot one time in the arm, and then about six or seven months later, he got shot again. The second time the bullet missed his heart by two inches. If it had gone any further, he wouldn't be here on earth today. I thank God that He saved my brother's life.

My brother and I rarely talk. We talk but it's not the same as how it used to be. When we were younger we used to play laser tag or hide and seek, and we could never find him. Then he would jump out of the closet and scare us. I miss those days, but now my brother is back on the right track. He has a beautiful daughter, my niece, and I love her dearly. It may sound crazy, but I love my brother more than I love myself.

I look up to my brother a lot because I know that he's been through a lot and is on the road to making a major change. Since I didn't always have that older brother that I really wanted, I looked up to my older cousins as my brothers. I used to hang out with them until my mom said, "You are a girl. There is no need for you to be out with a whole bunch of boys. It just doesn't make any sense that you act just like a boy." I told her it isn't my fault that I was raised around dudes.

My brother is currently enrolled at Santa Rosa Junior College, and I am so proud of him for going back to school because I know he will do well. To me my brother is my biggest inspiration. He has been through so much and still bounced back like nothing ever happened. I know he tries to stay strong for the family, not because he has to but because he wants to, and for that I love him dearly. It seems like every time we see each other he sits me down and gives me long lectures. In my head I'm like, *here we go again*, but I know he is telling me because he doesn't want me to follow on the path that he took. He wants me to do better and accomplish a lot. For that, when I get my first big job, he's going to be the first person I get something for just because he's pushing me to be better and better. He knows I'm able to accomplish what I believe in.

I think Obama being elected as president will make a change in this country. I think he will do something about all the tragedies that are going on in the world. But one person cannot do it all. We need to support the people that are trying to make a change. Those are the ones who are voting because they want to make a difference in their children's lives. Those who are being brought up who need a president who is going to provide help for them, make the school system better so that they can get the best education possible, and help the families in need who are struggling because they have no one on their side. We need a new president to make a change, and I feel that Obama will be great for a change. The economy is screwed up, and sooner or later the schools are going to end up shutting down because there's no funding.

I hate school, but I know I have to go if I want a good career. My brother always tells me that if you don't have a career then you don't have anything. He basically says that no matter how well your job pays, it still doesn't beat having a career. That's why I'm in school faithfully every morning even though I don't want to be there. I choose to because I want to make my family and myself proud. That's why it's so sad to know that one day there might not be any schools left. Once there are no more schools and they're all shut down, everyone is going to turn to the streets. When you turn to the streets you end up dead or in jail. That will really affect me because I've seen a lot of deaths as a young child. To see that happen will really cut me deeply, so deeply that I would feel it's my fault. Right about now, I feel like President Bush doesn't care at all about how the economy and the war stuff is affecting us. In my personal opinion, I think that Bush needs to fix the problems he created. Politically, I feel he needs to hurry up and resign from the presidency. With or without Bush, there is going to be a change, and it's up to us to make that change. With the help of our new and improved president, a change will come.

A HOPE FOR AMERICA
Wenbin Tan

Dear Mr. President:

Thank you for taking the time to read my letter. I'm a student at Mission High School. First, I would like to congratulate you on becoming the new president. As the president, every little action you take or decision you make can have a big impact on the world. There are many things wrong in this nation; I hope you can fix them. During your campaign you spoke about many good policies for this nation. Try them—no matter how hard it is—and don't be shy. Because you are our leader, we will always support you. You are the most important person in this nation; you are the one who can change things. Without you, we would lose direction and not know what to do about international issues, national security, or human rights. Ultimately, you need to try your best to enact laws and policies that are aimed at treating the citizens of our country as you yourself would want to be treated.

In my opinion, one of the major problems facing the United States right now is gun control. In the United States, we have the Second Amendment, which protects people's right to have guns. I think the Second Amendment is designed to allow citizens to have guns so that they can protect themselves and their property when they do not feel safe. However, that is not what is happening. Guns have become a major problem in this country. Guns are increasing problems with gangs and crime. I have been watching my peers—teenagers—getting killed by guns. Something is wrong! Without the Second Amendment, there would not be a problem. Mr. President, I am asking you to limit the Second Amendment so that only police officers and soldiers can have access to guns.

I moved to the United States four years ago from China. In China, only police officers and soldiers can have guns. Don't you think that is better than loose gun control laws that basically allow anyone to own a weapon and contribute to high murder and violent crime rates? With stricter gun control laws, we wouldn't even have to worry about this big problem.

There are many stories about parents who lost their kids because of guns. I was recently watching a father's speech about his son being killed at school, and he was crying. According to national data released in 2002 by the Children's Defense Fund and National Center for Health Statistics, 3,012 children and teens were killed by gunfire in the United States in a single year. That is one child every three hours; eight children every day; more than fifty children every week. That is the thing you will probably never understand, Mr. President, because you have never experienced one of your kids getting killed by guns!

Every year, there are many cases of five- to nine-year-old kids accidentally killing themselves or their parents by playing with guns. They are too young to use these weapons correctly, and many parents don't manage their guns safely. Parents often put guns in a place where their child could easily get them. Sometimes parents are too busy and don't have enough time to take care of their kids. They may leave their kid at home alone, and kids always like to play with new things. When they see a gun, they think it is a toy and fire at other people or themselves. Here's a true story: Recently, a toddler fatally shot himself after finding a gun in his parent's car. According to the authorities in Jackson, Mississippi, the three-year-old was sitting in the car at a gas station when he found the gun in the front seat and shot himself in the face. Police questioned the boy's parents, but no charges have been filed. These are not freak accidents. More than 500 children die annually from accidental gunshots. Some shoot themselves, while others kill friends or siblings after discovering a gun. I found this information on the Internet:

- On July 19, four-year-old Dylan Jackson shot himself to death after finding a loaded gun at a friend's home during a birthday party.
- A three-year-old Southeast Washington boy shot himself in the foot and grazed his hand while playing with his father's gun—which he found lying on the floor.
- A two-year-old Tampa boy shot himself in the chest with a loaded 9 MM he found on his parent's couch while playing.
- Last February, a thirteen-year-old boy shot himself with a semi-automatic handgun in the home of his guardian, a Maryland police officer.
- The ten-year-old son of a New York City police officer died after shooting himself in the face with his father's loaded revolver. The boy found the weapon on a shelf in the basement while looking for a ball his mom had hidden.

Is there a way to stop these senseless deaths? "The biggest mistake parents make is assuming their child doesn't know where the gun in the house is," says Matthew Miller, associate director of the Harvard Injury Control Research Center. "Kids are smart and if they know there's a firearm in the house, they'll probably figure out a way to get to it. We can't expect children to act like adults," he adds. "Parents monitor their kid's diet, curfew, and social life, but when it comes to guns, parents often just say, 'Respect the gun, it's off-limits,' or 'Guns are dangerous.'" That type of parenting just doesn't work. Mr. President, I hope you save these kids. I beg you, please. If you help to enact legislation that further limits Americans' right to own guns, kids would be much safer.

Along with children accidentally using guns, gangs are also a part of the problem of gun control. Gangs use guns as part of their drug businesses and to scare or intimidate civilians or other gangs. They use guns to expand their power and to increase the number of gang members. Most gang members get their guns from the black market. They kill different gang members to own the rights to sell drugs in their territories. This problem is not just between gangs—it also seriously impacts teenagers' and civilians' lives. There are many teenagers who are captivated by guns. They think that it is very cool to have a gun and like showing their weapons to each other. Unfortunately, teenagers often don't know how to control their anger, and when they get mad, sometimes they use guns without thinking. At other times, they fire guns by mistake and kill people. As a result, they could spend their whole lives in jail. Therefore, it is not just about one person's life being lost, it is two people's lives. Because the United States government follows the Second Amendment, almost any civilian can own and buy guns very easily. A person can pretty much buy a gun from the supermarket.

I have had a very personal experience with guns. One night, I was on my way home and there was a police chase on the freeway. At the moment when the police almost caught the person, he pulled out his gun, but the police killed him before the person was able to attack. There is a major reason why the United States police have a higher rate of firing their weapons in the line of duty than any other nation does. In the United States, police instinctively pull out their guns and point them at people who they think are dangerous. It makes people nervous and contributes to police killing by mistake, because when people get nervous, their actions become irrational.

Another night, I was on my way home. I remember it was raining, and I was listening to music on my cell phone when I suddenly noticed two unknown guys crossing the street. I didn't think about what they were doing, I just slowly walked on. One of them began walking right in front of me, and the other one was behind me. "Can I have a dollar, man?" the guy in front of me said. "Yes, please wait." I looked at my wallet. Suddenly, the one behind me used his arm to choke me very hard. At that moment, I knew what they were trying to do to me, but it was too late to run away.

Then the one in front of me said, "Give me anything, anything!" At first, I didn't give up my property. "Please, don't do that!" I said. My hands were holding my cell phone very tightly, because it was new and I liked it very much. They started to hit me. They hit my face and my body repeatedly and very hard. It was late at night and raining, so no one was around to help me. Finally, I had to give up my property because I could not keep letting them hit me. I would have died.

They ran away right after they got my property, and I kept watching them head to the bus stop. Then the only thing I could do was go home. So many things came to my mind: the first thing was whether there was a police station near the site where they stole my cell phone. The second thing was trying to find someone to help me. I'm a guy and I thought I should have fought for myself, but I was worried that they might have had a gun. I hated them and myself, but after a while I began to hope that they would forgive themselves. I also wondered if their families knew what they were doing and if they could help to fix them. After I got home, I called up 911 and told them what had happened. Then two police officers came to my house and asked me for details about the case, but they could not find the robbers because there was no witness at the location.

Because of my experiences living in China, I can see the differences between the two countries. Even though China is not as rich as the United States, I felt that I could spend my whole life in safety there without getting shot down. I remember when I was fifteen years old. I was a simple boy, still living in China, and I didn't know too many things about my community. I always spent nights out and sometimes I got into trouble with people. I used to get beat up or have property stolen by people. I even lost a couple of teeth during a fight. I was sure I would not lose my life because there is almost no way for a regular civilian in China to get deadly weapons. Guns, bombs, rocket-propelled grenades, and other dangerous weapons are all illegal to own or sell. If the government finds out that you have these types of weapons, you will go to prison or be executed. These laws mean that the people of China almost never get killed by guns, and students never bring guns into school to shed blood.

Earlier, I talked about United States police officers using their guns often. In China, the police officers would not use guns unless something extremely serious happened. For example, they would use them only if they knew a group of robbers was trying to rob a bank using deadly weapons, but the officers would have to go to the station first to obtain guns and bullet-proof vests.

The last problem I want to talk about is the United States economy breaking down. I believe there are many reasons for the recession, such as war, banks, and people's incomes. During the past eight years, George W. Bush has done many things wrong. He started two different wars in the Middle East. It has brought people here and abroad into a dark age. Sometimes the U.S. military has destroyed happy families by mistake, when soldiers think Iraqi civilians are terrorists and shoot them down without any warning. At times, the U.S. Army provides food and water for Iraqi kids, but when the kids go home, they get beaten up by their parents for accepting items from the military. This is not just about Iraqi civilians, but also about U.S. soldiers who are dying one by one. That is not what we wanted. Especially those soldiers who have just gotten married or had kids—some of them didn't have a chance to go back see their children or families. The place where we live is called the United States, but the reality of our country is the opposite of its name. We are not united. Too many of us are divided. Horrible things happen in this country and outside of it because of our actions. The United States has the most power, which means we are responsible for taking care of other nations. But have you thought about why the terrorists mostly attack us and don't attack China or other countries? Maybe our policy is wrong. It conflicts with some nations, making the terrorists hate us. Is it fair that the U.S. military stays in other countries? Other countries should have the right to defend themselves. Maybe they don't need the U.S. military.

Since the origin of the human race, we have had violence in many places at many moments. Haven't we had enough? I think it is time to stop. No matter what we are or where we are living on the earth, we have the same dream. That dream is for peace. We should improve our world. With this essay, I want to bring happiness to those people in the war.

Hopefully, President Obama, you will improve the state of our nation as a whole and individual people's bad situations. You are part of this nation, of us. When anything dangerously impacts us or threatens us, it is your business to deal with it. Please keep in mind how you would like to be treated by other people and by your government while you are leading us. Because of you, we are hopeful that we will have a better nation than ever before.

TRYING TO CHANGE A LIFE
Melvin Morales

My story is about how all people can help each other by giving support and help to each other when they need it. My first example is Mario. When I met him last year, I tried to help him. I saw him suffering, and I don't like to see people suffering when I know that I can help. He is from El Salvador, from a town called San Juan, where the schools do not have much support for their students because there aren't enough resources. He didn't know many things, like how to speak English. He didn't like to do homework and he didn't understand anything in his classes.

In the beginning, I gave him all my trust, my support, and my little knowledge to help him in his homework and life. When I first saw this guy, he was very quiet and afraid. I tried to change his life for the better, but it was too late. He didn't talk with anyone because he didn't know people in his classes. I was the first person who had a conversation with him because I could speak his language, which is Spanish. I told him to always try to understand the teacher when the teacher was explaining the lesson, but he didn't pay attention. He didn't want to learn English. He wanted somebody to translate what people were saying; he never listened to my advice. He always did what he wanted to do with his life and didn't want my help.

When I came to this country one year ago, I felt the same way he felt. My parents moved from my country, Guatemala, because the economy and the work were so bad. When I started school, I didn't speak English. I was afraid to ask what was happening in the class. Like my friend, I had the same very bad experience. I thought that I could help him and also make a new friend.

When I came to this country, I didn't know anybody—only my parents. My parents are good people who understand friendship, respect, and love, and they always taught me these things. They are my only family in this country. First, my mother came to this country eight years ago. This was really a big problem in my life because I was not used to living without her. My family was separated, and it was hard for all of us. She did this so that we could have a good life. Now I understand the sacrifice that she made. From my family I learned much about life, like all people should respect others and help when they can.

My parents have given me many examples of how to help other people. Five months ago, they gave help to a friend who was living in Guatemala. She didn't have enough support for her children, wanted a better life for them, and wanted to come to the United States. She had no money or resources, so my parents thought about it and decided to help. They sent her the money, and when she arrived here, they helped with many things—they bought her clothes, found her a place to live, introduced her to new friends, and found work for her. With these examples, I learned how I could help and respect people so that they would help and respect me. That is why I wanted to help my friend.

The culture in the United States is sometimes the same but also very different. I think the culture is the same because this country has a lot of Guatemalan food and people. Here, the climate is colder and access to work is more difficult, but, overall, life is easier. But there are many difficulties and changes. I remember the first day in school. I arrived in the classroom to see many guys sitting and talking one on one, so I sat down in the corner and felt very afraid. I sat in the back because it was the only place where I could sit and be like the guys in this classroom who spoke English. The communication that they had between friends was good. The people in the class spoke all the time, and I did not know who could speak Spanish. I tried beginning a conversation in Spanish, finally, to find somebody who could talk with me because I felt comfortable speaking in my language. I could not answer anybody who talked to me in English because I didn't know anything about the language. The experience that day was really unforgettable. I felt like crying. I wanted to go out of the classroom and go back to my house. I felt that the guys were talking about me, like I was a bad person for my appearance or the color of my skin.

When I came to the school, two friends really helped me. Maria De Leon and David Figueroa were the first two people who talked to me. Maria and David helped me every day. Many times they explained the homework to me when I didn't understand the teacher. When I went to lunch they would say, "Hey, friend, how are you? Come here and sit with us." They were my only friends. Maria continues to study here and we are both seniors. It is her last year, like me. David graduated last semester and I miss him because, with David, I always got to talk about soccer and man things. I can't talk about those things with Maria because she doesn't like soccer or other things like computers. Maybe we will graduate together. For me, that will be beautiful to do because she was the first friend that I met. In my heart I feel that David and Maria are true friends because they are two good people.

I had a similar experience to Mario's when I came to this school. I didn't know anybody. I was very quiet, and when I saw my classmates walking in the halls, I just smiled at them. Mario had the same attitude when he was in the classroom. I could relate to him. I couldn't laugh at him because he was like me. I helped him in the math class that we shared, but he didn't do the homework that the teacher gave him. For example, I told him to pay attention because the class was good, but he didn't want to. He said he didn't pay attention in this class because he was very bored and he wanted to be a mechanic. He thought numbers wouldn't serve him. Then he drew a picture on his hand because he was distracted.

Many times I had to explain the homework twice so that he understood better. Every day after school, I explained to him the new things that I had learned. I also told him that he needed to better understand how important it is to study, but he thought it was better to work than to go to school. After I did many things for him, such as translating, helping him with homework, and giving directions, we had a big problem. One day in math class, he left the classroom without taking his homework. So I picked it up from his desk to give to him. The next day when I gave him his paper, he became angry with me because I took his homework, and he said it wasn't any of my business. He said his things have nothing to do with me and I butt in where I am not wanted. He told other friends that I was a bad person because I could speak English better than him and could do more things than him. He thought that I thought he was stupid, so he was angry. I think that he was furious because he had a bad day, or he was nervous when other people tried to speak to him in class or any other place. He was so mad that our friendship ended just because he was so egotistical.

Several months ago, I saw him walking in the street. We never talked again, but I believe that he is the same person I knew in school—the type of clothes he wore were the same. I listened to some words that he spoke in Spanish with someone, and I recognized him. I didn't know if he had learned to speak English because I never knew about his life again. That day when I saw my friend, I tried to talk with him, but I think that he never wanted to talk to me again. He saw me but ignored me. I had forgotten the past and wanted him to talk to me again and be my friend. I felt bad when he ignored me because we had been good friends, but now, no more.

I take this as a good experience, but I am very sad. I did a simple thing to try and help. I'm satisfied that I was given the opportunity to help somebody without them having to give me something in return. It makes me feel good and I am at peace with myself. Bad things always end badly. Even if I do good things and am not recognized for them, I will know that my capabilities can always get better and I will be a better person each day.

BRAZIL
Ingrid Reis

I n Rio de Janeiro on June 12, 2000, tour bus number 174, full of vacationers, was taken hostage by an armed young man. On TV, I heard that Sandro Nascimento terrorized the people on the bus for five hours; the news media were there, telling us about everything that was happening. The police came to negotiate, but when Nascimento was ready to surrender a police officer took a shot at him and missed. Nascimento then reacted by killing an innocent female hostage. It is most likely that Nascimento came from the *favela* (the slums).

Brazil is a good country, full of beautiful places like beaches and mountains. Brazilian culture is great fun; there is a dance called the *samba*, food, like *feijoada*, happy people, the carnival, and warm weather. What you don't always see is the poverty, which causes violence and takes the innocent lives of many young people. When tourists go to Rio de Janeiro, they just go to the rich places like Copacabana, Leblon, and Barra, to drink coconut water, go shopping in the best places, and buy the best things. They go to the beaches like Ipanema, but they don't go to the poor areas, where the real life happens.

The poor area we call *favela* because *favela* means "on the top of the hill." The slums are located in the middle of the city on the hill and mainly poor people live there. Inside the *favela* there are a lot of poorly constructed houses, many made of wood, and all of the houses are close together. Nobody has to pay for electricity because they rig something up, but I don't know how it is done. Most of the time kids from the *favela* don't go to school and when they do, they don't have the right conditions for study—they are lacking good teachers, lunches, chairs, tables, books, and transportation. Often, families need the kids to work instead of going to school, to help with the food. People live there because they don't have the money to buy a house in the city or in a good neighborhood, but they are still good people, trying to do the best they can. When given the opportunity to show what they know, people from the *favela* work as hard as anyone else.

I have family who live inside the *favela,* who are good people and who are stuck there because they don't have the means to leave. I grew up in Rio de Janeiro outside the *favela,* but we visited my family there often. I remember seeing a lot people in the street, girls with skimpy clothes, a lot of motorcycles, and people in bars drinking beer and talking. Once I saw a little boy who couldn't have been more than six years old, holding a gun. Why was he holding the gun? Has the world gone crazy? Maybe he didn't have a family, but to me, seeing a kid with a gun is crazy. When I saw that, I felt like someone had knocked my legs out from under me. I stopped to think about what makes people violent. I stopped to think about the difference between the opportunities that my mother gave to me and the education that boy's family gave to him.

One of the causes of violence in the city is the divide of rich and poor: When the poor people go to the rich area, the rich people look at the poor people like they are nothing. That is why the poor people get so angry. They feel like revolting. That is why you see kids not much more than five years old with guns in their hands, using or selling drugs in the street or inside the *favela.* I can't say they never rob, because it happens all the time. The rich people don't give them jobs and they don't give them chances. The poor people need food to eat, so sometimes they are left with no choice but to steal. I think the violence also starts when people don't have food to eat. So daddies kill sons and sons kill daddies; people kill each other for money. There are gangs everywhere. In many countries we see kids living in the streets, and when gangs go to war, kids come back missing an arm or a leg. And do you know what happens? Families cry and cry. The government can help stop this, but they never really solve anything. Every month the government gives the poor children fifteen Reais (approximately five or seven U.S. dollars) each, but this is not enough to keep the poor quiet.

Let me tell you what the schools need in Brazil in order to give the students a good education. Kids attend school from age six until they are eighteen or nineteen years old, and then they go to college. We should wake up and pay attention and think about what we can do to help the poor people and take kids off the streets. What I want to do to help end the violence is give more opportunities to the poor. I would like to open new schools and businesses, and change the way the government works.

For example, in the schools there should be after-school programs that keep kids off the streets and out of gangs. Also, there should be more arts and sports programs to give the students something to look forward to. There should be local businesses in the community. This world needs more love and respect; it needs us to care for one another. I think if everyone thought the same way I do, the world and our lives could be much better. We could live in peace, but we have to think and act fast. I think then God would be very happy with us.

In the United States we can have everything we want—a good car, good jobs, and enough money to take care of ourselves. I like living here in San Francisco, California, because people can get good jobs with better pay than where I used to live. I think that is why many people come here. My family came here for that reason.

I go to work and school most days. Today I live on Alemany Boulevard, in a good neighborhood, where I never see strange things happening. The streets are clean, the houses look nice, and the people are relaxed.

My house has a lot of space and I have my own room, like in Brazil. The transportation in San Francisco is really fast, and we don't have to stay at the bus stop for too long. We can get anywhere at any time. I want to talk more about the opportunities that I didn't have in Brazil, and that can be found here in the United States.

Life in the United States is not perfect: We see people on the streets using drugs all the time. We also see a lot of crazy people. Two months ago, when I was on the J-train, I saw I man with a black coat sitting on the floor drinking juice, eating something, and playing a guitar. He smelled so bad and he was singing so loud. I think people use drugs everywhere, but in the United States, I have seen it happening often. I once saw a man smoking marijuana while he was driving.

People who come here from other countries sometimes become gangsters when they arrive. They start fighting in the streets because they are from different sides of town, or different sides of the world. This is stupid, but even when the police arrest some of them, they come back to the streets and continue using drugs and fighting with each other.

Now I want to talk about the war in Iraq and, of course, about President Bush. Why did he start the war? I think what he is doing is stupid. Every day he takes life away, he sends people to war and do you know what happens? Families everywhere cry, while Bush is drinking coffee. I am really angry and sad because he spends millions of dollars on bombs, money that could be spent helping poor people and other countries, like those in Africa. This is terrible and causes innocent people to die.

Life here can be difficult when you arrive and find out that you have to live with other people. My aunt told me that when she got here fourteen years ago, she had to live with four people in a bedroom for a year. Living here is not always easy.

In Brazil, the public schools are really for the poor, who don't have the money to pay for a private school with good teachers in a good part of town. The government never gives money to improve the public schools, or to buy equipment like computers. The schools need materials to build better buildings and help the students improve their lives, giving them a chance for a better future. If they are given more chances in life, they can get a nice job. In the public schools, students have to buy their own supplies and give them to the school. This is really disrespectful to the Brazilians. The government runs the schools but they force us to supply our own items, which they then claim as school property. When you purchase items, you have to pay a tax. However, the people have no idea where the tax money goes. We wonder what the government does with all of it. A lot of people my age don't go to school because they don't have the money to buy supplies.

I see all of these injustices happening and I can't do anything to help. I ask myself why people continue the cycle of violence. I don't think anyone knows. So I want to talk about and solve violence, because my life and this world mean so much to me. I can see that if a person does not have a family, he or she might end up on the streets. I want people to pay attention to what is happening around them.

THE GOLDEN HURRICANE
Ranon Ross

I want my president to be a leader who will do for his country whatever it takes. He should be intelligent, wise, and concerned. When Hurricane Katrina struck on August 28, 2005, what we needed was a leader who would take risks. The president should do what he thinks is the best thing to help his country. He should definitely not do what President George Bush did. Bush did nothing at all, except hope it turned out well in the end. I want my president to think of better, even if unconventional, solutions.

When Hurricane Katrina struck New Orleans, a lot of citizens died. Many others were seriously injured, and countless families were separated from each other. Many families lost their homes and belongings and were forced to live in shelters. I went to school here in San Francisco with a girl from New Orleans, and she told me a lot of interesting things about the situation.

She and her mother moved here from New Orleans right before Hurricane Katrina hit. Her grandmother, grandfather, and great-grandmother had wanted to stay in New Orleans and did not want to leave their homes because that is where they had lived their entire lives. She didn't tell me what happened to her grandparents, but if I were in her shoes, I probably would have made my grandparents come with me because I would fear that if they did not come with me, something bad would happen.

When the people of New Orleans asked President George W. Bush to help them, he did not give them enough assistance. In my opinion, he didn't care enough to help rebuild New Orleans when he needed to. Therefore, President Bush did not fulfill his duties as a president and a leader because he didn't do enough when it mattered most.

To me, this event signifies a lot. It was a very tragic situation in history, and a lot of things changed. As a result, people such as athletes and students from across the country helped the citizens of New Orleans in their time of need. Hurricane Katrina stuck with me because when it happened, I felt devastated. It makes me ridiculously angry that President Bush did not prepare to act when he knew the hurricane was coming—he did not respond sufficiently to the situation when it happened. I think that he didn't respond to the situation because he was too cautious and afraid to take a risk. It makes me embarrassed that Bush was our president. In my opinion, Bush could have made sure that the citizens of New Orleans were kept safe.

Being an African American, I am also worried that, as many people have suggested, Bush's lack of action was due to the race of most of New Orleans' families. It is not fair that the color of my skin means that I am discriminated against by my president, who is supposed to care for and be concerned about me. The color of anyone's skin should not be cause for discrimination, especially by the President of the United States.

The entire situation made me so angry. It makes me think about how easily it could have happened to my family and me. My family works extremely hard to make a living. They pay their taxes on time and they obey the laws. If a catastrophic earthquake hit San Francisco, I would be afraid, angry, sad, and devastated. If I knew about the earthquake before it hit, I would immediately tell my family to move out of San Francisco.

Katrina affected New Orleans in many ways. New Orleans experienced flooding because several Army Corps–built levees failed. There were several incidences of damage done in residential and business areas. Many blocks to the south of Lake Pontchartrain were under water.

In addition, the flooding stranded many people who remained in New Orleans after the hurricane. Some stranded survivors lived on top of houses and other buildings all around the city. Many who remained in their homes had to swim for their lives and tread through deep water.

Many people climbed up onto their roofs with hatchets and sledge-hammers, which residents had been urged to keep in their attics in case of such events. These citizens were trying to get noticed and rescued by helicopters, jets, and other such aircraft, as opposed to drowning inside their flooded homes. Clean water was unavailable, and power outages were expected to last for weeks. Some hotels and hospitals reported that they were running short on fuel for their generators. The National Guard began to set up coroners' offices in certain locations. Ninety percent of south-eastern Louisiana was evacuated. It was the largest evacuation in United States history. The Superdome was used as a designated safety shelter for those who remained in the city.

A lot of the major roads traveling in and out of the city were damaged. There was only one route out of the city, but it was not useful because the bridge there had collapsed.

The hurricane also affected citizens' health. There was a lot of concern that the flood would result in an outbreak of health problems for those who stayed in the city. A lot of different diseases had broken out, such as hepatitis A, cholera, tuberculosis, and typhoid fever, all of which were related to the growing contamination of the city's food and drinking water, which had been compounded by the city's characteristic heat and humidity.

New Orleans mayor Ray Nagin declared that the death count could increase to as high as ten thousand after cleanup had finished. Some survivors and evacuees said that they saw dead bodies just lying on the streets and floating in flooded sections, especially in the eastern part of the city.

Six deaths occurred at the Louisiana Superdome. Four of these were from unnatural causes, such as a drug overdose and suicide. One of these four is believed to be the result of a homicide. The locations of corpses were recorded, but most were not collected.

I would like to talk about the racial issues that Hurricane Katrina has brought to my attention. Katrina showed me that Americans are not unified as a people. For example, here is a quote from the blog of college student Morgan Griffith about this situation: "We aren't all in it together, and most importantly, catastrophes do not hit the rich and the poor nor the black and the white equally hard."[1] This quote opens my mind to a lot of interesting thoughts. I repeat this quote to myself, and I have concluded that it is completely true. This quote has also brought some other thoughts to my mind. One is the fact that the government tries so hard to make sure that white people are safe and happy. But it will not try as hard to make sure that African-American citizens are just as safe as white people. For example, say that an all-white suburban neighborhood is in some kind of danger. The government would do everything that it can do to help the white people. But if an all-black neighborhood were in the same kind of danger, government officials would not really bother worrying about it.

Now that I look back on all of the terrible situations that I have been through, they are nothing compared to what the citizens of New Orleans had to go through. Hurricane Katrina has actually changed the way I act. For example, I am more appreciative of the things that I have. It has also given me a political viewpoint. I hate the current political climate because it does not help the everyday person. Although I am thankful for everything that I have, I feel that because I am black, if the same thing happened to me I would be treated the same as the citizens in New Orleans, and that would make me mad because it is unfair.

---

1.   http://www.brockbrown.com/katrina/index.html

THE THOUGHT OF CHANGE
Angel Chaparro

Human societies, regardless of such factors as race or religion, have always had some sort of ruling structure. There were the pharaohs in Egypt, the Inca ruler Atahualpa in South America, and Leonidas the great Spartan ruler in Greece. A king, queen, or religious leader might tell his or her people how they should live, including what their religion, job, and pretty much every aspect of life should look like. Eventually, kings and queens were questioned by others, and as people started to think for themselves, these oppressive ruling institutions began to lose power. Philosopher and astronomer Galileo challenged the Catholic Church in 1633 with his heliocentric theory. He was persecuted, put in jail, and threatened by the powers that be. However, over time scientists proved that Galileo's theory was correct. Eventually new leaders emerged—ones who didn't necessarily decide how you should live your life.

More recently, there have also been negative examples: leaders such as Stalin and Hitler, who tried to take over the world by instilling fear and blind obedience. They used their power to put fear in the hearts of their people instead of inspiring positive change.

Change is a part of life and nature. And even though many throughout history have been scared of it, there have been great leaders, politicians, and scientists to show us that change, often realized in different ways, is the right way to go. Some people want change but others don't want to go through the pain of it.

Change happens no matter what someone says; even if we don't see it happening because our minds are focused on what we think and feel in the present. All people go through problems and some of those problems may alter their perspectives, changing things like religion, appearance, and personality.

Some leaders have changed the way people looked at the world. For example, two brave men who emerged in the twentieth century were Mohandas Gandhi who opposed British rule in India, and Reverend Martin Luther King Jr. in the United States.

These two men changed the way the world looked at race relations. Gandhi led the non-violence movement in India by instructing Indian protesters not to strike back at British soldiers. The Salt March to Dandi is one example of one Gandhi's use of non-violence to oppose taxation and British colonialism. Through non-violent protest, Gandhi showed the world that one could be a leader without being a dictator.

Reverend King led the American Civil Rights Movement, including the Birmingham bus boycott. When King was leading boycotts, he and his followers were beaten by police in the streets of Birmingham, Alabama, but didn't let this silence them or their message. The most devastating thing happened to these leaders: Both King and Gandhi were assassinated. Their deaths continue to open peoples' eyes and inspire them to join the revolution of change. King and Gandhi left their marks as two of the greatest leaders to ever change the world.

Now, more then ever, we need a new leader. People are scared of what's happening to our government and the economy. We need a new leader to dig us out of this hole. We are considered one of the most violent countries in the world, mainly because we went to war with Iraq. People from other countries think we did this just for oil and not because we were trying to find the people who attacked the United States on September 11, 2001.

The nation is also currently in an economic hole because we owe billions of dollars to countries like Japan, China, the United Kingdom, and Brazil. The recent housing market crash has also contributed to our economic decline. The war has also contributed to the economic situation because we have spent so much money on it. Money going to the war could have gone to schools and to helping people keep their jobs. The current deficit could lead to another Great Depression. It will probably take a long time for us to get out of this and restore our economy.

People are looking for someone whom they are proud to call their leader. People are looking for someone with ideas that can change the world.

That leader may be of any sex, religion, or race; people just want someone who behaves in a way that they can relate to. This leader should not be stuck up, or people will not look up to him or her. Even worse, they might not care anymore. The leader should work towards what society wants: keeping the government and economy strong so that the people are happy. The leader should have many good characteristics, such as patience—because the way the government is now, he or she is going to need it. The leader has to be calm because he or she is going to be dealing with a lot of frustrated people. Leaders must be willing to take a pretty bad beating now and then; Gandhi and King went though hell to fight for what they believed was right. I consider Gandhi and King great leaders because they had these characteristics and the willingness to lead.

Now that we are in a presidential election year, new leaders are rising. I believe this election has brought many new opportunities and ways of thought, the type of revolution brought forth by great and thoughtful leaders who inspire positive change in the people just as their predecessors did. I believe Barack Obama could change the United States and what the world thinks of this country.

The first time I saw and heard Obama speak was when he was in a presidential debate with John McCain. The moderator asked questions about the economy, government, health, and war. When it was Obama's turn to speak up about his ideas, he said things that I had thought of before. For example, I would sometimes say that the government should help the poor and the middle class. When I heard Obama say that, I knew he would be a good president.

People want change and I think that Obama will bring it, that he will actually see it through. People should be smart about who they elect. In my opinion, if they elect McCain they might as well say hello to another four years of Bush. I don't agree with John McCain because some of his ideas are poorly thought out. For instance, he talks about sending more troops to Iraq to fight instead of bringing them back to their families so they can be happy.

Obama has so many good ideas. He stated in one of his speeches that he would provide $50 billion to jumpstart the economy and prevent one million Americans from losing their jobs. This means giving $25 billion to growth funds to prevent state and local cuts in health, education, and housing and heating. The other $25 billion would include job and growth funds to prevent cutbacks in road and bridge maintenance, and also fund school repair. If people lose their jobs, how are they going to be able to support their families? Right now, a lot of people are losing their homes and their jobs. The mortgages on their homes are getting so high that people can't pay them.

If Obama is elected, I hope that he will keep his word and bring the change he talks about. I want to see the world look at the United States differently. I want to see him make life better for Americans—including those who are not citizens.

*   *   *

Last night—November 4, 2008—Barack Obama was elected the 44th president of the United States. Every citizen voted either for a person they thought will change the country or they thought would keep it going in the same direction. I would have voted, but I'm not old enough yet.

If I could have cast a ballot, I would have thought about the future: how things would be for my children and my children's children. The U.S. can do so many good things, but what's the point if it doesn't change anything? It's not worth anything if everyone in the world hates us.

THE RULE OF THE PAPER TRAIL
Jorge Pinto

remember the day of the meeting. With distance and time I see it differently. I understand now as a soldier, spy, and person how the Golden Rule can sometimes play out in a different way. Even in the military, we live by treating one another as the United States military treats its soldiers. However, sometimes people can manipulate the "rule" and use their power in a harmful way.

I waited patiently in the barracks around a wooden table for the meeting to begin. I joined the Marines at age seventeen, about ten years ago. I joined because the Marines gave me a rank and skills that I couldn't acquire in the world of Cartersville, Georgia. After enlisting, I spent the next five years taking different specialized trainings while going from base to base. Altogether I was at eight different camps, including Camp Pendleton, Camp Parks, and Camp Pinole (all located in the United States). I am now stationed at Camp Dragão in Germany, where I've been since—at age twenty-two—I signed up for the Special Forces. Before I could get here, I took three years of rigorous training at Fort Bragg, but joining a Special Forces unit meant better pay, better health care, more specialized work, and the best part of all: the green beret.

Now I am thirty years old, and everything I've known is challenged. I have discovered a breach in security.

I find myself following District Commander Mark Kirkland. Commander Kirkland holds the rank of Lieutenant Colonel, and there's also a man with us that I recognize but cannot yet identify. As I trail behind them to the other side of the base, past the smelly bathrooms, we reach our destination: the meeting rooms.

Commander Kirkland carries nothing, and the other man is carrying a big stack of files. I'm biting my nails, worried about what they're going to do with the files. As they sit down, two more people walk in, and I quickly identify them as the Battalion Commander (BC) Lieutenant Colonel Miles Freeto and the Command Sergeant Major (CSM) Kevin Tran, who are from my own battalion.

The unidentified man quickly stands up and calls everyone to attention, and then says, "At ease, take your seats." I finally figure out the man's identity: He is the General of the United States Marine Corps, Marion Perry. I remember him from when I first started out as an unranked soldier. Then— out of nowhere—in walk four NCOs (Non-Commissioned Officers), all with sergeant ranks, who want to be a part of the general's plan.

The meeting starts. General Perry talks about documents. Documents which were reported missing last week but are now in the hands of this corrupt general. He plans to turn these documents over to the North Korean government. When I hear that, I immediately think, "What are these guys up to?" The general continues on, discussing intentions and plans. The documents surface. They discuss the United States' national defense systems, troop locations, and the plan to amass more soldiers around North Korea.

"What can I do? What can I do?" I say to myself. "What would make them do this?"

I slip out the window unnoticed, run over to my barracks, and grab my camcorder to record what they are doing. I run all the way back to the corridors only to find no one there.

That night I don't sleep well. I am constructing a plan. The next morning in the barracks I wake up to an alarming and very disturbing drill sergeant calling PT (physical training)! Ugh. Not again. I'm sleeping.

I go outside and see the Battalion Commander (BC) acting as if nothing has happened, requesting orders, and telling people what to do. If only everyone knew what he and the rest were up to. "I'm not listening to orders," I tell my lifelong friend from the 32ND, Sergeant Murtoff. The drill sergeant calls me over to drill and PT along with the other drill sergeants and First Sergeants with their companies. *Fine—I'll do it,* I think. I do the training for four hours and finish PT.

After, I notice that the Company Commander is missing along with the CSM and BC. Then the men pass, and I learn that meeting went on again in the corridors, this time with the Company Commander. The men look suspicious: They have all of their belongings, and the general is guarded as he carries the big stack of documents and files.

I run into my barracks, grab a duffle bag, put some clothes in along with the camcorder, and radio Sergeant Murtoff to tail the general and his men. I take a shower and put on my class-A uniform (a formal uniform used only for ceremonies), grab my stuff and go over to my Chevrolet Tahoe, and quickly get on the road. I radio Sergeant Murtoff and ask him his location. He says Berlin-Schönefeld International Airport, three hours away from camp Dragão.

I radio sergeant Murtoff again; he says the men are at the airport. I tell him to follow them wherever they go, even if it means behind enemy lines. He agrees. "They are on a plane leaving for North Korea," Sergeant Murtoff says, then adds, "I'll go along." I continue my way toward the airport.

When I arrive at the airport, I contact the SecDef (Secretary of Defense) through a call to General Matthew Lombardi from the Navy who I used to train with when I was training for the Special Forces Unit. After waiting on hold with the SecDef to verify my story, he tells me to hold again so he can go brief the President on my message. Amazingly, I am connected with President Walter Sullivan. When he answers I recognize his voice and strongly present myself, "First Sergeant Damien Jones from the U.S. Marine Corps 14TH Brigade, 135TH Battalion down in Germany, sir."

"I know," he says.

"I'm informing on General Marion Perry and his men; they've just left Germany's International Airport. I have a peer tailing them, and report is they've left to North Korea with classified documents."

"Are you sure of this?" the president asks.

"Yes, sir. Will you support Sergeant Murtoff and me on this mission? We need to inform the special forces troops, the Rangers, and our allies in North Korea."

"You've got my support, one hundred percent," the President replies.

In North Korea, the General and his men have arrived along with the disguised Sergeant Murtoff. Sergeant Murtoff radios and informs me that they have landed, and I tell him to stay low and out of sight.

Back at the airport in Germany, I'm waiting for the next flight to North Korea. I'm informed that all flights to Korea have been cancelled until next month. The cancellation is due to the North and South Korean governments' decision to close the borders. I can't wait that long. At the same time, I think, "Why the South Koreans?" Then I put it together: The North Koreans would have all this power, and the South Koreans would be left out. That meant that the South Koreans are desperate, vulnerable, weak, and willing to accept anything for some power and dignity. With all of this going on, the South Koreans would now have reason to go over to the enemy. The SecDef calls and puts me back on a flight to Washington, D.C.

On my flight, I sit next to a man wearing a German military staff jacket. He smells like left-out fish and perspiration and is carrying a metal suitcase. We take off and thirty minutes later he makes a call from the seat phone and starts speaking in German. I translate and learn that he is talking to General Marion Perry and his men, plotting to destroy the United States. I wonder if there's a possibility that this man could know my identity.

I guess not, because the German man is still talking, and he says that the company commander has noticed that someone is following his team. I think that I need to radio Sergeant Murtoff in the airplane restroom on a closed frequency and inform him that he's been made. He needs to go change and hang low until I get there.

When we arrive in D.C., I follow the German man talking on his cell phone to a house. He and his men are getting ready to leave for North Korea on a private jet. I charge into the room. The German man grabs his gun and points it at me. I outsmart him, escape with his duffel bag, and find the private jet on the landing strip behind the house. I change into his clothes and disguise myself as the German. I successfully get on the plane alone.

In North Korea, Sergeant Murtoff is tailing General Perry, even though I instructed him not to. They approach a checkpoint which belongs to the North Koreans, located at a base somewhere outside of United States territory. The base is actually a camp known as Camp Chapultepec. After General Perry and his men cross the checkpoint it is Sergeant Murtoff's turn to act like a local. The Korean sergeant askes Sergeant Murtoff for his documents. Stupidly, out of habit, he shows his United States Marine Corps Military ID. Fifteen soldiers come out of nowhere and aim guns at sergeant Murtoff and take him captive.

Hours later, Sergeant Murtoff wakes up in a black, empty room. The humid environment is affecting his body and mind. Being locked up in an isolated room with no view of life and no light just adds to the pain. Sergeant Murtoff struggles to break free but he can't. With a strong push to the door, in walks General Perry, accompanied by Lieutenant Colonel Kirkland. General Perry questions Sergeant Murtoff. He then has the audacity to ask him to join his men. Murtoff refuses the offer. Unlike Perry and his men, Murtoff keeps the real meaning of the Golden Rule in his soldiering. He thinks of the country he is protecting and will even risk his life to defend his people.

When I get to North Korea, my first order of business is to find Sergeant Murtoff and the documents while making sure no one sees me. I'm looking through numerous rooms and offices. I enter a strange room in which I find a safe that is open. I run towards it as fast as I can, as if it were a hundred yards away even though it's only ten feet. I find all of the files and documents and shove the stacks of files into my duffel bag. I quickly leave the room to look for Sergeant Murtoff. When searching earlier, I hadn't noticed that there was a basement. I look for the nearest elevator and take it down to B-3, the lowest basement. As I'm running through the halls, I hear Sergeant Murtoff struggling from behind a closed door. I grab a weakened Murtoff and we escape. He passes away en route to D.C.

In D.C. I land the jet. As I get off, reporters and military officials approach me. Confused, I take quick pictures with the press until President Sullivan arrives and takes me over to the White House, congratulating me for my heroic valor. I tell President Sullivan that I would like a hero's burial for Sergeant Murtoff. He agrees. I clean up and prepare for the frustrations of writing up my report.

Days later I receive a phone call at my house in California from President Sullivan who tells me to meet up at the White House at twenty-one hundred hours. I get ready and take a flight out to D.C. again and take a taxi up to the White House. When I go inside I pass Marine guards and police officers—getting many thanks here and there. I ask for President Sullivan. He comes down the stairs saying, "You're late for your next mission."

I groan. He leads me up a flight of stairs to a dark room. Suddenly the lights turn on, and many people are there from across the nation and the globe to give me their appreciation for treating them with the respect of doing unto them as I would have them do unto me. I receive such a warm welcome—then I receive awards, all on national television. But I start to cry at the mention of Sergeant Murtoff, a man I'll never forget.

RESPECT

Yong Chang Chen

I stood on the 45-MUNI bus and saw the old woman slowly get on. She looked very tired. She had white hair, white skin, and blue eyes with glasses. She wore a beautiful checkered dress and old sandals on her feet and was holding a cane. Her bright red and yellow checkered cotton dress fit her big body loosely. Her makeup was neat, with rouge color on her cheeks, and she had mild body odor.

The 45-MUNI bus looks like a normal bus except it has two lines one the roof attached to cables above that make the bus move using electricity. It is usually white on the outside and has about thirty seats inside. This bus is very busy anytime because it goes downtown, and some people use it to transfer to other buses. When I got on the bus that day people were sitting, talking to each other about whatever they knew, reading, and receiving text messages. Some were looking at the newspaper.

"Can somebody give me a seat, because my leg hurts me, please?" the old woman loudly demanded. Everyone was baffled when the old woman stopped talking. No one offered their seat immediately even though they heard her talking. The old woman was upset and exhausted. She had expected people on the bus to be kind. No one was thinking the same thought as her, however, because they didn't want to stand up. The bus driver drove slowly, wondering if anyone would offer a seat to the old woman. He wanted the people who were sitting on the bus to be respectful.

The old woman remembered another time when no one offered a seat to her. The event had happened a few years ago, after she had broken her leg in an accident while shopping. She was on her way home from the hospital, but when she got on the bus everyone thought she was a healthy senior and no one offered a seat. The old woman just stood on the bus and held the handrail. All the passengers sat on the bus and talked with their friends, forgetting about this tired woman still standing on the bus.

On the bus that day, I started thinking about what the woman's life might look like. When she was six years old she moved to Jackson, Mississippi and went to school until she was eighteen years old. The woman graduated from high school. Then she got a job taking care of babies and met her husband at a party. They were married when she was twenty-eight years old. They were poor but still happy. Jackson was a wonderful city. It was a nice place to live because people were kind, and there were many options for places to live. The residents of Jackson were happy to work and live there.

Maybe the woman and her husband had two children, one son and one daughter. When the children were young, they had energy and sometimes would make trouble for their mother because they were always dirty when they played around inside the house. The family lived in a small house, but they were happy.

The woman still has a job taking care of babies and cleaning houses. When her children were born, she stayed at home and took care of them. She was happy to see them grow up and find great jobs. Sometimes she played with her children and taught them how to be good people in the future. Because she wanted her children to become good people and find great jobs, she always told them that her job was hard and that she wished she could learn more skills so she could find another job. Her children were clever and wanted comfortable lives, so her daughter became a teacher and her son became a successful businessman. Now the son is thirty-eight years old and the daughter is thirty-six.

Maybe the woman also has a sister, who lives somewhere else now. The woman remembers playing with her sister when she was young, and she misses that time now. She misses her sister so much that she visits her in San Francisco every six months. Sometimes she goes with her husband and her children, but normally she goes by herself.

The old woman has been visiting her sister in San Francisco for twenty years. She is glad to visit and discuss what she has done during the past six months. Her sister wants to visit her, but she cannot because she has to work. She is doing three jobs so she does not have time.

San Francisco, California, is a big city, and a lot of immigrants live there. People love San Francisco because it has nice weather, people are kind, and the schools are good. But the old woman thought San Francisco had changed a lot in the twenty years she had been visiting her sister.

On this trip, for example, a lot of taller buildings had been built since her previous trip. Some of the streets and bus stops had changed, and a few of the houses had been painted. Also the bus map changed once a year. But the biggest problem for the woman now was that she had Alzheimer's. She tried hard to understand the new bus map but some of the routes had changed. A Safeway grocery store had moved to an empty lot. Some other buildings had changed colors and different companies had moved in. She felt confused and angry. She worried that she wouldn't be able to find her sister. During her walk, the old woman had just picked up a map to ask people how to get to the 45-MUNI bus stop. When she felt hungry, she had gone into Burger King to buy a hamburger to eat and a Coke to drink. Then she continued trying to find people who knew this bus stop and walked until she found the stop. By the time she got on the bus she felt tired, lonely, and upset because nobody had helped her.

I also saw a young boy sitting on the bus. He looked like he was vigorous with black hair and white skin. He was wearing a colorful sweatshirt with a white hood and black pants. He was listening to his iPod. I imagined that the young boy was born in San Mateo, California, and grew up there. San Mateo is a small city in California, and people like to live there because they have more opportunity to find jobs, nicer houses to rent, and better schools. Maybe the boy had a sister that was younger than him. And he was studying at the biggest high school in San Mateo with his sister. He lived in a big house with his family. He was sixteen years old and a tenth-grade student. He liked to travel because he wanted to see new things in other cities. He also liked to play video games and sports, see movies, and watch TV. These things helped him to relax when he was tired from studying at home after school. He was a good basketball player and had joined the school team.

Maybe his parents worked in San Mateo. They thought they were in a great place, and they didn't want to move anywhere. His father was a successful businessman in an international company. His mother was a middle school teacher, and she taught science. They also liked to travel.

The boy's sister was younger than him, fifteen years old and a ninth-grade student. The boy always paid attention to his teachers in school. As he sat on the bus that day, he thought, *I should offer my seat to this old woman because our teachers always teach us that we need to respect seniors.* His teachers had taught him to be kind and respectful, just as his friends and his parents were respectful towards him. He knew this was the way to show his respect.

I stopped thinking as I watched the young boy. He said, "Please take my seat!" The old woman slowly sat down and said, "Thank you! Thank you! Thank you very much! My leg hurts me because I walked to this stop from a hotel to here for about five hours, and I wanted to take this bus to visit my sister, but I got lost when I transferred to the 45-MUNI bus. I did not take a break for five hours, so my leg hurt me." The old woman was happy, and the young boy was glad because he understood that this was the way to show respect to seniors. Everybody knew it was horrible that they had not offered their seats to this old woman immediately. They thought the young boy was doing the right thing for her and hoped that all people would show respect for everybody, not just seniors. The old woman would be remembered by everyone.

Respect is a part of the Golden Rule and showing respect is one way to show my Chinese culture. Chinese culture teaches kids to respect teachers, parents, and seniors—even your friends. That is a main point in Chinese culture. Respect is a traditional virtue that we need to learn as children to use in our lives. I agree with this because it affects whether I can become a good person or not in the future. Everyone needs to follow the rule to respect each other in the world, no matter what language they speak and what country they live in. The Golden Rule is very important to us.

LA NOCHE OSCURA

Johana Yanez

Un rayo de luz traspasaba por la ventana de su recámara, trazando su cuerpo extendido sobre la amplia cama, envuelto en sábanas blancas y lizas. El verano había comenzado. Violentamente Mariana se empezó a retorcer. Luego abrió sus ojos, tan negros y brillantes como dos escarabajos, bostezó un poco, se sentó, y contempló el clima. Sus ojos se empañaron de lagrimas. No pudo, ni quiso ver más. Dentro de su corazón sabía que ella no era una buena madre.

Durante tantos años había tratado a su hija Clara con indiferencia y ahora Clara le respondía con la misma actitud. Se vistió, tomo sus llaves, y salió de casa. ¿Cuantos viajes y paseos prometidos se quedaron sin realizar, cuantas caricias y palabras de amor volaron en el aire antes de ser dadas? Ella siempre estaba ocupada. Era una mujer de negocios, que siempre quería darle lo mejor a su hija, pero se olvidó de esos simples y pequeños detalles que hacen de la vida algo hermoso. Clara prometía ir a visitarla pero al final nunca cumplía, ni siquiera se despedía de ella en las escasas veces que se veían.

Se hacía tarde y empezaba a oscurecerse. No pudo más. Se dejó caer

THE DARK NIGHT

Johana Yanez

A ray of light trespassed through the window of her room, tracing her extended body, wrapped in white, flat sheets over the ample bed. Summer was beginning. Violently, Mariana began to twist about. Then she opened her eyes, so black and brilliant like two beetles. She yawned a bit, sat up, and contemplated the weather. Her eyes fogged with tears. She couldn't, nor wanted to, see more. In her heart, she knew she wasn't a good mother.

During many years she had treated her daughter, Clara, with indifference, and now Clara responded with the same attitude. She dressed, took her keys, and left home. How many promised trips and tours were left unrealized, how many caresses and words of love flew away in the air before having been given? She was always busy. She was a business woman who always wanted to give the best to her daughter, but had forgotten those small, simple details that make life into something lovely. Clara promised to visit her, but never came through. She didn't even say goodbye the scarce times they saw each other.

It was getting late and it was begging to get dark. She couldn't any-

al suelo encima del pasto, húmedo y con olor penetrante, enfrente de una casita aislada. Empezó a llorar.

"¿Qué es lo que te sucede, mujer?" preguntó una señora.

"Nada," contestó Mariana muy apenada con la situación.

"Si no me quieres contar, está bien. Allá tu, pero permíteme, por favor, contarte mi historia. Aunque no necesites ayuda, te quiero contar por que simplemente hoy es verano y los veranos me traen recuerdos."

*   *   *

Todo siempre era igual durante todos los veranos. Por el día el sol era un torbellino de calor y las noches se hacían claras y largas. Nunca imaginé que ese verano fuera a ser completamente diferente. En aquel tiempo papá había propuesto ir de vacaciones rumbo a un pueblo llamado San Marcos. No se me hacía tan mala la idea, después de todo, a qué podría quedarme en casa, así que acepté.

Claro que ese viaje implicaría no ver a Demetrio. Lo cual provocaba que me deprimiera un poco. Demetrio era el hombre más maravilloso. Era alto, delgado, serio pero simpático. Al sonreír se le formaban dos hoyitos en sus mejillas sonrosadas. Lo conocí en una de las tantas juntas a las cuales papá me llevó. Por miedo a no ser correspondida, yo nunca le había mencionado nada a Demetrio acerca de mis sentimientos por él. Él tampoco a mi. El miedo a no ser correspondido era mutuo. Yo lo miraba desde lejos, según yo sin que él lo notara. Tan solo mirarlo me colmaba de alegría. Él, al sentir mis miradas, volteaba hacia mi. Yo no podía dejar que él me descubriera, instantáneamente quitaba la vista, y sentía como con el mismo amor él me miraba.

Todo marchaba de acuerdo al plan. Mamá estaba muy contenta y papá no paraba de sonreír. Incluso a mi hermano, Toribio, le gustaba la idea de vacacionar en el dichoso pueblo. Y salimos.

De repente el carro se detuvo y mi papa me dijo que abriera la puerta a mi derecha. Demetrio cortésmente me saludó, yo le respondí con un hola, y los dos nos miramos directamente a los ojos. Él se sentó junto a mi. "Estoy seguro de que le va a encantar San Marcos Demetrio," escuché

more. She let herself fall to the grass—damp and with penetrating odor—in front of an isolated little house. She began to cry.

"What's going on with you, woman?" asked a lady.

"Nothing," answered Mariana, grieved by the situation.

"If you don't want to tell me, that's alright. That's up to you. But let me please tell you my story. You might not need help, but I want to tell it to you simply because today is summer and summers bring me memories.

*   *   *

Everything was always the same during the summer. In the day the sun was a whirlwind of heat, and the nights were long and clear. I never imagined that that summer would be completely different. In that time, dad had proposed going on vacation toward a town called San Marcos. I didn't think it such a bad idea; after all, what would I have to do at home?

Of course that trip would imply not seeing Demetrio, which depressed me a little. Demetrio was the most marvelous man. He was tall, thin, serious, but nice. When he smiled, two pits formed in his rosy cheeks. I met him during one of the many get-togethers my dad took me to. For fear of my affection being unrequited, I had never mentioned anything to Demetrio about my feelings for him. He didn't mention anything to me either. The fear of unrequited love was mutual. I watched him from afar without him noticing, or so I thought. Just to watch him topped me with joy. He, sensing my looks, turned toward me, and I sensed that he watched me with the same love.

Everything marched on according to plan. Mom was very happy and Dad didn't stop smiling. Even my brother, Toribio, liked the idea of vacationing in that happy town. And so we went.

Suddenly, the car stopped and my dad told me to open the door. Demetrio greeted me with courtesy, I replied with a hello, and we looked at each other directly in the eyes. He sat next to me. "I'm sure that you'll love San Marcos, Demetrio," I heard my dad say. That's when I understood that Demetrio would travel with us. I though the idea was enchanting.

Once on the road, the five of us were very anxious to get there.

decir a mi papa. Entonces comprendí que Demetrio viajaría con nosotros. Me encantaba la idea.

Ya en el camino, los cuatro estábamos muy ansiosos por llegar. Aun recuerdo que íbamos cantando para calmar nuestras ansias. Al oscurecerse un aguacero repentino nos atacó e hizo a que papá se desviara del camino. Más tarde papá concluyó que ya estaba perdido y que era mejor parar el carro y preguntar por direcciones. A lo lejos de la nada, pudimos observar un rancho. Nos acercamos y preguntamos a un viejito llamado Don Carlos si él sabía donde se encontraba San Marcos. Desgraciadamente no nos pudo ayudar, pero nos invitó a pasar la noche en su rancho. Todos aceptaron encantados menos yo, pues aquel señor se me había hecho un poco extraño y más cuando se nos quedaba mirando a Toribio y a mí con una mirada profunda y vacía. Toribio y yo éramos muy unidos. En él siempre encontraba la paz que en ningún otro familiar podía adquirir. Sentí la obligación de alertarlo de cualquier cosa que nos pudiera suceder si pasábamos la noche en ese lugar. "No te preocupes hermanita. Yo voy a estar siempre a tu lado, cada ves que me necesites, para defenderte." Con estas palabras de aliento una vez mas Toribio devolvía la paz a mi espíritu.

Yo estaba muy exhausta, así que decidí ir a descansar al cuarto que el señor Carlos me había autorizado. Aquel cuarto no era muy acogedor, olía a humo, era frío, oscuro, sólido, y las maderas del piso viejo rechinaban demasiado. Me recosté sobre la cama y me puse a pensar en Demetrio, en lo guapo y inteligente que era. Sin querer perdí la noción del tiempo y me quede profundamente dormida.

Rancho Girasoles, 1973

No prendió la luz del patio, ni hizo ruido. Abrió la puerta y entró al cuarto donde Juanita y Héctor casi dormidos aun seguían esperándola. "¿Qué es lo que pasa, mamá?" preguntó Juanita, pero no hubo respuesta alguna que le aclara sus dudas. Su madre solamente fue por el rifle que colgaba en la pared tras la cama de Héctor. Tan pronto como tuvo el rifle entre sus manos salió apresurada para verificar que Don José aun no regresara. Por

I even remember that we were singing to calm ourselves. When a sudden downpour darkened the sky, my dad made a detour from the road. Later, Dad concluded that he was lost and that it would be best to stop the car and ask for directions.

Far away in the darkness, we could see a ranch. We approached it and asked an old man named Don Carlos if he knew where we could find San Marcos. Unfortunately, he couldn't help us, but he invited us to stay the night in his ranch. Everyone accepted, charmed, except for me—that man seemed to me a bit strange, more so when he paused, looking at Toribio and me with a deep and vacant look. Toribio and me were very close. In him, I always found the peace that no other family member could give me. I felt obligated to warn him that something might happen to us if we stayed the night in that place. "Don't worry, sis. I'll always be at your side to defend you." With those encouraging words once again returned peace to my spirit.

I was exhausted, so I decided to go to the room that Mr. Carlos had allotted me. That room was not very friendly—it smelled of smoke and it was cold, dark, and solid. And the planks of the old floor screeched too much. I lay down on the bed and thought about Demetrio—how handsome and smart he was. Without meaning to, I lost the notion of time and I ended up profoundly asleep.

Rancho Girasoles, 1973

She didn't turn on the light of the yard, nor did she make any sound. She opened the door and found the room where Juanita and Hector, almost asleep, were still waiting for her. "What's happening, mama?" asked Juanita, but there was no response to clear her doubts. Her mother only went for the rifle that hung on the wall behind Hector's bed. As soon as she had the rifle in her hands, she left in a hurry to make sure that Don José hadn't returned. She came back a second time, left the rifle on Hector's bed and ordered the children to put on a sweater because that very night they would run far away from the monster that they had for a father. A

segunda vez ella regresó, dejó el rifle sobre la cama de Héctor, y les exigió a los niños que se pusieran un suéter porque esa misma noche huirían lejos del monstruo que tenían como padre. Una puerta azotada hizo que los tres se detuvieran inmediatamente. Era Don José que había regresado, rápidamente la madre cogió el rifle, "No voy a permitir que nos mates," dijo ella con voz exaltada. "Me espiaste," dijo Don José, riéndose como un loco. Luego se lanzó sobre Cristina y de un jalón le quitó el rifle. Juanita y Héctor miraban.

La niña quiso detener a su padre pero no pudo hacer nada. Solo se sentó lentamente sobre la cama y dejó que el tiempo transcurriera. Cada abuso que su madre recibía dejaba al descubierto una lágrima más en su piel canela. Ya ni siquiera quería seguir mirando pero algo la impulsaba a seguir haciéndolo. Volteó a ver a su hermano. Estaba lleno de lágrimas, lleno de miedo, y dolor. ¿Dónde es que había quedado el muchachito, aquel que era valiente y más fuerte que ella? De ese muchachito ya no quedaba nada. Juanita con tristeza agachó la cara. Por un instante pudo hacerlo. Más luego la subió para seguir mirando. Esperando por un milagro que rescatara a su madre, porque ella simplemente no podía.

La cama había sujetado sus pies, la cama, y el temor. Juanita, completamente fuera de si, trató de gritar pero ni siquiera eso pudo hacer. Después de algunos minutos su madre cayó al suelo inconsciente. Después de un forcejeo la madre se pudo liberar y corrió en busca de una salida. Como respuesta encontró la puerta trasera y pudo escapar. Héctor reaccionó y se levantó a asegurar la puerta para que Don José no pudiera salir fácilmente y su madre aprovechara para huir lejos. Don José abrió la puerta para ir en busca de Cristina, su presa.

De repente desperté y allí estaba ella parada, observándome como me retorcía de miedo al verla, mirándome como una sombra más. Con su pelo negro y largo cubriéndole el rostro murmuró, "Ayúdame por favor." Luego prendí la luz para poder mirarla mejor. Ya no estaba. No obstante la busqué debajo de la cama. Cuidadosamente dije, "¿Juanita donde es que te has metido?" Ella no contestó, pero al asomarme por la ventana la vi corriendo por el trigal. De pronto un escalofrío me envolvió. No sabía

door thrown open made the three stop for a moment. It was Don José, who had returned. Quickly the mother grabbed the rifle. "I won't let you kill us," she said in an angry voice. "You saw me," said Don José, laughing like a maniac. Then he lunged at Cristina and grabbed the rifle from her. Juanita and Hector watched in shock.

The girl wanted to stop her father but could not do anything. She just sat slowly on the bed and let time pass by. Every abuse her mother received resulted in one more tear on her cinnamon skin. She didn't want to continue looking, but something pushed her to do so. She turned to look at her brother. He was full of tears, full of fear and pain. Where was the little boy that was braver and stronger than her? Nothing was left of that little boy. Saddened, Juanita put her head down. A bit later she raised it to continue looking. Waiting for a miracle to rescue her mother, because, simply, she could not.

The bed and fear held her feet. Juanita, completely beside herself, tried to scream, but she couldn't even do that. After a few minutes her mother fell down on the floor, unconscious. After a struggle the mother freed herself and ran looking for a way out. She found the back door and was able to escape. Hector reacted and got up to lock the door so Don José wouldn't be able to go out so easily, and so his mother could take the opportunity to get very far away. Don José opened the door to chase down Cristina, his prisoner.

Suddenly I awoke and she was standing there, observing me as I convulsed in fear from seeing her, looking at me as just another shadow. With long dark hair covering her face she murmured, "Help me please." I turned on the light to see her more clearly. She was no longer there. I looked for her under the bed. Cautiously, I said, "Juanita, where did you go off to?" She didn't respond, but when I looked out the window I saw her running through the wheat field. All of the sudden I felt chills all over me. I didn't know whether I was awake or dreaming. I looked at the clock. It was one in the morning. I stood up and stepped on something. It was the same rifle, but it wasn't the same room. Could it be I was in Juanita's room? There was a timid knock at the door. "Who is it?" I asked, taken

si estaba soñando o si ya estaba despierta. Miré el reloj. Era la una de la madrugada. Me paré y sin querer pisé algo. Era el mismo rifle, pero no era el mismo cuarto. ¿Sería acaso que estaba en el cuarto de Juanita? Tímidamente alguien golpeó la puerta. "¿Quién es?" respondí desconcertada. No me contestó nadie. Volvieron a tocar nuevamente. Esta vez abrí la puerta inmediatamente, al hacerlo no podía creer lo que mis ojos estaban viendo. Era el pequeño Héctor o lo que quedaba de él. "¡Corre Juanita, corre!" En ese instante realmente yo no sabía que estaba tratando de decir, pero sabía que tenía que correr e ir por ayuda. Tan rápido como pude empecé a correr lejos de aquel rancho. Tropecé con algo y me golpeé en la cabeza.

Juanita y Héctor no lo pensaron dos veces. Salieron en busca de su madre. Estuvieron buscándola por horas hasta que la encontraron. "¿A dónde creen que van?" dijo nuevamente Don José. Tomó a Héctor y a Juanita de sus brazos delicados y suaves, y los llevó hacia la casa.

Cristina lo trató de detener pero él con el rifle, la paró a ella.

Entonces, sin consideración, vació gasolina alrededor de toda la casa y le prendió fuego. Héctor y Juanita lograron saltar pero ya el fuego había comenzado. Iban corriendo los dos juntos, cuando una viga cayó sobre Héctor. "¡Corre Juanita, corre!" dijo Héctor. Juanita no quería abandonar a su hermano pero sabía que tenia que salir por ayuda. "¡Ayuda! ¡Ayúdenme por favor!" Nadie escuchó sus ruegos, excepto él que, parado a la par de un árbol, la observaba y se burlaba de ella. "¿Por qué papá? ¿Por qué? ¡Te odio!" le gritó con desesperación a Don José. Luego con furia se lanzó sobre él.

"Suélteme Don Carlos," fue lo primero que se me ocurrió decirle a Don José cuando me había sujetado igual que a sus dos hijos. "¡Ayuda! ¡Ayúdenme por favor!"

"Si tú me odias Juanita, yo también te odio."

"Yo no soy Juanita," le respondí asustada.

"Mi Juanita, tu si eres mi Juanita. Perdóname Juanita, yo no quería matarlos. A mi nunca nadie me quiso."

"¿Dónde están mis padres y mi hermano, que les hizo?" gritaba.

"Suéltala," los hermanitos desde un rincón gritaron reclamando su muerte.

aback. No one responded. They knocked again. This time, I opened the door immediately, and couldn't believe my eyes. It was little Hector, or what remained of him.

"Run, Juanita, run!" In that moment I didn't really know what I was trying to say, but I knew that I had to run and get help. I started to run away from that ranch as fast as I could. I crashed onto something and hit my head.

Juanita and Hector didn't think twice. They went looking for their mother. They were looking for hours until they found her. "Where do you think you're going?" said Don José again. He took Hector and Juanita from her soft and delicate arms, and began to take them to the house.

Cristina tried to stop him but he had the rifle so he stopped her.

Then he thoughtlessly dumped the gasoline around the house and set it on fire. Hector and Juanita were able to jump but the fire had already been lit. They were both running, when a beam fell on Hector. "Run, Juanita, run!" said Hector. Juanita didn't want to abandon her brother but she knew she had to get help. "Help! Help me please!" No one heard her cries, except for him. He mocked her while standing next to a tree. "Why, father? Why? I hate you!" she screamed desperately at Don José. Then, full of rage, she lunged at him.

"Don Carlos, let go of me," was the first thing I thought of saying to Don José when he held me the same way as he had held his two children. "Help! Help me please!"

"If you hate me, Juanita, I hate you too."

"I'm not Juanita," I replied, scared.

"My Juanita, you really are my Juanita. Forgive me, Juanita I didn't want to kill them. No one ever paid attention to me."

"Where are my parents and my brother? What did you do to them?" I screamed.

"Let her go," screamed the little siblings from a corner protesting their death.

All of the sudden Don José didn't know what to do. He was awash in remorse. Meanwhile, I took advantage and escaped, seeking out my parents,

Enseguida Don José no supo que hacer. Se vio acorralado de remordimientos. Mientras que yo aprovechaba el tiempo para huir e ir en busca de mis padres, de Toribio y de Demetrio. El hombre al darse cuenta corrió tras de mi. Juanita y Héctor esta vez no se quedaron sin hacer nada. Aun siendo sombras del pasado lo lograron detener. Lo confundieron e hicieron que se cayera. Los demonios del infierno oscuro no se apiadaron del alma de José y tan pronto como murió se lo llevaron. Entonces pude entender que yo había sido parte de la venganza de Juanita y Héctor. Salí del cuarto y busqué a mi familia y a Demetrio, quienes para ese entonces ya habían amanecido y estaban esperándome en el carro para seguir con nuestra ruta.

Yo les conté lo que me había pasado pero ellos no me creyeron. Al llegar a San Marcos Demetrio se me acercó y me dijo: "Toribio y yo vimos como se lo llevaron. Te amo." Sujetó mi mano y me abrazó.

*   *   *

Tal vez no me creas, al igual que mis padres, pero sabes, a estas alturas de mi vida ya no me importa. Creo que lo que me pasó me ayudó a valorar a mis padres y a mi hermano. En cuanto a Demetrio, siento que lo amé cada día que pasaba y se lo demostraba y él a mi.

Si te encuentras en tu camino a un niño o a una niña, cómo Héctor o cómo Juanita, ayúdales y aun siendo tu un extraño, dales tu amor. No dejes que se conviertan en el mismo reflejo que sus padres, como Don José que era malo o cómo Cristina que era cobarde. Recuerda que el niño es el futuro y una sonrisa a un nuevo y mejor mundo.

Si ves en un hombre a Don José, siente compasión. No dejes que se apodere de ti el coraje y la rabia encontrada dentro de él, porque si no, poco a poco, sin darte cuenta, llegarás a ser exactamente igual o peor. Mejor dale el ejemplo de saber amar y probablemente él aprenderá. Si él no aprende es mejor que te alejes de él y que ayudes a aquellos que lo rodean para que no salgan afectados por su crueldad.

Nunca de lo nunca seas cobarde. Si logras no serlo trata de ayudar al que si lo es. Da tus consejos por más pequeños que sean. Una sola palabra hace la diferencia.

Toribio and Demetrio. When the man noticed this he ran after me. This time Juanita and Hector did not sit idly doing nothing. Even though they were shadows from the past they were able to stop him. They confused him and made him fall. José received no mercy from the demons from the darkest hell, and as quickly as he died they took him. It was then that I understood how I had been part of Juanita and Hector's vengeance. I went out of the room and looked for my family and Demetrio, who at that time had already gotten up and were waiting for me in the car to continue our journey.

I told them about what happened to me but they did not believe me. When we arrived in San Marcos, Demetrio came close to me and said: "Toribio and I saw how they took him. I love you" He took my hand and hugged me.

*   *   *

You might not believe me, just like my parents, but you know, at this point in my life I don't care. I think that what happened to me helped me to appreciate my parents and my brother. As far as Demetrio, every day that went by I loved him and showed it to him, and he to me.

If you find a little boy or girl on the road, like Hector or Juanita, help them and even though you may be a stranger, give them your love. Don't let them turn into mirror reflections of their parents, like Don José who was evil or like Cristina who was a coward. Remember that the child is the future and a smile towards a new and better world.

If you see Don José in a man, be compassionate. Don't let the anger and fury inside him take you over, because if it does, little by little, without you noticing, you'll end up exactly like him or worse. It's better to show him the example of love and maybe he'll learn. If he doesn't learn it's better for you to get away from him and help those around him so that they don't end up infected by his cruelty.

Never, ever be a coward. If you succeed at not being one try to help those that are. Give advice, no matter how small. Just one word makes a difference. It doesn't matter what the day is, whether it is day or night, always tell the person that you hold in high regard that you really appreciate

No importa el día que sea, no importa si es día o si es noche, siempre dile a ese ser que estimas lo mucho que lo aprecias. Si son tus padres diles que son únicos y que los necesitas, si es tu hermano o hermana dile que lo quieres, si son tus hijos diles lo importante que son para ti, si es tu pareja o esa personita que te hace sentir como en las nubes, confiésale tu amor. Pero sobre todo nunca esperes nada a cambio. Siempre da lo mejor de ti y verás como todo eso que diste regresara a ti como el verano. Si no regresa, no te preocupes, piensa y comprende que no todos tuvieron la suerte de tener un corazón que supiera amar o perdonar y querer nuevamente.

Mariana le bastó con escuchar este relato, se paró del suelo, le dio gracias a la señora, y después se fue caminando muy de prisa, hasta llegar a la casa de su hija. Tocó el timbre pero no le abrieron. Al parecer no había nadie. Abordó el primer taxi rumbo al trabajo de su hija. Le iría a decir cuanto la quería y cuanto le dolía que estuvieran separadas una de la otra.

Desconocidos atónitos miraban un cuerpo ensangrentado en medio de la carretera. Mariana no distinguía muy bien quien era. Todo parecía indicarle que era Clara, la forma de su cuerpo y el color de su cabello. Mariana aun no conciente de lo que pasaba se bajó del auto, le pagó al chofer, y se acercó a mirar, siendo una extraña más entre la muchedumbre. "Un momento," se acercó llorando amargamente. Abrazó y besó a ese cuerpo pensando que era su hija.

"Mamá, mamá, ¿la conoces?"

"Clara, ¡eres tú! Yo pensé que tú eras…" Las dos se abrazaron y por fin se dijeron lo mucho que se querían.

them. If they're your parents tell them they're unique and that you need them, if it's your brother or sister tell him or her you love them, if they're your children tell them how important they're to you, if it's your partner or that certain someone that makes you feel like you're up in the clouds, confess your love. But don't ever expect anything in return. Always give the best you have and you'll see how all that you give comes back to you like summertime. If it doesn't come back, don't worry, think about and understand that not everyone had the good luck of having a heart that knows how to love, or forgive and love again.

For Mariana it was enough to hear this story. She got up from the floor, gave thanks to the woman, and then walked away very quickly, until she reached her daughter's house. She rang the doorbell but no one opened the door. Apparently no one was home. She got in the first taxi heading to her daughter's workplace. She was going to tell her how much she loved her and how much it hurt that they were apart, one from the other.

Shocked strangers looked on at a bloodied body in the middle of the road. Mariana couldn't really tell who it was. Everything seemed to indicate that it was Clara, from the shape of the body to the color of her hair. Without being quite sure of what she was doing, Mariana got out of the taxi, paid the driver, and got close in order to look. She became one more stranger in the crowd. "Hold on," she got, close crying bitterly. She hugged and kissed the body, thinking it was her daughter.

"Mom, Mom, do you know her?"

"Clara, it's you! I thought that you were…" They hugged and finally told each other how much they loved one another.

—Translated by Abner Morales

THE GOLDEN RULE
Tifani Fuentes

This is a story about me, my life, and who I am. People have problems
with many things, including school, the future, social status, and
even the people they're surrounded by—the people they live with,
the people they love, and their families. I am telling this story about all
these things to let people know how hard life can be, how to see past the
negativity, how to be able to see the bright light at the end of that long
narrow tunnel, how to see and feel hope, how to change, how to build
character and integrity, how to start from nothing and end up with something. This story is about the problems in my life, the things I endured,
and how they shaped me into a stronger person. It is also about how
people helped along the way in making me the person I am today.

For me to fully understand my life, my choices, and my future, I needed
to grow up. When I was five years old, I had not a clue in the world about
what life really meant. I started thinking about my actions and the actions
of my mother. I had a hard time at school. I didn't care to listen or behave.
My mother wasn't very responsible most of the time. My grandmother
watched over me when my mother wasn't there. I grew to learn the dif-

ference between love and hate, right and wrong. Eventually I stopped seeing my mother, and was more attached to my grandmother than I ever had been to my mother. It was hard growing up without my mother. I had to relearn everything I knew—about how to act and what's right and wrong—from my grandmother.

When I started middle school, I was overwhelmed, but my grandmother always tried to do what was best for me. This made me feel that I had to be a good role model for my younger sibling. I feel like my grandmother gave me a lot of tough love. When she was my age, her parents had done the same thing. She had to take responsibility and watch her actions growing up in a family of eight. I can relate to that because everything I do can affect how my younger sibling might act. I want him to know how to make good choices on his own and know right from wrong. I think the reason my grandma is the person she is today is because of the things she did in her life. These things molded her into a wise and kind person. "Tough love," my grandma always says. She only shows it to me, though, while my younger brother gets everything he wants. I sometimes wonder why I have to work so hard and take on so many responsibilities.

One day in middle school I started to think of all the things my mother had done and what my grandmother had done—two opposites. I began to care, and I began to change a great deal. It's hard to name all the details that can greatly impact your life. It's impossible to stop changes from happening to you and to your life, but it is possible to make them good changes. Before I lived with my grandmother, I had one picture in my mind about how life could be—one dull black and white picture. Now, thanks to my grandmother, I have not one but many vividly colored pictures in my mind. I have overcome what I was taught at first and learned what I now know. I have come so far, and my attitude and appearance have morphed so much that sometimes I'm stunned to think that I could have turned out a totally different person. Sometimes it's scary to think of being someone else, but in a person's life there are so many different paths to take and it's hard to know which one to take. I am very thankful to my grandmother to have put up with me through my rough times. I even thank my mother because, if it weren't for her actions, I wouldn't have learned from her mistakes, and I would have made them on my own. This part of my life really sticks in my mind because I feel that my experiences then are what made me strong and helped me to do great in life and not become someone who makes bad choices.

There were good days and bad days in middle school, days with their ups and downs. I remember some of the hardest times were when I was undergoing embarrassing and humiliating teasing at school. It was hard. I was a fat, short girl then, mostly quiet and shy. People talked nonsense to me, and they laughed and looked at me. I always wore a light blue sweater and carried a rolling backpack around. I walked around the school alone and had chubby red cheeks. I was really nice to anyone who spoke to me, even kids who had nothing respectful to say. I focused in school and stayed after class a lot. Many called me a teacher's pet, but I was only concerned about my grades. My grades weren't *A*s or *B*s, but it wasn't because I didn't understand the work; it was just really hard for me to put myself out there in a very judgmental place. I was very self-conscious and didn't enjoy school a lot.

One ordinary day, I was walking down the school stairs. I was focused on going to class, when I felt something land on the top of my head. I heard people laughing, but it didn't faze me much. It wasn't until later, when I was in class doing my work, that I touched the top my head and noticed a huge ball of sticky splattered gum in my hair. My jaw dropped to the floor, and I ran to the girl's bathroom and looked in the mirror. I was so embarrassed and mad that I went home crying. I was shocked that this could ever happen to me.

When I got home, still crying and upset, I went straight to my grandma's room. I mumbled as my grandma sat on her bed wondering what was going on. She said, "Calm down, I can't understand what you're saying! What's the matter?" I told her what had happened, and she found the huge clump of gum in my hair. She had to cut my hair that day. I cried all day but she comforted me by telling me about things she had endured in school and how hard it had been for her too. She told me how the girls made fun of her because she was so skinny and dressed differently. Her words made me feel somewhat better because it was like her problems were my problems.

Those small moments I shared with my grandma were very meaningful because she was always there to listen. If my grandma hadn't been there to talk to, or to give me a hug when I needed one, or to laugh and share stories with, I'd have felt very alone. Talking to her that day made me feel that, even though my hair had been cut and my feelings were hurt, I was loved. Every day at 4 PM when I got home, I knew I would have open arms to walk into. I think that's what people need: just someone they can trust and talk to. That's what I needed to get through what seemed to be the hugest problem. I feel that it was those moments that made me feel special and the people that helped me made me who I am today. Learning from my grandma, listening to her stories and her problems, made me feel like everyone has problems and everyone deals with them in their own way. It made me feel equal, like I was connected to another person.

Another thing I remember is walking home from school the day I was elected president of the eighth grade. When I heard that I was the new president, I was overwhelmed with joy. I couldn't ever imagine winning something. Every time I think back on that moment, I remember telling myself how far I'd come and how far I had passed my mother in the race to succeed. Not only did I feel proud of myself, but the people around me were congratulating me, and it made me feel very special too. I literally ran home to tell my grandma the news, and her face was all pink. She smiled with her cheeks high up by her eyes, and I felt so good because she was so proud of me. I felt like I wasn't what my grandma had expected me to be but something that my grandma *wanted* me to be, someone that enjoyed life and did well in it. I felt that I had finally proven myself as a person to my grandma. Her respect and encouragement meant so much to me because, before that, I had never won or had a chance to shine.

There were bad days, too, when I just wasn't as happy. Sometimes I still get these lost, lonely feelings. It's something inside me that I can't seem to pinpoint. It's a sort of confusing feeling, like there is a part of me

I still don't quite get. There have been days when I've told my feelings to my grandma. I've told her on many occasions that I felt insecure and very alone in life, confused about who I am and what purpose I have. I have told her that I love her but sometimes wonder how I would feel or what I would be like if I lived with my parents. Would I have a close relationship with them like I do with her? I have asked myself those questions and even brought them up to her in numerous talks.

When I talk to her about these problems, I know I can trust her because she doesn't lie and she doesn't sugarcoat the truth either. She's very straightforward. I think that's why I love talking to her. She tells me about some of her perspectives on life, how things back in the day worked, and how throughout the world everyone has the same problems. She tells me things that she thought about as a teenager and how she'd see her mother every day. Sometimes I get sad about that. But I feel like my grandma is my mother and father all in one, and realizing that the two of us share a lot in common makes me feel at ease inside.

My grandmother has helped me through rough times and times when I needed her. Without her I would feel very different than how I feel now. One big way she impacts my life is by having long, detailed conversations with me about life and problems. She tells stories about how hard it was for her to grow up in a family of ten. Sometimes I wonder how she came to be so knowledgeable about things and how she handles them so perfectly. I feel like she's already raised her kids, seen it all, and dealt with so many problems in her life that my problems are things she has already faced. I am dedicating this story to my grandmother who has always been there through the bad and the good, through the funny times and the crazy times. I'm writing this story of my life in dedication to her for never giving up on me, for making me believe in myself, and for giving me the tough love she does. Without her, I probably would have a lot of unanswered questions and no one to talk to. I feel that I know her and myself a great deal because she has always been there for me.

Tell me, what's the point of watching a soccer game played without friendship? Imagine a game with friendship and character. If one player fouls another, he can help the player get up, or shake his hand and say sorry. It isn't that big of a thing to do, but it can make a big difference.

But if your favorite team is playing dirty, the opposing team is going to get mad, and then that's when the ugly game comes out. Playing dirty means a team hurts somebody from the other team. Most dirty players go for the physical abuse, like giving their opponent a hard kick in the ankle. Some players can say something that may hurt another's feelings, like, "You should have let me shoot that, not you," or, "We lost because of you," or, "You're ruining it for everybody."

Another example is when you see a player trying to fight somebody from the opposing team, and the other players on his team show him a good example by telling him not to fight, to do what he really came for—to play the beautiful game of soccer, have fun, and make friends. Wow, that's what the fans want. That's a sports game with character and friendship.

To play the game beautifully, you need to know the history and the rules of soccer. The history of soccer started back in the nineteenth century, when it was still combined with rugby. Then, in 1863, the London Football Association split the two sports and banned carrying the ball with hands, as in the modern game. The objective of soccer is to get the ball into the opposing team's net. There are twenty-three players on each team, but there can only be eleven players on the "pitch," or field, at a time. The rest are on the bench. Some of the different positions are the goalie (the person who guards the net), three or four defenders, four mid-fielders, and two or three forwards. Throughout the game, the ball is worked up and down the field.

There are a lot of rules for soccer. For example, only the goalkeeper is allowed to touch the ball with his hands. Another rule is that a player cannot play dirty, like I mentioned earlier, or else they will definitely get a yellow card or a red card. A yellow card is a warning from the referee, but if a player does another bad thing on the field, and gets another yellow card, that adds up to a red card, and he gets kicked out of the soccer game. To get a yellow card, the offense committed is not that serious. For example, a player might slide tackle their opponent in order to make the play. A red card, on the other hand, is either for a repeat offense or a direct physical attack. An attack would definitely get a player kicked out of the game by the referee. Another rule is that a player can never argue with, talk back to, or scream at the ref, or else the ref can kick that player out of the game. Also, if the offense is great enough, the referee may suspend a player from the next match or matches. Another rule of soccer is that a team can only substitute three players throughout the entire game.

This sport, soccer, is changing the entire world because soccer socializes people. In soccer, there is no racism—it is a game with respect. That's why it is a sport that could bring a whole nation together. People from all races, from every country, go to watch their favorite teams. The World Cup, a tournament that happens every four years, moves to a different country each time. There are thirty-two national teams, from six continents, that qualify every four years to compete to win the cup.

Thousands of people come from all around [...] World Cup. People have a lot of passion, an[d ...] to be there—to feel it—and to be aroun[d ...] ing the same thing they are thinking. [...] want to see who wins the cup and ha[...] goal Diego Maradona scored with his han[d ...] 1986 World Cup in Mexico, which has become [...] God." Or when Pelé did two *sombreritos* (a soccer [...] flips the ball over their opponent's head). With that mo[ve ...] the winning goal that took his team, Brazil, to the final in 1[9...] Italy. Those are examples of this tournament socializing people [...] different cultures.

A lot of people think soccer is a very boring sport, but in my life, soccer is one of the things that keeps me alive. I play soccer, and I know what it feels like to play soccer. It is a sport that one plays with passion, with heart, with all one's strength. It is a battle between a team and its opponent, but it's also a sport that is played with honor and respect toward that opponent. For example, if a team wins, those players don't make fun of the other team. Instead, both teams shake hands to say "good game" to each other, because the game isn't easy, it's a battle over who has what it takes to win. That's what soccer is about. Also, the fans on the benches leave happy when they see both teams shake hands and say nice words to each other. That's when the fans get happier; even if their favorite team loses, they feel proud of them. More people come to see those kinds of games.

Since I was four years old, my passion for soccer has been amazing and great. It is something that has helped me with my character, and with the way I think about life. When I play soccer, I always tell myself, "Don't hurt anybody physically or with words. Just play the beautiful game of soccer, have fun, and make friends." When a player from another team fouls me, they always help me to stand up, and I tell them, "Thank you." That's how everybody should treat each other—with kindness. If everybody would be like that, this world would be a lot different. That's because two people are always better than one person. For example, if you need help, and you ask for help and somebody helps you, then two people is better than one person.

A lot of people think that soccer is just a bunch of kids running after a stupid ball. That's not true. It's about controlling your character and having good times with your friends, or even with people you don't know. After a game, the people you didn't know can become your friends. That's what soccer is about. I know, because I have been playing soccer for a very long time—almost my whole life. That's how soccer could change your way of thinking too. Soccer is a sport that can bring people together—not just together physically—but also in one spirit. I love it when I play soccer and all the fans are enjoying a beautiful and friendly game. Soccer players respect everybody on the pitch, as well as the fans.

I bet you if you ask anybody who likes to watch or play soccer what the game means to them, they are going to tell you the same thing that I mentioned before—that soccer is a sport that brings thousands, or millions, of people together. They are going say it is like that because in soccer, we treat everybody like family. It is like a family because we all love the sport, and we all enjoy playing and watching.

All I'm trying to say with this is that soccer could bring peace between nations. For example, let's say two people never got along before. Let's say both of them like soccer, and let's say that they also have the same favorite team. Just like that, they could be talking about soccer, and out of nowhere they become friends. Wouldn't that be nice, if two people who never got along before became friends because of soccer? I know that sounds funny, but I'm saying this because that experience has happened to me before.

The story goes like this. I have known Jimmy since sixth grade, but in that year I didn't get along with him. Then, when we both moved to seventh grade, I heard him talking about soccer, and I got into the conversation. The two of us started being friends, and now we are best friends. Imagine—if soccer didn't exist, I would not be friends with my best friend right now. What I'm trying to say is that soccer can change people—not only me, but a lot of other people too. Soccer could also bring countries together. That's why I love soccer, because it teaches us to respect and get along with everybody in this world. Wouldn't it be beautiful if two countries were fighting and then imagine them getting along, just because of the beautiful game of soccer. I think two countries getting along would look beautiful.

So that's why I am trying to tell everybody that soccer is not just a stupid, boring game or just players running after a ball. Soccer is more than that. It is about character and a will to change the world. That's a benefit for us, the people in this world. When the World Cup—the biggest tournament of soccer—comes, oh my god, you will see hundreds of thousands, or millions of people from the entire world go and appreciate the soccer games.

Well, now you know why I like soccer so much. Soccer is a big festival that allows a lot of people to get together and get along. I know that if we could support soccer even more in the future, soccer could bring nations together in peace.

Soccer is a beautiful sport to play. People all around the world play soccer, and it is, in fact, the number-one sport played. A survey in 2001 by Fédération Internationale de Football Association showed that "more than 240 million people play the sport of soccer in over 200 countries across almost every part of the globe." One of the greatest legendary soccer players was Edison Arantes do Nascimento, best known as Pelé. In his autobiography, Pelé refers to soccer as "the beautiful game." To me, this means that the game should be played with respect, character, and friendship. The sport of soccer shows us how to act in the world: life should be played with respect for the opponent, and with character and friendship. And that's how I want all people and myself to remember the sport of soccer—as the beautiful game. By approaching life with this mindset, people can change the world by treating all people of all nationalities with respect.

LOVE DOES NOT HAVE A GENDER

Sylvia McClain

Some people say we should stand up for what we believe in, but it depends on the situation. Many times we feel like we can't make a difference or help someone. That's when we have to look inside ourselves and fix our insecurities. In order to stand up for someone else, we must have confidence in ourselves. When we stand up for something we strongly care about, it's not something we take lightly. Insecurities are often caused by our peers, and we have to break away from the notion of what people might think of us. We cannot worry about how we are going to appear to others. This builds character and shows what type of morals we have—it kind of gives a pictorial description of the Golden Rule, if you will. The situation that I am going to describe is a real test of someone's character.

The day started off like any other day. My friend and I were on our way downtown. We were having a normal conversation; everything was normal. We got on the 22-Filmore bus, and immediately I could feel a different vibe around me. Something didn't feel right. My friend didn't sense the vibe, and I didn't want to mess up the ride and the moment, so I continued to talk to him. We talked about fashion, the upcoming election, and many other things. My friend is such an optimistic person, and I can talk to him about anything. There was a group of people that had just gotten on the bus. It sounded like they were continuing a conversation about homosexuality.

There are many points of view on this controversial subject, but that doesn't mean that you should have a discussion about it on the bus. Some people say that it is our First Amendment right to speak freely. On the other hand, the tables can turn, and people can hurt and affect the person or group that they are referring to. People have to have consideration for the many people that ride the bus. And people should watch what they say.

In the conversation, I heard, "This is an abomination, having gay marriage legal." In my head I thought, *How could people be so closed-minded? Do they not know that they could be offending someone on this bus right now?* My friend looked at me and smiled as he tried to ignore the comments that were being thrown back and forth. Sometimes that's what you have to do. You can't let things get to you. You have to be the bigger person and let things go. But when you have to go through life thinking that what you are doing or how you are living your life is wrong, it gets old after a while. It gets old, and you just want to live your life. This goes for anything that you decide to do with your life. It's your life, and it shouldn't have to be critiqued by society.

I was just sitting there listening to their closed-mindedness; it was disgusting. My friend tried to make conversation with me so that the time would go by. By this time, you may have figured out that my friend is gay, and to me, there is nothing wrong with it. It does not change the way I feel about him, nor will it ever. I felt him getting uncomfortable, and I wanted to do something. I wanted to let those people know that what they were doing was not OK and that they needed to have consideration for the people around them.

"Do unto others as you want them to do unto you." I believe this. If you have that respect, that kindness, and that common courtesy, and you are aware of your surroundings, you will be able to accept individuals. Another thing people need to have is acceptance. They don't have to agree with everything that people do—in fact, you can strongly disagree—but just respect the other point of view.

The people continued to talk, and one of them said, "There must be something wrong with them. What they are doing is not of God and should not be legal."

When I think of something that is not of God, I think of murder or rape, something heinous or horrible. They were talking about someone loving someone and describing it as wrong, just because the two people are the same sex. You cannot control who someone loves. Whether it is a man or woman, they should be treated the same and have the right to be married. Marriage is a symbol of love and a big step in the majority of people's lives. Everyone should have the right to love someone and be able to show it.

The comments made my friend seem like he was doing something wrong by being gay. The way they described homosexuality made it sound like he should be locked away. I don't think that you should talk about anyone like that. People are different; everyone is different. You can't judge them before you get to know them, because then you will miss out on some wonderful people. That's what I learned.

The strength was building up inside me, and I told my friend that I was going to say something about this. What they were doing was wrong. He told me that I didn't have to say anything, and that he goes through this all the time. I was appalled. People need to have respect for any and everyone. You give respect to get respect. Thinking this gave me more strength to say something to the group. I got up and went to where they were sitting, and I listened in closely to what they were saying.

One person said that there must be something mentally wrong with someone to be gay. I was thinking to myself there must be an epidemic going around of mentally ill gay people. That's when I said, "How dare you say that about the gay community? Do you know that they are regular people, and that this doesn't change because of their sexual orientation? You are so closed-minded."

They just stood there, looking blank. They looked sorry, but I wasn't done yet. "You have to see a person's personality, not what they look like or their sexual orientation. Being gay does not define a person—their character does. And don't be so sure that you're his type, because that is your real insecurity. You have insulted me and my friend on this bus. He happens to be gay, and he was offended by what you said."

They said they were sorry, and we got off the bus. I felt better after that. My friend was embarrassed, but he said thank you. I think that it's wrong to judge someone because they are not from the same walk of life as you. Everyone in the world is not the same, and you have to go through life and meet different people. If you go through life thinking that a group of people are a certain way, you will not get very far.

Since early Christianity, homosexuality has been considered immoral. This has heavily influenced the way people think about homosexuality. They say that it is wrong and that it is an abomination to society for people of the same sex to get married. Most Christians believe that marriage was meant for a man and a woman. It's not surprising that the most common argument against gay marriage is that it undermines the traditions of marriage, family, and society. Almost all religious figures tell you the Bible says that homosexuality is wrong. This country is based on democracy, and yet we have problems with letting many people do what they want to do. Most people growing up have some type of religious background that teaches them homosexuality is wrong; these people are entitled to how they feel. What makes it wrong is when you question someone's character. This subject is touchy because it really has to do with someone's personal life, and it should not have to do with public society. There are plenty of things that people do that a lot of people disagree with, but those topics are not in the media in such a big way as homosexuality is.

The conservatives believe that homosexual behavior is innately sinful, disordered, abnormal, and unnatural. It is an offense to God. God intends everyone to be heterosexual. It is a liberal argument that sexual orientation is a part of one's being—some people are born homosexual. And it is a conservative argument that it is one's sinful choice to become homosexual, which is against conservatives' beliefs. These theories are held by people who believe heavily in the Bible and live strictly by what it says.

Sacred texts don't have an opinion about question of gay marriage, since they were written before it was an issue. However, those same texts do have strong opinions on homosexuality itself. "If a man lies with a male as with a woman, both of them have committed an abomination: they shall be put to death: their blood is upon them" (Lev. 20:13). But the Bible clearly explains that homosexuality is wrong. Though God chose people to write his words, those people had their own opinions. The Bible is like a rule book or a religious Constitution that people use to live their lives. The Bible is something that you should take bits and pieces of. Take the parts of it that inspire you. Some religious scholars believe that references to homosexuality in the Bible have no real relation to same-sex relations at all—for instance, the gang rape in Sodom had nothing to do with homosexuality. The intent was for a man to humiliate others by treating them like women. This Bible verse has nothing to do with the love or relationships between homosexuals. So people can take whatever they want out of the Bible and combine it with what they were taught when they were growing up.

The government saying that people of the same sex can't get married is like telling someone who they can love. The First Amendment is supposed to protect that. The First Amendment protects the rights of freedom of religion and freedom of expression from government interference. The Ninth Amendment of the Constitution says that you cannot deny the rights of the people. We use this amendment, but do we abuse it? Can we say what we want? The answer to me is yes, of course, you can say whatever you want. But you need to know that the things you say can have an effect on people.

Now we have Proposition 8 in California, which is going to eliminate people's marriage rights. Most experts believe that the same-sex marriages that have already been performed will remain legal regardless of what happens with Proposition 8. However, this issue has never been tested.

We say what we want because our rights are protected, so it can be a win-win or a lose-lose situation. It's somewhat of a free country—you just have to know what to say and when to say it. There is a lot of bigotry in this society. In the dictionary, *bigotry* is defined as prejudice and/or discrimination against one or all members of a particular group based on negative perceptions of their beliefs and practices, or on negative group stereotypes. This is exactly what people in society are doing to gay people: discriminating against them because of their beliefs and practices.

I live my life by the Golden Rule: "Do unto others as you would like them to do unto you." We go through life crossing other people's paths, and we have to have respect and kindness. The world is based on respecting others. This is what determines what kind of person you are. We need to be able to look at all people for their character and not their sexual orientation, nor any other differences they may have. People have the right to their own beliefs. Taking that right away from one group is wrong and immoral. We should have more acceptance in our society. We have come a long way, but still have a way to go in treating people with equal respect.

Kindness plays a role in life. The way you talk to a person and the way you interact with a person can determine how you adapt to things. You don't always have to get along with a person or agree with a person's beliefs, but as long as you have kindness and respect for that person, then there's an even balance. If everyone respected each other, then there would be little to no conflict. People don't really have to agree on homosexuality, but they should respect it. On November 4, 2008, Californians should have voted "no" on Prop. 8 because it takes away people's fundamental rights. However, Proposition 8 passed, and now it is up to the courts to decide if it is constitutional.

Standing up for people is just part of the fight. Respect is key. Homosexuality is a sexual orientation; love does not have a gender. I believe that what people do with their personal lives is their business. When it comes to society, people should respect and tolerate everyone, no matter what race, disability, or sexual orientation. I believe that there is only one person who can judge you: That is God, and no one else. However, people still comment on other people's lives. People can believe what they want, but they should respect other people's beliefs. You can do this by treating others in the way you want to be treated. If we all live by the Golden Rule, people will respect each other even if they are different.

THE ONE WHO CHANGED MY LIFE

Eduwiges Rivas

A few years ago, I came up with a question when I was watching *The Justice League*, a cartoon that is supposed to represent ideal human qualities or traits. Should a hero be strong, handsome, smart, cool-headed, big-hearted, and tall? .

TV programs mostly depict heroes as white people with blue or green eyes, who are tall, rich, and strong: Superman, Batman, Ironman, and Spiderman. It seems as though they never pick a brown or a black person, and almost never a woman. Maybe the people who make these shows believe that women are only able to do chores and have children. I believe a hero should be different from the ones we see on TV. They should have radical changes in mind to end violence, work to create a huge difference in the world, and expand the real meaning of life and love. They should be able to help anybody, be there at any time, and know what someone needs without being told. A hero can be the oldest person ever or the ugliest—if this person has a big heart and is a compassionate human being, his or her age and appearance do not matter.

My hero is different from those on TV. She has a different skin color, black eyes, and is short. She is beautiful inside. She has the biggest heart I've ever known, is compassionate, and is not a racist. Most importantly, she is always there for people. I didn't realize how important it was to have a hero, a person you admire the most, until I met my own personal hero.

I'm an immigrant student who arrived in this country almost three years ago. I was pretty scared of everything on my first day of high school. I was worried because of the language barrier. I was afraid of the teachers because I couldn't understand what they were saying, and of the students because they were different from my friends in México. The classrooms, books, and places looked different to me in every way.

I remember it like it was yesterday. On the first day of high school, my English teacher gave me an English book to read. The book's title was *Out of the Dust*, and my teacher asked us to write an essay about it. I was shocked and didn't understand what was happening or what she was saying. I sat in silence and frustration. I don't remember how I overcame this challenge, but I managed to pass with the help of a Spanish-English dictionary. It was a creepy experience because I was alone. I felt like I was going into the jungle without any tools. I was also concerned because I was about to graduate from high school and go on to college. I didn't know what to do or how to achieve my goals. I think God knew and saw how much I was struggling, and he sent an angel in the form of a teacher to guide me.

There she was, sitting at her desk, waiting for the students to come into class. She is someone I never imagined I would meet, much less like. She looks mean but is not; she is short, has a deep voice, and wears old-fashioned glasses. I would have never imagined that she would do anything for anyone else. I know it sounds ridiculous, but it is true. I never imagined a stranger would help me without demanding something in return, but I was wrong. All this person wanted was for me to succeed, overcome my fears, face my truth, and reach my dreams.

One day I was in my hero's class looking worried; she saw my expression and asked me to stay after school. Usually I'm always laughing—that day was the first time she saw me worried, sad, and mad at the same time.

After class she asked me if I was OK. Right away I said, "No, I'm not." I didn't want to say why, and she didn't ask; she understood and stayed quiet. Then she changed the subject, asking me if I wanted to go to college. I said yes. She was happy that I wanted to go to college. I still remember what she said: "If you want to go to college, I'll help you. If not, that is your choice. But if you want, I'll even fight for it. Because you can do it, and everyone has the right to attend college." Another time when we were discussing my future college plans, she discovered that there were some criteria to meet in order to apply to either the University of California or California State University. Since I am an immigrant, under the AB 540 Law (which was created for immigrants who wish to attend college but can't afford it), I need three years of high school in order to apply to any university. I had only two years of high school. She told me that if I finished one more year of high school I could apply under this law. She also told me that I needed to take the ACT and SAT to fulfill the criteria for college, and she gave me a waiver to reduce the fees for both tests. After that I applied for my first SAT and she helped me study for my test. This was the most amazing thing that anyone has ever done for me. It will forever stay in my heart and mind.

Sometimes we think that life is hard, but we don't realize that sometimes we get in our own way. I have learned from this experience that there are heroes who want to help us understand what our mistakes are in order to succeed and achieve our dreams. I don't really know why my hero did what she did and continues to do for me. I'm happy and feel more comfortable and confident with her around. As a student who comes from a different background and culture, I don't know if there will always be people with integrity in this new place, people who are willing to share and teach others. Sometimes we don't realize that we will be treated the same way we treat others. I have learned from life that you always need to be *you*—authentic, compassionate, and whole—in order to succeed and be treated well. My hero must have been treated very kindly, because she treats other people so well.

My hero also comes from a different background. She isn't white, but she grew up adopting United States ideals. Her skin color is different from the heroes shown on TV, and she is female. But the most important thing is the courage she has to stand up and fight for her beliefs, never worrying if she'll get into trouble. This is what I like most about my hero. I think this has influenced my future plans: I want to be a science teacher and a doctor, like her. She is a wonderful chemistry teacher not just because she knows science, but because she teaches chemistry in a different way. This might be because she loves what she does, and she knows that science is an interesting career where you can discover what the world is made of. My purpose and goal once I become a doctor/teacher is to help everyone, especially people of color, like my teacher does. She is always there for anyone, even if they come from a different background. She doesn't care about background details, all she wants is to teach others that when we work together, we can change the world for the better.

Life has taught me that what makes you trip and fall can also make you rise and succeed. A few days ago, I was really upset and sad. Someone had said a lot of offensive words, things that I didn't want to hear. I was in shock and I went to my hero's classroom feeling frustrated. She told me to sit down, then she asked me what was going on. I told her that I was sad, because life is never fair. At times life makes you feel bad. People are always saying dumb things to make others feel bad. She told me right away to stop saying what I was saying, because life is the most beautiful thing God ever created. She sat next to me and told me to believe and trust. She said, "I will help you and be there for you." She told me that if someone hurt my feelings, she would do something right away, because she wanted me to feel safe. "Tell me," she said, "and I will talk to this person and fix the problem." But I rejected that option. If someone is mean to me, I don't want to be like that person—I want to be better, to show them I have integrity, that I'm kind, and grateful for what I have. I think that is something I learned from my hero. She is kind and compassionate to everyone. She is a hero because she knows how hard it is to fight for a structure and for thoughts that differ from those belonging to the majority. She has a different idea of the model American citizen.

I don't want to sound racist, but it's true that people judge you based on who you are and what you look like, not for how you think or what your feelings are. But my hero doesn't care about what other people say or think, she stands up to defend her beliefs, because she wants everyone to have the same rights.

I really admire this person; she is just tremendous. I'm not allowed to give details about her life because she doesn't want me to, and I want to give her space and respect. I can say this: she has been faced with lots of challenges. This might be because she doesn't look like George Bush, but she wants the rights Bush has. Many people don't like the way she thinks. But I do, and I agree with most of her ideas. When I was in her class, she told us, "If you don't look like George Bush, you'll be treated with racism. But if you know your rights and you know how to use your voice, nobody, not even me, will treat you badly. Learn how to use your voice, talk to me in English, practice, and I'll help you to succeed." This helped us a lot. I know it might sound dumb to you, but for people like me who are immigrants and don't know the United States' education system, this sounds real. Sometimes people lie to make you feel better, but she was authentic and truthful. She told us about the realities of life, and to me that's what a hero should always do. Sometimes I don't like the way she expresses her thoughts, but I know she does it because she wants us to understand that if you want something, you have to fight at least twice as hard for it.

You might already know that most immigrants come to this country seeking a better life, but teenagers like me come to this country following in the steps of their parents, not because they wish to come here. You might not know how much we struggle to obtain what we want, to reach our dreams. Sometimes I think that life sucks, but then I think of my hero and what she has faced, and I am reminded of what we have overcome together. I realized that even if you trip while following your path, you still can look forward, because there will always be people like my hero to support you. You'll always need someone to talk to, to cry with, or to share stuff with, and this is who my hero is for me. And one day when you need help, someone will be there for you. I also know that one day,

I'll do something for my community; I would love to help change the way we treat each other.

A hero is not just a person who protects you, it's also a person who always tells you the truth, who never lies to make you feel better, even when he or she knows that this might be the easiest way to comfort you. A hero is fair, but also kind. As you walk through life you'll find that life is like a roller coaster. Sometimes you are up and other times you're down. My hero knows this and applies her knowledge as she moves forward. She never looks back, but she is always willing to stop in her path to help others. Normally we think that heroes are like magic, that they don't exist. I disagree: heroes may be the minority of the population, but they exist. They are there waiting for you to scream, "Help me!" I have my own hero because I screamed and asked for help.

Do it. Don't be afraid to open your heart and mind to people; trust me, you will learn more than you already know.

I know that it will be hard for you to share, or trust someone you don't know that well with your feelings, but if you don't try, you'll never know what can happen to your life. Sometimes taking the quickest way is the easiest thing to do, but if you struggle a little more to reach your dream, you'll learn to appreciate the world in a different way. If you open up to others, they'll open up to you, and you will form a bond with them. That is a real reward in itself. My advice to you: always be real, authentic, kind, and truthful, and you will be treated with respect.

KINDNESS
Gwenisha Collins

On Sunday night, after I got off of work, I was walking through an alley when I met this really hot guy. He had light brown eyes with dark brown hair. He had, like, a caramel tone to him. I remember standing right next to him. He was robbed by some punks, and they took his money, so I ran after them with my mace. They ran, of course, and so the guy ended up running too. They got away. I never got to see him again.

OK, it's May 22, 2008, two days away from prom. What am I going to do? I've got no dress. No shoes. The most horrible thing of all is I've got no date! Oh my god, I just found out that the prom is going to be at the new Hilton hotel. It's supposed to have a huge water slide and a chocolate fountain. Now how am I going to get all this stuff done in two days?

I went home crying. My mom asked me what was wrong and I told her prom was in two days and she told me not to worry about it because she had a plan.

"Mom, what kind of plan are you talking about?" I asked.

"Well, first I want you to call your auntie and we'll all figure out a plan together."

Later that day I called my auntie to see what kind of dresses she had, so I could see which one I wanted to wear to prom. She told me to come around four o'clock. Soon as I walked in I was overwhelmed by how many pretty dresses she had—colors from pink to turquoise. So I tried on two dresses that I really… really… really liked, one being orange with different little rhinestone designs on it. It was cute. But I liked this purple one—it tied around the neck with the back cut out. My auntie and I decided that this would be my prom dress. I still needed to get some sandals to go with my dress. I stopped by Zara's, my favorite place to shop, because I knew they would have the perfect pair of shoes.

The next day I still had to get my nails, hair, and make-up done.

"Oh my god… What am I going to do? Mom, how are we going to get all this done?"

"Relax dear, no one goes to prom early. You want to be fashionably late."

My mom took me to get my hair done at Simply Fabulous, when I got there, it was closed.

"Oh no, what am I going to do?" Tears began to roll down my face.

I waited until five o'clock. I phoned the store again. No answer! Again! I stomped my feet on the ground and punched the wall. This homeless man looked at me like I was crazy. I was mad, really upset, that this lady just flaked on me.

My mother came and got me and I went back home, trying to think of who could do my hair. I began to cry again and lost hope that I would ever go to prom.

I called my favorite cousin. She said she would do my hair for me and I felt so relieved because I was going to have a heart attack if I didn't get it done. It didn't take long for her to do my hair. From there I went to the nail shop to get my nails and feet done. I picked out this really cool color, but I had my friends with me, and they were saying that I should "get pink," "get yellow," or "get blue." But I got the color I wanted, which was purple. And I got a design with the letters G and C, to stand for Gwenisha Collins.

On my way home to get dressed and get all cute for prom, I called my stepdad because he has his own limo company. He said he could pick me up in about two hours. I jumped in the shower for an hour and a half. My hair was done, nails were done, feet, eyebrows—done! I was fresh out of the shower, smelling like a dozen roses—ha! I loved myself.

The limo arrived. My stepdad, Dennis, opened the door for me. I felt like Cinderella getting into her carriage.

Finally, we were off to prom. Crossing the Bay Bridge we had the music bumping so loud that we couldn't hear anything. Then, some way, some-how, we got a flat tire. The limo driver pulled over. We were just waiting for a good thirty minutes. The driver was standing by a ramp, trying to flag people down. Finally, a grey Pontiac pulled over. I ran to the car and the man gave me this weird stare, as if he knew me. He had light brown eyes, and dark brown hair with caramel-toned skin. He offered my friends and me a ride to prom.

As we got in the car he asked me, "Aren't you the girl from the alley?"

"Yes."

"I knew you looked familiar. I just wasn't sure until now. You know I never got to say thanks for helping me that night."

"You're so welcome. I haven't seen you since."

"What's your name, pretty girl?"

"Gwenisha. Those guys were real jerks you know. Hey, I never got the chance to tell you that you dropped your wallet when you ran. And ever since then, I haven't seen you. Oh, and I still have your wallet too. After you ran I had those punks right in my sight. I wasn't letting them cowards get away."

"I can't believe I ran. I guess I was scared."

"The police came and filed a report. At first I didn't remember how the police were even contacted. Some old man named Richard, who owns the ice cream shop down on 30th Street, said he heard us yelling, so he called the police immediately. And they came in and took those young men to jail. Not to mention, one of those supposed-to-be-men was a woman!"

Why was I lying to this really hot guy? *Oh my gosh*, I thought to myself, *why does he have to be so cute? Maybe I should get his number.*

Finally, I got to prom. I thanked the hot guy for dropping us off.

He said, "No problem. Anytime. Here's my phone number, call me anytime."

Then we walked into the hotel ballroom and they were playing very loud music, it happened they were playing my favorite song, "Whatever You Like," by T.I. We ended up standing around for a good minute, then I started dancing with this really good-looking guy. He was real tall, like six-foot three, with an all-white tuxedo and some all-white Air Force Ones. He was looking really good.

I wasn't too worried about not having a prom date because I knew that once I got to prom I would have had to leave him anyway to go party with my friends. My friends and I, we took a group prom picture.

After the prom was over we went to Denny's restaurant. It was about 1 AM and we were all tired and ready to go home. After I arrived home, I stretched out on my bed, called it a night, and fell asleep. I had a really good dream; that I was on the phone with the really hot guy. He repeated what he said in the car, "What's your name, pretty girl?" And then I woke up.

In my dream, my family had helped me out when I was in need. If it wasn't for my family, I wouldn't have ever gone to my senior prom. They showed me kindness, which is the moral of my story. Kindness goes beyond treating others the way you want to be treated. Kindness is about doing something from your heart without expecting anything in return. This shows love.

I'm glad I am able to share my story with you because the world would be a better place if everyone shared kindness and could do stuff for others without expecting anything in return.

CARE
Yanhong Yang

One day, I wanted to go to bed when my mother said her leg was very painful. She wanted to see the doctor. I was very tired at the time, and it was so cold outside. I really did not want to go out. However, I had seen my mother. I knew that she was suffering. There was pain on her face. I thought about how hard my mother worked. If I did not help her, she would be tired out. I felt so hard in my heart. My mother always cared for me but didn't do the same things for herself. At that time, I thought I should care for her, too. So I took my mother to the hospital.

When the doctors told us that my mother needed hospitalization, I felt very sad. So every day after school I would go to the hospital to see my mother, sometimes to chat with her and sometimes to help massage her sore muscles.

Mom said: "My child, you have become thoughtful, concerned about me." When I looked at my mother's wrinkled face, I decided I needed to take better care of her. Even though it was cold, I felt happy.

Maybe you are wondering: Why did you feel happy—your mother was ill—are you crazy? No! I felt happy because my mother said to me, "You have grown up, I feel very gratified." To care for parents is a great thing, an indispensable part of life. As I heard these words, I felt happy, too. I don't think many young people take care of their parents, but it is important for you to learn it. Have you done it? Parents give you life. They needn't care for you, but they give you care in every possible way. If you are a good person, you will want to care for them. Some people will only accept their parents concern and are not concerned about them, even when they are old. I think this is not right.

This incident made me think a lot. My mother is a great mother. She is very diligent. She would work while I was usually at home doing nothing. I would finish my homework, then watch television until I went to bed. I did fewer household duties. In fact, my mother's life was very hard. She was at work every day until seven o'clock. After returning home, she would cook something for me and my uncle. My mother's leg was injured two years ago, but she works hard. At the time, I couldn't empathize with her and would give her trouble. Once, my mother asked me to help her take some dirty clothes to the laundry, but I was watching a movie. I did not help her and I think that made my mother very sad.

After beginning to care for my mother, I began to ask myself, *Could I change to be better?* I really wanted to help every time I saw my mother in so much pain. I wanted to give up the habit of being lazy. People said I was like that because I have been spoiled. They said I did not care for others and did not respect my parents. In fact, every time I heard those words, I was very sad. I even thought that the reason I was acting this way was because my parents divorced early. I thought that they were never properly concerned about me, and that I would become like them. Instead, I now understand that my parents were very concerned about me. Maybe they were busy with their work, and I just had a lack of communication with them. I think they realized they had to change to become concerned parents and respect their children.

I remember when I was in China there was a television advertisement that showed a daughter-in-law wearily helping her mother-in-law with a foot bath. There was an enjoyable smile on the old mother-in-law's face, and then I thought, *What do I do for my parents? What can I do to make my parents smile?* When I saw the part about the children taking a foot bath of water to their mother, their mother was brought to tears, and I was moved by this heartwarming moment. The mother was sincerely happy.

If I do the same for my parents, they would be happy like that mother, right? Just like the children on the advertisement, I also want to take some water to wash my mother. When my mother gets off duty and comes back home, I will make a cup of tea for my mother. I think she would be very happy. Mother thinks work is hard but worth it, and now I can do something for her. I can care about her and protect her.

After seeing that, I changed. My mother is recuperating at home now, but her leg has not improved, and it is hard for her to walk. The doctor checked my mother's leg by taking an x-ray, but they could not find the problem. The doctor said that if the pain in her leg continues, it will be necessary to undergo an operation. Now that I know this, I'm very distressed.

Every day after school, when I come back home, cook something to eat, and do household duties, I'm not worried about me anymore. When it is time to take medicine, I take a cup of hot water and administer medicine to my mother. I tell her, "In the future, you are not allowed to do housework. Leave it to me, while you rest in bed."

Everybody grows older, and there must be children to care for the old. When the children get older, there will be another generation to care for the children. After the passage of time, elderly parents are returned to their original state. They are the same as children and need care. They don't demand a lot, they just hope that we will spend time with them. Just like the Chinese commercial showed, respecting the elderly is a virtue.

Parents care for their children by nature, and they don't expect anything in return. Can we really understand the inner world of older people? Sometimes older people could be thinking differently than you might. At this time, you need to help them. They need your caring. When you are older, you may need caring for. One day, when you have lost your parents, will you have some regrets?

These experiences made me realize many things, such as: Don't give the excuse of being busy with work; know that the work can be done later. Money is a bottomless pit, it can never be enough. However, our days with our parents are numbered. Once our parents are gone, we can take the time to do work. Money can be earned another day, but old parents cannot wait.

When people are hurt, they desire comfort; when they are confused, they want guidance; when they are sick, they hope to be taken care of. None of us are philanthropists. However, we can do the same and show concern for others. We don't need to deliberately find people to help as long as we help others. This I will keep in my heart.

I have learned that, in order to care for others, first you need to learn to be considerate. We have the Chinese saying, "One person's heart, the heart of tens of millions of people." That is how a person's heart, and ten million of people's hearts are alike. Learning to care for others does not mean simply to indulge others. When friends encounter frustration or depression, be sympathetic and show your concern. But it doesn't help to share their depression. So, why not a different attitude? You should use an optimistic attitude to cheer them up. You can tell them that setbacks are inevitable, but there are many friends that are concerned for them and will help. What difficulties cannot be overcome with help? When they feel good again, full of confidence, they will more deeply realize that you were sincerely concerned. This will motivate them to continue an active life.

I remember one cold winter night at 2 AM. I was sleeping when suddenly my friend called me. She was crying and said to me, "I'm very sad now. My boyfriend and I broke up, and I do not know what to do." I said to her, "Don't be sad. Maybe he does not fit you, and you will find better. You should go to bed, tomorrow is a new day. You still have a lot of things to do." I was with her every day after that to remind her to look to the future. She got well slowly, became cheerful, and was grateful that I had been with her to help her out of the predicament. I felt gratification that my concern for other people helped her feel good.

When you learn to care for others, you also help others in their hardship.

One can always pay attention to small details, like a good man showing concern for others. Know how to care for others and help others who are happy, because one should be concerned with other people's well-being. Showing concern for others is a virtue. I hope everyone can develop it.

Dear readers, have you done it? Have you tried to show concern? I wrote this article because too few people understand the importance of this. It is important to care for parents and to care for others. Concern and caring can improve one's growth.

LOVE TAKES OFF MASKS THAT WE FEAR WE CANNOT LIVE WITHOUT

Ashley Peurala

You know that fairy tale romance most of us girls wish for? I thought I had found my soulmate, someone who completely filled my heart with endless love. Later on, I found out I was wrong; people use masks to hide parts of them until you discover the true side of how they act, feel, learn, and love, and how complex they are. You don't understand them until the mask is completely removed. This is my story.

It started out two years ago when I first met Cameron. I was living in Lincoln, Nebraska with my mom, and it was the start of my freshman year of high school. Everyone in Nebraska is isolated, family oriented, and loves football. My family life there was a disaster, and I hated football.

It was a nice fall morning; the air was fresh and the sun was peeking out of the clouds. My friends liked to hang out on this corner in front of school, which was just outside of school boundaries so they wouldn't get hassled by teachers. While at the corner, I saw this perfectly good looking guy. He had ice blue eyes, dark brown hair, and was just the right height. I just kept staring at him, and I had those stomach butterflies that everyone talks about. My heart was racing. A friend of mine, Connor, introduced him to me. His name was Cameron. We didn't say anything to each other. Cameron just opened up his arms and expected me to hug him. At first, I looked at him like he was crazy, but then he looked at me like a girl has never rejected one of his hugs. Puzzled, he said, "What, I can't have a hug?"

"Well, I guess, but I don't even know you," I replied. We hugged each other, and (oh my god) I didn't want to let go, but I did anyway. After that morning, we didn't see each other for a couple of days.

When I met Cameron, I thought I didn't have a chance to be with him. So when this guy Ben asked me out, I said yes. The next week, I walked down to the corner. Cameron ran up, hugged me, and said, "Where have you been?"

"Actually, where have *you* been?" I said. Then my boyfriend Ben walked up to me and grabbed my hand. Cameron's face looked shocked and confused. But it didn't stop him from walking up to school with all of us together. As we walked, Cameron was on my left and Ben was on my right. I took a step back and looked at both of them. I realized that I liked Cameron way more than Ben.

Shortly after, Cameron found himself a girlfriend named Tiffany. I was upset because I thought he liked *me*. I was flat out jealous of Tiffany. I kept thinking, *Why her?* Then again, why should I think I had that possibility to begin with?

A while later, I broke up with Ben because he was kind of two-faced. And finally, Tiffany broke up with Cameron! I never found out why. I remember being down at the corner when Cameron came toward me. I turned away because I didn't want to be the "rebound." That next morning, while at the corner with some friends, Cameron walked up to me, hugged me, didn't let go, caught me completely off guard, and kissed me—a moment I'd been waiting for. Still wrapped in each other's arms, I leaned back and asked, "So… are we together now?" He smiled and replied in the sweetest voice, "Yes."

The following day Cameron and I decided to skip school with a few friends (I know, not a smart idea). We went to someone's house to play cards, eat, talk, play video games, and watch television. Cameron and I were inseparable that day. After a while, we all caught the bus back to school. We cuddled in the third row. I remember how at peace and relaxed I was that day. His friends at the back of the bus were giving him BS because they could tell he was being loving, caring, and honest with me. Cameron used to have the reputation of a party animal who never stopped. He had that reputation because he had insecurities, but with me, he took off his mask and showed his true self. He would talk to me about his life and include me in everything that he did. He was never like that around his friends because they would make fun of him.

The next two days we didn't see each other. I wondered where he was and if he was OK. On the third day, while I was walking to the corner, I was so happy to see him. When he started to walk toward school, I felt like he was running away from me and my heart sunk. When I got to the corner, Connor came up to me, and from the look on his face, I could tell he had some bad news about Cameron. I had just gotten dumped.

Connor said that it wasn't my fault; Cameron was about to get locked up for a long time. He said that Cameron didn't want to hold me back. When I asked why Cameron was getting locked up, Connor explained that Cameron had been defending a girl from getting beat up by a guy. Cameron didn't stand for that because he had grown up with six sisters. Cameron ended up breaking the guy's nose and was charged with assault. I was heartbroken. It was the first time I ever cried over a guy.

A year later, my mom forced me to move to my dad's in San Francisco. I started at Mission High School halfway through the year. It was a rough start for me at a new school trying to catch up to the other students. Amazingly, I made ten friends in the first week and the number just kept on growing. As I became settled and comfortable, Cameron was off my mind. I never forgot about him, though. I just didn't think about him as much.

One time I got onto MySpace and happened to see one of my old friends from Nebraska on there. I sent him a message that said, "Here is my number, give me a call so we can catch up." A couple of days later, I got a phone call from my friend, Chris. He told me that Cameron was sitting next to him and asked if I wanted to talk to him. I paused and said, "Sure."

When Cameron got on the phone, I thought it was going to be awkward, but it was surprisingly easy. I guess because we hadn't talked in so long. We ended up talking from 7 PM till 5 AM. I asked him if he would give me a second chance. He said he would! He told me, though, he wouldn't blame me if I didn't forgive him. He was sorry that he had left me, and he promised he would never do it again. We ended up falling in love with one another all over again. After that night we talked day after day.

We started a long distance relationship. It was great, at first. We would go online and talk to each other, and he would call and text me. We would tell each other why we loved the other and talked about having a future together. We would talk about our past and explain how much we both had changed. He would tell me I was the most beautiful, perfect girlfriend ever. We made this plan in which he would drive to California and take me to live with him in Nebraska. We were both excited about it and couldn't wait!

I couldn't help but think if I were to run away with him, then five years later I would still be depending on him. I couldn't do that to him if we were together. It would be too much of a burden. I wanted to be something in life. I had plans to go to culinary school and become a pastry chef. Cameron planned on going into the bricklaying business with his friends. I would have felt responsible for possibly ruining everything that we both wanted in our lives. So when I called him up one night and told him that I wanted to finish school he got quiet on the phone. With Cameron that means he is mad. So I told him to call me later. He called me the next day and said that he was sorry and that it was better if I finished school.

After that happened we didn't really talk that much. He stopped calling and texting and I got really depressed. He started to accuse me of cheating on him and of not loving him. We started to get into a lot of fights and arguments. I told him a couple of times to forget everything. He wouldn't let me go, though. We managed to stay together.

As I started my junior year, Cameron and I talked about how hard it would be and how we weren't going to be able to talk to each other as much. We used to debate if we should stay together or just break up. We decided to stay together and it was a real struggle; it just seemed hopeless a lot of the time.

One night I called him and told him that we should break up and just be friends for a year to see how that would play out once I moved back to Nebraska. He told me that he couldn't be my friend because he wanted to be with me. I told him it wasn't going to work because I didn't even have any time for myself. I wanted to join sports and keep my grades up. He got mad again. I didn't blame him for getting mad this time because I also would've been mad if I were in his position. We didn't talk for a couple of days. He called me and said that I was right and that we should break up. I got mad and started to yell at him. "Oh, it's OK for you to tell me this and break up with me?" I said. He said that he had a really bad day with his mom being drunk and the state determining if he should be taken away from his mom. He didn't have the ability to listen or understand, even if he had wanted to. He said that I didn't need to worry about what was going on with him, but that he was here for me and I came first. After that conversation, we didn't talk at all.

When I look over this whole situation it makes me upset and think a lot. It takes me back to when I first talked to him again on the phone. I could have said no, but why did I say yes? I could have saved myself all of this pain and regret. When I realized something was wrong, we ended up not talking to each other for two weeks. I started to message him on MySpace and he would reply "I don't know" to every question that I had. It annoyed me after awhile, and I decided to end it completely. I asked him if there was anymore "us" and if he loved me anymore and what was going on. He just gave up and gave me no reason. He broke his promise and broke my heart again! I felt like an idiot, but people told me that it was not my fault and not to blame myself for anything.

That is the sad ending of my story.

You are probably wondering what the mask has to do with it. We all wear masks that we use in our own unique ways. There are ways that you act in public and different ways that you act around certain people. It is like a target with a bull's eye and four rings. The first ring is your closest friends; they have known you forever and know everything about you. The next ring is the people that have known you for a while but don't necessarily know everything about you. The ring after that belongs to people that know your name, maybe, but you only say "hi" to them. The last ring is people that you see but you don't talk to. See what I mean? You have your mask on with everyone except the people in the first ring. You only show your complete true self to people you know you can trust.

I cherish my mask because it can protect me if I don't feel comfortable around someone. I can just say to them, "You know, I don't feel comfortable talking to you about this." The person that you don't wear the mask with is a person who you feel comfortable telling all your problems to, the person you can run to if you need help, the person you always know will be there for you no matter what, the person who is reliable, the person you know who is trustworthy. Don't take off your mask unless you know that the other person will do the same for you.

Cameron's mask functions to hide his insecurities and his true identity. At first he came off as this cool guy who likes to party, get into a lot of trouble, and not have a care in the world for anything. He was very good at making you think that this is actually who he is. When I got to know him, he showed this caring, loving, mature person that no one else ever discovered. That is when I knew that he had removed his mask. People would see that Cameron was kind and sometimes they gave him a hard time, so he decided to put his mask back on. And this is what breaks my heart. Cameron wears his mask like a security blanket because he isn't ready to not care what other people think about him.

At first, Cameron and I both had our masks on, and after getting to know one another, they were slowly removed. Some people don't know at this age, or even when they are adults, when to learn from their individual insecurities and to acknowledge when someone is real. It's a hard thing to know what people want with you and if they are real with you. I am not saying it's a bad thing; it's just something that is hard to learn but it can really come in handy. Cameron has a lot of insecurities and hasn't grown from them, and he let that ruin the relationship we had. It is fine if he isn't ready to completely get rid of his mask; at least I know I am ready to get rid of my masks when someone is going to be there for me—someone who will be by my side for the rest of my life. Someone who will love me just as much as I love them. Someone who understands me. That is the fairy tale story I am still waiting for.

HOW I CAME HERE
Luis Serrano

Many innocent people have been accused of doing things they didn't do. The law often hurts innocent people instead of helping them. If every police officer treated people with kindness and fairness, innocent people would not have to pay for the crimes of others. I have seen many events that happen in my country, El Salvador, and also in the United States, where the police are allowed to hurt people and arrest people who don't have problems with the law. This is the reason I want to be a police officer: to change the way officers treat people.

The history of my family that my daddy told me is the reason that I dream of being a police officer. He told me that he worked when he was nine years old. He started to work in agriculture, and this work was hard. The people would pick tomatoes, sweating in the sun. Sometimes the people got sick because they were exposed to many chemicals. In many cases they got leukemia. One of my uncles died because the chemicals gave him leukemia. My grandfather went crazy after that because he blamed himself for my uncle's death. When my uncle died, my father had to go to work, and that is why my daddy couldn't go to school and didn't have a chance to set a better goal. That's the reason he wants to support me in my goal.

My father doesn't want me to be like him. He works in construction, but he told me that that work is hard to do, and sometimes people lose their fingers because they use many types of machines. Also, some of the metal beams fall and can break bones or cause other damage. This work is hard, but the people do this work because the company pays well, and they want more money. My father does not want me to work like him, and that's why he supports me in my goal to be a policeman. The help that he gives me makes me feel I can make my goal. My family is the main inspiration of my life and is the best thing I have. That is why I want to help my family. I especially want to help my daddy because he is the person who has supported me in my life. He has shown me the way that I can act on the street and has helped me to treat people on the street with respect.

My father's opinion is the most important because my father wants all my brothers and me to be professionals and have different jobs than he does. I want to make his dream real for me and my brothers. Also, my father tells me how to solve my problems without getting into trouble. I have other goals for after I become a police officer. I want my father not to work because it is my obligation to help him and my mom with money, housing, food and other things. Also, if my grandma and my grandpa are alive, I want to help them, too, because they are like second parents to me. By that time, I think I will be ready to be a dad and have a wife. I want that life because that is special.

When I was in El Salvador I had goals, but I lost them when my uncle was killed by the gangsters who were trying to steal my family's land. When I saw my uncle on the ground with fifty machete cuts to his body, I started to cry. My family didn't recognize him because he had so many cuts in his face. That type of violence is terrible. At that time I wanted justice. The people who killed my uncle were free. Uncle Marcial was a good person to me and to other people too. I think he died because another person wanted my family's land. The police got the gangsters who killed my uncle, and the court found them guilty and gave them forty-five years in prison. The gangsters escaped, but after a month they were caught and went to prison again. This time they went to a prison in La Paz, which is nicknamed Alcatraz because they have strong security. My family left El Salvador because my uncle was murdered, and we were afraid the gangsters wanted to kill the rest of the family. I didn't want to come to the United States because I didn't want to leave the country that saw me grow up. It was difficult for me, but I needed to come here because the rest of my family was already here, and only my little brother and I were still in El Salvador.

To get here I walked with my uncle and my little brother across the border between El Salvador and Guatemala. Then we took a bus from the border to the capital of Guatemala and a boat from Guatemala to Mexico. We walked in the mountains and took another bus to the United States. On the bus, the Mexican police came inside to ask for documents. They knew that I was an immigrant, and we had to pay them because if we didn't pay the money we could be deported. We paid them to continue on the bus and reach our goal here.

While we were in a hotel in Mexico with the rest of the people that came with us, two people came and knocked on the door to our room. My friend opened the door, and the two people took out a gun. I was scared. They said that they needed to go to another room where my cousin was. They wanted money from my cousin, but my cousin didn't have any. My cousin told them that he would collect the money for them. He asked my brother and me to go to the room with the girls, and the rest of the people went with the two men from the gang. The next day, a person that my cousin had sent came to the hotel and took all the girls and me. For the rest of the trip I was with only five people and this one person. This one person helped us in many ways and gave us money for food. I never forgot this thing that happened in Mexico.

When I crossed the border, the ICE (Immigration Customs Enforcement) took my brother, but I ran to the ICE because I didn't want my brother to be alone. I spent that day in a room that was very cold. My little brother started to cry, but afterward he slept. The next day the ICE took my little brother and me to a house where only immigrant boys lived. It was like my own house because the people who cared for us were so special and that made me happy. I forgot that I was in an immigration house. There were teachers, and in the afternoons we played soccer or basketball. I spent twenty-eight days there, but then my mom came for my little brother and me, and we took an airplane to the United States. I had to go to court where a judge would say if I could stay here or go back to my own country. If you have problems in your country and you have evidence, the judge will say you can stay here. I only went to the court one time. I was scared to go back to my country, but the judge told my mom, my brothers and me that we could stay here because he had so much evidence that gangsters killed my uncle, from the news from my country and from photos that showed how my uncle was killed. That is why the judge gave us residence documents.

That changed my life. I have the opportunity to have any job, and I want to seize that opportunity. I can't go to my country because the gangsters are angry with my family, but now the United States is my new country. I want to teach people that it doesn't matter where you're from; if you want something, you need to try for it. Because I suffered from gangsters, I want to help people with problems. I will try to do something about gangsters who want to make more problems, and I will meet with them and show them there are other ways to work because the way they are living is terrible. They are bothering and stealing from people, and I don't want that for this beautiful city. I will fight against any type of violence in this city because I want the people to walk wherever they want to in San Francisco and not be afraid. I will work hard to better this city. This community will be the best in this country because of what the police of San Francisco can do, and that will make me happy. This is why I want to be a policeman in this country.

People need police. For instance, two weeks ago two people got into my uncle's house and told him they wanted to kill him. My uncle was scared. My cousin escaped with her daughter and raced to tell my other uncle, who called the police. The two people left the house, but the police didn't get them.

I also want to be part of the police force because I don't want people who have done nothing wrong to get hurt by police or other types of law enforcement. For example, in October of 2008, the ICE went into many houses in San Francisco, throwing gas bombs because they thought that there were gangsters living in these houses. The ICE said that they were looking for drugs, gangs, and other things. At the same time, they arrested many people they found in these houses. Some of the people were deported; other people were put in prison. That is OK if they have done illegal things, but the thing that makes me so sad is that innocent people also got arrested just because they lived in those houses.

There are many people from other countries who want to work and send money back to the rest of their families, but they can't because they need a social security number. This causes some of the violence and forces some to go back to their own countries where other gangsters might kill them. This makes me sad, and I want to help these kinds of people. I think that will be the first time that someone helps these people.

Another thing I want to do when I become a policeman is to help the people who live on the streets and don't have family because of drugs and other problems. I want to help them with food, clothes, and other things that they need. My family taught me that when other people need help, I can help them. If someday a person in my family became homeless, other people might help, and that would make me very happy. It doesn't matter where these people are from, I can help them.

The goals of people can come true if they really want them and work at them. My auntie is trying to achieve her goal. She is going to the university in El Salvador even though she has two children. Other people try to help the community where they live because they don't want violence in their community. My father is a person who, throughout his life, has tried to do things that help his community. He is the person I admire most, and he supports me in my dream. I want to be a policeman in this country, but if I don't get this profession, I will look for a profession that helps the community and other people. I could go to the army and be a soldier, or to the navy, or some other way that helps the country. I could join the FBI. I could be a lawyer. Whatever I do, I will do it with the help of my family and the people who love me.

STRUGGLE FOR A BETTER LIFE
Brenda Madero Cuevas

To anyone who has gone through what I have: you're not alone. There are people, such as your loved ones and family, who love and care about you. Let your experience make you stronger. Don't let anything get you down.

People say that you should treat others the way that you want to be treated, but there are some who don't follow the rules. I don't believe you have to go through bad situations to understand how a person should be treated. I want to share my story with the world so people can relate to it and learn from my mistakes. Everyone makes mistakes, nobody is perfect. We live in an imperfect world. We are born to make mistakes, but it's on each of us to decide if we want to learn from them or just let them lead us to failure.

At the age of fourteen, I was having trouble at school. My grades had dropped because I started going out with friends and I stopped caring about classes. My parents and I decided that the best thing was for them to send me to Los Angeles to live with my uncle. They thought that it would work out because I didn't know anyone there and it would be a fresh start. If I put more effort into school I would do well.

I remember I was very upset and scared because it was going to be a really big change for me. I've never liked the idea of being a new student at a school where I didn't know anybody, especially not a new school with a new family in a new town. The idea freaked me out. But I was willing to go and give it a try.

Going to a new school wasn't as bad as I thought it would be because I got to go with my cousin. In the beginning I missed my family and friends a lot, but I couldn't complain because my uncle treated me as if I were one of his daughters. I liked it.

Then, after having lived in Los Angeles for ten months, everything turned bad. I stopped getting along with one of my guy cousins. The situation is too sensitive for me to go into further detail here, but I no longer felt safe living there. It was as if everything had gone downhill. I needed to call someone to get help. I thought, *Who better than my sister?* I called her to let her know what was going on and how I felt. She understood and the next day she and my dad came to take me back home to San Francisco.

After that, my family and my uncle's family stopped talking to each other. I was with my family again, but they didn't seem to care. I knew they were hurt because of what happened, but they never bothered to ask me how I was feeling. I was really sad and depressed. I felt really guilty, even though most of the time I knew I had done the right thing. On my own, I started to look for help. I got counseling at school and it helped a lot because I just let everything go. The only thing I regret is that both of my families don't speak to each other. But I realize I'm in charge of my own destiny and can't let any obstacle interfere.

I finally decided to change, to be the person I really wanted to be. I decided to be happy in spite of everything that had happened. I remember saying to myself, "I'm going to change for good. I will do things my way. I will not let anything get me down."

One person was there for me and I was there for him. Omar is my brother, my best friend, my buddy who listens and gives me good advice. In the very short time he lived in San Francisco with me, my mom, and my dad, he became a very important person in my life. He helped me realize that nobody is perfect, everyone makes mistakes, and we all deserve a second chance. What it took for us to get that close was playing video games and watching movies at night, talking, and sharing our personal experiences. We learned from each other. We went from crying ourselves to sleep to crying from laughter. We both knew we had done things that were not right. We knew we were never going to stop making mistakes. But we can decrease the number of mistakes we make. Becoming my brother's best friend brought me one of the most happy and memorable periods of my life.

Even when you are having a great relationship with someone, bad things still happen. My older sister has two daughters, ages twelve and four. A few months ago my four-year-old niece was diagnosed with leukemia. This was very shocking for the whole family.

It all happened when my niece started complaining that her foot hurt and she couldn't walk. We thought that maybe she had broken her ankle and immediately took her to the hospital. After being there for several hours, the doctors had no clue what was wrong and all they gave her was baby Tylenol. We took her back home, but when she still couldn't walk days later, my sister decided to take her to a different hospital. That's when the doctors said it might be something serious; they transferred her to the UCSF hospital, where they took really good care of her. They found out she had blood cancer. It was very scary for us to find out that a baby can be so sick, and at any time she could die.

The family grew close. We all had hope and faith that she would get better. We forgot about the misunderstandings and problems we had with each other. We all felt the pain and went to visit her at the hospital often. Having to see her there—so small and little, lying down in bed—was really hard for me. She cried herself to sleep from the pain she felt. She was so skinny and most of the time she was in a really bad mood because of the medication they gave her. But we still went and played with her so she wouldn't feel so lonely.

At some point they gave her medicine that restored her appetite and she gained a lot of weight. It was really funny to see her eat so much. She would even eat a little too much. She would get really mad when we hid food from her because she wanted to eat every thing she saw. But the doctors told us they weren't sure if her body would accept the medicine that could cure her. So we were still worried.

My family realized that our niece could die at such a young age, and here we were not talking to each other for worthless reasons. Finding out that she was sick changed us and the way we treated each other. We realized that every thing we do affects everyone around us. Now we try for her sake and for our own to treat each other with love and respect. Yes, like everybody, my family still has problems. But now we know how to deal with them. As long as the family is together, has hope, and has faith in God, things will get better.

This event changed my life and the way that I treat my family and friends. I used to be a very immature girl. I never cared about school. I was never proud of myself. Now I know what I want and how I want to get it and I will not let anybody stop me from getting there. I do not let my past and bad experiences interfere with my life anymore.

All I ever wished for was to have a happy and stable family. But at times that has been really hard to obtain. Now I believe that we can accomplish anything. I know we will always have problems. There will always be an obstacle in the way. We will always make mistakes, but we have to learn from them.

Allow your mistakes to help make you a stronger person. Everyone is different and everyone has different points of view. This is mine. And as long as I feel good about myself and know that I'm doing the right thing, I'm happy. Being happy and making the people around me happy is all I ever wished for. Now I just have to work hard to get where I want to be.

Before these things happened, all I wanted was to go out with my friends and have fun. I was in my shell of fun. I never thought about the danger that was out there or realized that while I was exposing myself to all kinds of bad, my family was worried about me, not knowing if I was OK. I just expected to get things without giving back or earning anything.

To my family, education is one of the most important things in life. They always used to say to me, "You will have time to have fun and go out with friends. Trust us, you will have fun, but save it for later. For now, what you need to do is focus on school and get an education. Later on in life you will be happier doing what you love to do. You'll be older and you will see things differently. You still have a long way to go."

Now I can finally say that they were right, when I used to think all they wanted was to bug me and make my life miserable. I can say that they cared about me and they just wanted the best for me. I know my family will be by my side, willing to do anything to help me achieve my goals in life. The saying "You don't know what you have till you lose it" doesn't apply to me. I can say that I know what I have and I don't need to lose it to understand it.

Today I know what I want to do with my life: I want to graduate from high school. I have classmates who don't seem to take school seriously, and think things will come to them without effort. I take school seriously because you can't get anywhere without an education.

I see myself now as a very smart, wise young lady who thinks with her head and wants the best for herself. I am caring and willing to sacrifice anything to get to where I want to be. I feel very strong. I've been through so much and instead of letting it get me down I've allowed it to make me stronger. I feel very proud of myself for having used my pain and weaknesses to guide me to be the person I want to be.

Other people who have been through what I have, have used the experience to make themselves weaker and weaker. It's like drowning in a glass of water. They get into drugs and start drinking alcohol. Some even lose their jobs and family because they feel they're alone and there's no solution to their problems. Some are just scared to talk about it, scared of letting it all out of their hearts, or embarrassed that people will know and find out what they're going through or have been through. They feel they're the only people who have gone through what they have and that they're alone, when really they're not.

I have not let my past and bad experiences interfere with my life, instead I feel more mature and I know what and where I want to go. This makes me feel very proud of myself. I will not let anybody stop me from getting there. The word "impossible" is gone from my vocabulary. I have set goals for myself that I will achieve. This is my story.

WHY ARE WE FIGHTING MOST OF THE TIME?

Julian Montes-Luna

I think that she doesn't understand me.

I grew up in a life of violence, especially in my house. My parents were always fighting. Between them were not just words. There was also hitting. I was the one who always stood between them to stop the fighting. I'm not throwing the blame on my mother or my father, or saying that because of them I am very violent. I'm not justifying. I just want my mom to understand the violence in me.

I grew up with this instinct of violence, and so I get angry easily, but you can ask all those who know me and I bet you they will say that I'm a good person, that I am funny, that I like to have fun. I almost never show aggression because I know that it is not necessary, but when people do things that I do not like, all that laughing and having a big smile on my face changes instantly. I understand why I am this way, why that great smile disappears.

I believe that the majority of our mothers do not understand the concept of being young today. For me, it is very difficult to stay home all day. I like to go out with my friends and have fun, but I think that in this country, it is very difficult for our moms to give us all the freedom that we want. Here it is very easy to get into drugs and gangs. In Latin American countries it is very easy to get into the same things, but not in the same way. In the United States we have more freedom and so we are in the streets more and can get into more trouble, just by the way we dress. In my case, I have often chosen roads that are not good. I have often focused on bad things. Sometimes I acknowledge that I am doing things that I should not do, and then I change for a while, like a week, and then I start doing bad things again.

I am always in trouble. To show you, I am going to tell you about just one day of my life. I wake up at six in the morning to take a shower, and my mom starts yelling, "Hey, Julian, hurry up." I tell her to hold on because I have one hour to get ready to go to school. When I am ready I walk my little brother, Jesus, to an elementary school that is just two blocks away from my house. I leave him, and I make my way to school. As soon as I get to school in the morning, all I want to do is leave because everything about it frustrates me. When my school day ends I have to go home early because I have to pick Jesus up at 5 PM. Sometimes I have to cook for him because my mom comes home tired from work. I also have the responsibility to clean up my house and other odd jobs like that. I do all of it because I want my mom to be happy with me, but often she doesn't appreciate it. She's always nagging me for little things. My brother's always bothering me, saying things like, "You want to fight?" I do it because he wants to play with me, but then he starts crying, and my mom thinks that I'm fighting him for real and starts screaming at me, saying, "Why are you making your brother cry? He's younger than you." I say, "If he wants to play with me he shouldn't cry. He knows that I'm bigger and stronger than him, but he still wants to play." I have fun play-fighting with him, and I keep doing it even though I know I am going to get in trouble.

I want to change. I have been trying to be more responsible because I want to graduate from high school and get a good job. I have tried to get all my school work done, and I am doing better in history. The teacher is always pushing me to do better and better and better. He talks to me and says, "Come on. Move away from your friends and get focused." This works. I get focused and get the work done. Just the other day in that class I completed an assignment to make a wanted poster for a slave-owner. I liked the project because I believed in it.

In the beginning of the school year I was doing all my work in my English class. Then we started this project where tutors, people I had never met before, came into the class and worked with us to write an essay. At first, I did not like having a person who I did not know sitting behind me in the computer lab, pushing me on to tell him what I thought about this or that. I have not been doing as well—but I *want* to do well. I see hope for all my classes. I have hope.

I want to write a letter to my mom. I have never talked to her about all the things I am thinking, because I am kind of shy. I hope the letter will make my mom realize that I care about her.

Dear Mom,

I'm going to tell you things that I have never been able to talk to you about. I know that I make you mad sometimes. I have done things that I never thought I would do. I have tried to hurt you. Because of me, you lost a job that you were dreaming about. I broke my ankle and then, because you had to take care of me every day, you could not go to work. I did things with my friends which got me sent to jail. But you know what I have lost—forgiveness. Many times in my life I say that I am going to change; I have tried many times. I try to change my way of being and I'm still the same as always.

I have always complained about things that I dislike, but some-times I start thinking that you were all alone trying to get us to move ahead in life. I know that you are already tired because you are always working, and I try to understand you, but I am always displeased by all the things you say. I think you are always saying these things to me because I am not the son that you expect me to be and you want me to change. You always say that I am like my dad, or even worse than him, and I do not understand why you say that to me. I didn't choose him to be my dad—you were the one who chose him to be your husband. My dad is not my fault. I just want you to know that you are the reason for my life even though you don't believe me. You were—and continue to be—the woman who gave me life. You have been teaching me what is good and what is wrong and how to treat others the way I want to be treated.

Once you told me what you did wrong as a mother and that was when I said, "You didn't do anything wrong." You did, and are still doing, good as a mother. We learn what you teach us. But we children make our own decisions, and if we choose a wrong path, it does not mean that you were not a good mother. You always say that you do not expect even a glass of water from me but always you give me what you can. Never in my life will I leave you alone. They say that when I marry my wife she is going to have to be first and not you, my mom. I say, in my life you are always going to be the first. You spent your whole life taking care of me, and nobody will come and take away your position, which is my one-and-only lady. And I want to thank you for everything you have done for me even though I did not know how to appreciate it.

Te quiero mucho, mi nega,
Julian

ABOUT THE AUTHORS

 ***María Alfaro*** was born in Mexico and moved to San Francisco one year ago to join her family. Her inspiration to write her essay came from a bad experience she had in the United States. She wants to share her story so that readers learn the same lesson she did. She found that writing about her experience was challenging but rewarding. She hopes her readers find it rewarding themselves.

 ***Catalina Almeida*** comes from a very diverse family. Having parents from two different countries makes her life extraordinary. From a young age, she was being thrown big responsibilities. Moving back and forth between Brazil and the United States has made her culturally aware and a more open person. In the United States, she faced many new experiences, and she based her story on one of them.

 ***Ravon Anderson*** is a creative person who enjoys reading and writing short stories for fun. He also enjoys going out with his friends and having a great time. He even takes time out to think and write about things like his community, school, and family. Sometimes, he writes short poems about things that are getting to him. He is a caring person and likes to be known as helpful to people, especially when they are feeling down. He likes to make them smile and not worry.

Idalia Beltran is a sensitive person, full of dreams and goals to reach. She is always responsible with her work and, even when she doesn't understand something, still gets through it. She dedicates this essay to her grandma—a special person who Idalia will always have in her heart. Even when her family has hard times, her grandma's help and examples make the family come together again. Idalia loves her mother and brother and says that they are everything in life and she will always be there for them.

Daarina Berry was never really a writer until her freshman year of high school. She began to write after being given a poetry homework assignment. This story is her first to be published in a book, and she was excited to finish it. She really likes to write poetry, but this essay has been her favorite so far.

Dante Calonsag wrote about the presidential election and our country's political issues because he is affected every day by these issues and wants to see change in this country. Dante loves to play basketball. He plans on playing for the Mission High School basketball team. He also loves to spend time with his family and friends. He enjoys listening to R&B and hip-hop music because they put him in a positive mood for most of the day.

Angel Chaparro was born and raised in San Francisco. He enjoys buying and watching DVDs and chilling with family and friends. His main love is eating his favorite foods: pizza, burgers, French fries, cheese steak, and anything else enjoyable. His main goal for writing a story for this book was to open people's eyes—to have them see his point of view and to make them realize what is important in life and what is not. Angel dedicates this story to his lovely father, who has kept him motivated and encouraged him to keep working and reach for what he wants in life.

Yong Chang Chen is writing a real story for the first time in his life. He is learning how to write a good story from reading books and newspapers. He came to the United States a year ago and enjoys playing basketball, playing video games, watching TV, and learning a second language. He is always thinking about the future because he wants to become a successful businessman.

Gwenisha Collins was born and raised in San Francisco and has lived there her whole life. She wants to grow up to be a hairstylist and do big things in life. She dedicates this story to all the Mission High School students who support her in life.

Angelica "Angie" Marisel Colon-Chin is a unique individual with her own ideas. For example, she gives thought to how things are done and doesn't do things exactly how they are taught to her; instead she adds a little twist to them. She asks, "What is the point of being like everyone else?" Angie thinks the world would be boring if we were all the same, and she wants the world to know that she is full of surprises.

Brenda Madero Cuevas thinks big. She reflects on her life and changes things when she thinks they need to be changed. Even when things seem bad, she tries to look at them in a positive way. She has gone through a lot of hard things, but she always learns from them. She has grown as a person and is no longer afraid. She is strong and no one will get her down. *Ahora yo soy fuerte y solo veo para adelante, que ya para atrás dolió bastante.*

Dewayne Davis has a dream of what he really wants to do in life: play football for USC. He knows it's not going to be easy and he will have to work hard for it. Dewayne didn't think of himself as a writer until this class started to open his eyes.

Maynor Escalante has been in this country three years. He never thought that he would write a story about his life or write a story that would be published in a book for everyone to read. He enjoyed writing this story because he likes to read autobiographies. This story is dedicated to his mother, the person whom he loves the most in this world, and also to all people, even the young, who like to read.

Miguel Espinoza loves to read. He has liked reading since he was a little boy. His favorite author is Stephen King. His favorite novel is *Misery*. While writing his story for this book, he learned that helping people is not a waste of time.

Alejandro Flores started writing like a madman because he didn't know how to write an essay. Now he feels that he can write whatever he likes because he has so many ideas. Alejandro chose his topic because he wants to be treated with respect. He dedicates his story to everyone but especially to all the tutors from 826 Valencia who helped him. Without them, he would not have been able to tell his story clearly. He is grateful for their help.

 **Tifani Fuentes** lives with three of her siblings, her grand-mother, and her aunt. She is well loved and gets outstanding support from her family in whatever she does. When Tifani was about seven years old, she had dreams of becoming a veterinarian and an artist. Today, she continues with her art and hopes to go to college to major in animal health care. Having her story published has greatly encouraged her dreams.

 Kelvin Funes Gomez grew up in El Salvador. He came to the United States four years ago. In his free time, he likes to play video games and soccer with his friends. Kelvin is ex-cited to see his story published and would like to dedicate it to his teacher, Ms. Ramirez. He hopes to become a police-man or work for the Drug Enforcement Agency one day.

 **Christian Gomez** is a good person, a hard worker, and a very friendly guy. He loves to help people and never gives up. He likes to hang out with his friends after school, play video games, and play soccer any time of day, even if he is sick. He chose his topic to help the new president take care of those problems that affect the country and avoid making the same mistakes that President Bush made.

 **Victor Greene** is intelligent and likes working with the tutors from 826 Valencia. He enjoys playing basketball and football. His favorite positions are wide receiver in football and low post in basketball. When he is not playing sports, he likes to listen to Lil' Wayne. He hopes to become a chef and cook for his mom every day.

 *Ruben Gutierrez* likes to play soccer, and his dream is to one day be the best professional soccer player ever. He also likes to play video games and is proud to be Mexican. His favorite soccer team is A.C. Milan. He likes girls, listening to hip-hop music, and going to the movies.

 *Jayson Icaro Jr.* is a young, talented person. He came to the United States from the Philippines to get an education. He eventually wants to get a good job as a lawyer, and have a family in San Francisco. In the meantime, he plays sports, especially basketball, which he played in middle school and high school. He wants to be a good basketball player like his uncle, who was the MVP for his city's team in the Philippines.

 *Jesus Henriquez* spends a lot of time thinking about his future and how he can become a man who stands out in his community. He lives with his parents and two siblings. His family is kind of weird and funny, but he loves them. He is respectful to his elders and loves romantic writing. He is afraid of violence and of dying. He usually enjoys spending his time playing soccer.

 Josué Henriquez was born in San Salvador, El Salvador. He grew up with a lot of dreams and many thoughts about life. Josué is a musician. He loves to talk about the world, its problems, and his dreams of one day ending those problems. As a guitar player, he now finds himself a writer of not only music but also poetry and prose. Being a dreamer, Josué aspires to speak out for all those in search of hope, love, peace, and truth.

Dorrian Lewis is a thoughtful person who is a survivor of T-cell lymphoma. While battling cancer, she found a passion for music, from R&B to rock, which led to her own inspiration as an avid, talented choir performer. Music and singing are two things she holds dear, but her true passion is being on her computer. While she enjoys MySpace and Facebook, she has found a computer-savvy talent for designing pictures and backgrounds.

Kaya Lewis has always enjoyed reading the Urban Books series and writing poetry more than prose. This is the first time she has written a story by herself. Kaya enjoys writing a lot of poetry because it clears her mind and thoughts. Kaya is dedicating this story to her family and to herself.

Eryn-Rose Manzano is a simple teenager who has dramatic and fun moments that make her life feel like a roller coaster. She is a risk-taker because she doesn't want to have regrets. She really loves writing in her journal. She decided to write about her own story because she wants people to realize how important happiness is and that whether your memories in life are good or bad, you need to keep them as a part of who you are today. The story she wrote is like a journal that she has allowed the public to read.

Sylvia McClain is an intelligent human being. She grew up with many hardships, mostly without her parents being around, and had to grow up very quickly to learn how to be tough-skinned and independent. Living in San Francisco, she has learned how to love everybody, how to be tolerant, and how not to judge. Because she didn't have much family that lived in California, she formed her own support system. She refuses to throw her intelligence away to drugs. She dares to be different. Her school friends and family are her priorities.

Genesis Miranda is a really good dancer, especially salsa dancing. Genesis enjoys reading fiction books and likes writing love stories. She would like to become a marine biologist or a translator. Genesis chose to write about her family, because they have taught her to live with good values.

Julian Montes Luna is a "*desmadroso*"—a joker—who never thought he would be published in a book. Writing his story was a long process because he is used to keeping his problems to himself and doesn't talk to anyone about them while trying to figure them out for himself. During the writing process, he found out how to express his feelings.

Melvin Morales loves his family very much. One of his big hopes is to be able to help his mother. She is always loving and joking when she speaks to him and his two brothers. Maybe one day he can help her so she doesn't have to work and can make life easier for her. His other important dream is to go back to Guatemala and see his grandparents. He misses them very much.

Jae-Del Nazareno was born in the Philippines and is 100 percent Filipino. He came to the United States in 2006. His favorite sports are basketball and billiards. After finishing high school, he wants to go to college and to join the navy. His favorite book is *Life in Prison* by Stanley Williams because it is a true story.

Jose Nolasco has played soccer since he was four years old. The sport he loves most in the world inspired him to write his story. He plays midfield wing for a local soccer club. This project gave him the chance to show how soccer can bring people together. His dream is to become a professional soccer player and play for Manchester United.

Don Pacia was born and raised in the city of Zamboancia in the Philippines and immigrated to the United States only a year ago. He is going to San Francisco State University to study nursing. Don is someone who loves to hang out with friends and play basketball after school. Eventually, he wants to travel to the historic cities of Europe and the beautiful beaches of Latin America, sky dive, bungee jump, scuba dive, snowboard, learn how to surf, and fly a Blue Angel's airplane.

Ashley Peurala was born in Reno, Nevada. Ashley loves sports, friends, conversation, and food. She wants to attend Le Cordon Bleu of Las Vegas to study cooking. Eventually, she wants to become a pastry chef and own a bakery in Napa Valley.

Jorge Pinto was born in San Francisco. His mom is from El Salvador and his dad is from Peru. His two brothers and three sisters all have diverse backgrounds. He loves soccer, is interested in politics, and aspires to a career in publishing. He wrote his story to illustrate what effect the Golden Rule can have, even in the military.

Karla Poot-Polanco was born in Quintana Roo, Mexico. She began to write essays, fiction, and nonfiction about three years ago. She prefers writing essays and fiction and enjoys everything about reading. She dedicates her time to her family and studies, mostly for English class. She wants to be someone important in her life. She wants to be someone helpful to people, maybe a doctor.

 **Mayra Ramirez** lives with her mom, and her dad lives in Mexico. After her parents separated when she was eleven years old, her way of life changed. She realized that life was hard. Her big dream is to be a psychologist. She wants to help others with their lives, especially children who have experienced parents divorcing. Also, Mayra wants to make her mom proud. She admires her mother because she thinks that her mom is strong and is the kindest person that Mayra knows.

 **Ingrid Reis** is a native of Brazil who has lived with her family in San Francisco for about two years now. She likes to write about her life and also about the world. She enjoys staying with her family and going shopping on the weekend with her friends. She likes to play soccer and always tries to do her best. She is religious and respectful of other religions. She is sympathetic, simple, humble, funny, and smart.

 **Justo Reyes** is kind of tall and a really nice guy. He is a good artist and has mad drawing skills. Justo likes to make jokes and make people laugh all the time. He is a very loving person, but don't get on his bad side because he will snap at you. Justo can be very emotional when he is feeling serious. He is considered a wise person and a good friend.

 Eduwiges Rivas is an immigrant student who arrived in the United States almost three years ago. She decided to write her own story about how her ideal hero should be. In the story, she describes her own hero and how this hero is always there for her. As Eduwiges wrote her story, she found that heroes are real as life, but they are hidden waiting to help you. The story is dedicated to her real-life hero.

 **Ranon Ross** is an intelligent person. He is also tall and enjoys playing basketball with his friends. He chose to write about his topic because he likes to help people in need. He dedicates his story to the people affected by Hurricane Katrina.

 **Jian Pei Ruan** is from China. He came to the United States two years ago and now lives in San Francisco's Chinatown. His story is unique and shows how swimming can help people. He chose to tell his story because it was about the first time he helped other people. He dedicates this story to Leonard and Philip, his tutors.

 **Luis Serrano** is from El Salvador. He came to the United States when he was sixteen years old. He dreams of being a police officer when he grows up. He is also trying to get good work to help his family now. He likes to play soccer when he has the time. He chose his topic for this essay because he thinks it is a way to help his community. He dedicates this story to his family because if they didn't support him, he couldn't accomplish his dreams.

 **Wenbin Tan** is from China. He is a nineteen-year-old guy who gets shy when he talks to the girl he likes. He cares about money but is lazy because he has never had a job in his life. He is trying to find a job now because he feels he is old enough. His favorite subject is math, which he wants to be his major in college. After he finishes college, he hopes to find a job in the business world. He tries to take things seriously when he really cares about them.

Van Tran is Vietnamese. She and her family moved to San Francisco in 2007. She loves all the members of her family because they raised her well. She wants all the best things for her family and for them to be happy. She wrote this story to thank all the people who have already helped her in her life. She wants people to know that helping people is a good thing that will make the world a better place.

Cindy Tuala was having a hard time at first writing a story for this. She stopped coming to class for a while, but when she did come she wrote about what she has been going through in her life. When she let out her thoughts in writing, the project became easier and she was proud of her work. When she is not struggling, she likes to go to the mall and shop for shoes and clothes. She also likes to watch girly movies like *The Notebook*.

Johnny Valencia is quickly becoming interested in books such as *Scorpions* by Walter Dean Myers. He is also becoming interested in computers and art. After taking art classes, he soon began to develop a hobby of sketching and painting. He dedicates his story to his parents and to his teacher, who is always leaving him helpful comments and questions on his school work.

Kenia Vanegas came to the United States three years ago from El Salvador. She likes to write and learning how to tell her story. She is working hard to graduate from high school and go to college. She dedicates her story to her family, which is always on her mind and in her heart. She is a friendly and respectful person who always likes to help others.

Ruth Cinto Velasquez was born in Guatemala and moved to the United States with her sister when she was fifteen years old. When she got to the United States, it was hard living far from her family. She misses them all every day. She decided to come to the United States so that she can go to college to become an architect—something she has wanted to do since she was five years old. Ruth is a positive, friendly person who is active and loves school and its programs. One day Ruth will go to Italy and eat gelato and lasagna and visit all the ancient buildings and write a book about it.

Juan Luis Omar Villamar is from Mexico. He has lived in the United States for almost three years. He likes to play sports and exercise. He plays soccer for the Mission High team and also likes to write. However, he doesn't like to read because he falls asleep. He loves his family and dreams that one day his parents will not have to work so hard. He hopes to continue his studies and become a professional, maybe a doctor, one day.

Vicky Wu is unique because she has different style. Her friends in China gave her the name "black horse" because she wears black and can run very fast. When she is with her friends, she is hyper and always laughing and having fun. She tries not to be wrong about things in her life. She also has a very good relationship with her grandma, just like a very good friend. She wrote her essay about a relationship and is thankful that people helped her write it, for if no one had, she would never have finished.

Johana Yanez is from beautiful Hidalgo, Mexico. She moved to the United States three years ago. Johana wrote this story because she wants to show people that how you treat other people is how they will treat you back. She sometimes likes to write stories for fun. She dedicates this story to everyone who enjoys reading.

 ***Yanhong Yang*** is a nice girl. She was born in China and moved to the United States on July 13, 2007. She lives with her mother and, although life is hard, they are happy. She likes to help people and wrote this story because she wants to tell people about caring for one another. She hopes many people know that it is important to learn that. She hopes everybody can read this story and change for the better.

 ***María Zapotecas*** is a good friend and has a strong and sensible character. She can cry for any reason but also knows when it is time to maturely confront the problems in her life. She dedicates this book to all the women of the world, especially her mother, because her mother was the main character of the story. She wants everyone to know her story because it is also the story of many other families and because she wants women to stand up and face anybody and fight for their liberty. Maria also dedicates this story to her grandmother, who gives Maria the courage to face her father because she would do the same thing if she were here with us.

ACKNOWLEDGMENTS

A publication of this size takes the devotion of a large community. 826 Valencia would like to recognize all the people who poured their time and hard work into producing this collection.

826 Valencia is honored to work with awe-inspiring educator Pirette McKamey on our biggest annual student publication. We first met Pirette years ago while she was teaching at Thurgood Marshall High School and are lucky to have worked with her on several large publishing projects and college essay workshops at Mission High School. Throughout her twenty-year teaching career, Pirette has taught middle school history and high school English, has spent four years at the University of San Francisco instructing future teachers, and is a Bay Area Writing Project teacher consultant. We felt fortunate to know such a strong and innovative teacher and last spring, at the onset of the project, it was clear that the time had come to work with Pirette and Mission High School on this grand endeavor.

What would the world look like if everyone lived by a set of values based on love, integrity, character, humility, and patience? This world exists in a big way inside Pirette's classroom and among the students you have gotten to know through this book. Expectations are high, so students work hard to accomplish their goals with determination. She has a way of creating joy and trust in both students and tutors. She teaches with the Golden Rule, and when students feel supported, loved, and honored, they take their education seriously.

During class, she spreads this feeling not only amongst the students, but also to 826 Valencia tutors. After leaving a session at Mission High, tutors will often thank us for the opportunity, even though they are the ones who have given their time. They talk endlessly about the excitement and inspiration that comes to life in Pirette's classroom, and what an honor it is to be a part of it. It's a gift that we hope readers experience as well. It was her commitment and support that made this book possible.

826 Valencia tutors spent seven weeks working alongside students as their pieces developed. Student and tutor partnerships formed extraordinarily quickly and lasted through the entire project. Tutors visited Mission High up to three times a week, over seven weeks, working with the same student— what commitment! We would like to express our immense gratitude to this dedicated group of tutors: Pat Allbee, Erin Archuleta, Renee Ashbaugh, Alanna Baumert, Deanna Beach, Jessica Beard, Zoe Brock, Ryan Browne, Melissa Caldwell, Leonard Cetrangolo, Tracey Cooper, Aisia Davenport, Meg Donohue, Adrianna Ely, Nelson Graff, Chris Greeley, Jessica Hansen, Jared Horney, Benjamin Kim, Elizabeth Kohout, Ryan Lewis, Michele Lobatz, Mercedes Logan, Maricel Manglicmot, Tiffany Marquez, Michelle Martinez, Shane Michalik, Sarah Million, Brian Moss, Ryan Noll, Jessica O'Connell, Kirsten Peterson, Arnold Posada, Stephanie Pullen, Rachel Sadler, Jennifer Saltmarsh, Jasmine Schimek, Ana Soriano, Henry Souder-Arguedas, Lena Timrott, Gabrielle Toft, Andrea Torres, Veronica Vasquez, Nancy Ware, Jessica Weikers, Kehinde Whyte, Matthew Wirgler, and Philip Wong.

We would also like to thank Professor Nelson Graff of San Francisco State University. He created a class that asks future teachers to volunteer with 826 Valencia for forty-five hours during their semester. We could not have done this book without the dedication and talent of his students.

We had the pleasure of inviting Joe Loya, author of *The Man Who Outgrew His Prison Cell*, to write the foreword to this book. Because Loya believes in the power of telling one's story and creating change, we were both honored and excited to have him join us. He visited the students and shared his poignant story and gave advice as a published author to a room of very excited, soon-to-be published authors. Loya spoke about the importance of writing for an audience, and how it is one of the hardest yet most powerful things they can do as they put together their book. After class, when one of the students brought up her copy of Loya's book for him to sign—and other students crowded around him for a handshake and a hello—it was clear that he inspired something new in them. Loya's memorable visit kept the students focused as they finished their pieces. We would like to thank him for bringing his engaging personality and humbling story to the project.

We also owe appreciation to the 826 Valencia community members who contributed their editorial support over several draft-editing weekends in the early stages of student writing: Joseph Borrelli, Joe Brown, David Brownell, Victoria Buonanno, Amy Cohen, Kate Cunniff, April De Costa, Dustin Delaney, Eamon Doyle, Lara Fox, Linda Gebroe, Walter Green, Ryan Lewis, Michele Lobatz, Nicole Lutton, Ryan Noll, Emily Parker, Cynthia Patricia, Kirsten Peterson, Dustin Platt, Heather Rasley, Karen Schaser, April Shimshock, Christine Shin, Elizabeth Stevens, and Loretta Stevens.

After all the writing was completed, an editorial board comprising students and adult volunteers worked evenings to discuss edits, determine the organization of the book, and write the introduction. They are responsible for turning fifty-four separate essays into the polished book you are holding today. To this group we are profoundly grateful: Mena Adlam, Ravon Anderson, Ashley Arabian, Erin Archuleta, Henry Arguedas, Renee Ashbaugh, Elissa Bassist, Idalia Beltran, Zoe Brock, Kate Bueler, Sarah Buishas, Leonard Cetrangolo, Angel Chaparro, Angie Colon-Chin, Tracey Cooper, April De Costa, Eamon Doyle, Andrea Drugan, Adrianna Ely, Victor Greene, Jessica Hansen, Josue Henriquez, Rebecca Kaden, Lucy Kirchner, Dorian Lewis, Kenya Lewis, Ryan Lewis, Michele Lobatz, Mercedes Logan, Eryn-Rose Manzano, Sarah Million, Ryan Noll, Cynthia Patricia, Whitney Phaneuf, Jorge Pinto, Dustin Platt, Karla Poot-Polanco, Heather Rasley, Ingrid Reis, Eduwiges Rivas, Ranon Ross, Linsey Sandrew, Karen Schaser, Cynthia Shannon, Karen Siercke, Ana Soriano, Nancy Spector, Loretta Stevens, Andrea Torres, Kate Viernes, Nancy Ware, Kehinde Whyte, and Vicky Wu.

And for their support during the production process we are indebted to: Elissa Bassist, Joe Brown, Lachlann Carter, Lucy Kirchner, Mia Lipman, Shane Michalik. Cynthia Patricia, Eliana Stein, Kate Viernes, and Jenna Williams.

Thanks to 826 volunteer Abner Morales for translating Johanna Yanez's story into English on page 250.

826 Valencia interns were also essential in completing this project. We're extremely thankful to Ryan Browne, Cameron Clark, Tracey Cooper, Adrianna Ely, Walter Green, Elizabeth Jones, Elizabeth Kohout, Ryan Lewis, Ryan Noll, Kirsten Peterson, Karen Siercke, Joanna Sokolowski, Shakema Stoney, and Andrea Torres.

This book marks 826 Valencia's first time recording an audio CD for a publication. The voices and stories that come to life on this CD were made possible with the generosity of Jason Mateo and Youth Speaks, who let us use their recording studio, and Molly Samuels, who lent her expertise and time to record, edit, and produce the CD.

Finally, we wish to extend an enormous thank you to our primary fiscal sponsors for the 2009 Young Authors' Book Project: The National Endowment for the Arts, a local anonymous fund, Mary Schaefer, Nancy Spector, and Mark Dwight, not only for his financial sponsorship, but also for ensuring this book's inclusion in the welcome bag of all 2009 TED Conference attendees.

We asked students to look at their experiences through the lens of writing. Many of them named a great change in their lives and the people who helped them reach a place of happiness. You would never know it by walking into their classroom, but among these bright faces are histories of hardship. You wouldn't know, because they have already gone through a change, they have already learned to move forward and live a life of compassion. We would like to thank all the student authors for taking on a challenge and for sharing their stories.

One student said that although she will always encounter tough situations and trying times, she could be happy and get through it all if only her family and friends treated her better. Because we learned the Golden Rule as children, it's easy to forget the impact it has in our relationships and experiences. We hope that through these stories it becomes clear that moments of thoughtful kindness can truly change the world.

ABOUT 826 VALENCIA

826 VALENCIA is a nonprofit organization dedicated to supporting students, ages six to eighteen, with their creative and expository writing skills and to helping teachers inspire their students to write. Our work is based on the understanding that strong writing skills are fundamental to future success and great leaps in learning can be made when skilled tutors work one-on-one with students.

HOW WE DO IT

826 consists of a writing lab, a student-friendly pirate supply store that partially funds our programs, and two satellite classrooms in nearby middle schools. More than 1,400 volunteers—including published authors, magazine founders, SAT-course instructors, and documentary filmmakers—donate their time to work with more than six thousand students each year. These incredible volunteers allow 826 Valencia to offer all its services for free.

Students thrive when they receive one-on-one attention from trained and caring tutors, and they work hard when they know that the community at large will read their writing. Our project-based approach allows students ownership over the learning process and empowers them to express themselves clearly, confidently, and in their own voices.

PROGRAMS

826 Valencia offers a full schedule of free programs that reach students at every possible opportunity—in school, after school, in the evenings, and on the weekends. Here are a few of our most popular offerings:

In-school Support

We dispatch teams of volunteers into local high-needs schools to support teachers and provide one-on-one assistance to students as they tackle school newspapers, research papers, oral histories, college-entrance essays, and more. Our in-school visits are a great way for us to support students who wouldn't, on their own, reach out for our help.

Writing Workshops

826 Valencia offers free workshops designed to foster creativity and strengthen writing skills. They focus on everything from cartooning to starting a 'zine. All our workshops—from the playful to the practical—are project-based and taught by experienced professionals.

Field Trips

Up to four times a week, 826 Valencia welcomes an entire class into its writing lab for a morning of high-energy learning. Students may participate in a roundtable discussion with a local author, enjoy an active workshop focused on journalism, or, in our most popular field trip, write, illustrate, and bind their own class book—all in two hours.

Tutoring

Five days a week, 826 Valencia buzzes with neighborhood students who come in after school and on Sundays for one-on-one tutoring in many subject areas. We serve students of all skill levels and interests.

Summer Programs

During the summer, our tutoring program caters to English language learners. Our project-based curriculum focuses on basic vocabulary, phonics, reading, and writing skills. We also host an intensive writing camp for high school students, in which campers write all day every day and work with celebrated authors and artists like Michael Chabon, ZZ Packer, and Spike Jonze.

Writers' Rooms

Our Writers' Rooms at Everett Middle School and James Lick Middle School are warm, in-school satellites where our volunteers serve every student in the school over the course of the year. These spaces allow teachers to reduce their class sizes and students to receive the one-on-one attention that leads to success.

STUDENT PUBLICATIONS

From our various programs, 826 Valencia produces a variety of publications, each of which contains student writing. These projects represent some of the most exciting work done at 826 Valencia, as they expose Bay Area students to publishing experiences otherwise largely unavailable to them. The book you are holding is the most recent in our Young Authors' Book Project series, which represents the most involved publishing project we undertake each year. Below is a list of previous Young Authors' Book Project publications, all of which are available for sale online and at bookstores nationwide.

Seeing Through the Fog: A Gateway to San Francisco, 2008
This collection of stories and essays written by seniors at Gateway High School will guide locals, tourists, and armchair travelers alike to new places and new ways of seeing through the San Francisco fog. It incudes a foreword by San Francisco Mayor Gavin Newsom.

Exactly: 10 Beavers, 9 Fairies, 8 Dreams, 7 Knights, 6 Princesses, 5 Dogs, 4 Otters, 3 Old Men, 2 Robots, 1 Traveling Shoe & Everything Else It Takes to Make a Great Children's Storybook (More or Less), 2007
This showcase of fifty-six children's tales written by students at Raoul Wallenberg Traditional High School includes vivid illustrations by professional artists, resulting in a delightful storybook for readers of all ages.

Home Wasn't Built in a Day: Constructing the Stories of Our Families, 2006
Essays by students at Galileo Academy of Science and Technology offer insightful stories that explore the myths and realities of what makes a family a family. The book includes a foreword by actor Robin Williams.

I Might Get Somewhere: Oral Histories of Immigration and Migration, 2005

This compelling collection of personal stories by Balboa High School's class of 2007 reflects on the problems and pleasures of life in new surroundings. It includes a foreword by author Amy Tan.

Waiting to be Heard: Youth Speak Out about Inheriting a Violent World, 2004

This anthology by students at Thurgood Marshall Academic High School offers passionate, lucid statements about personal, local, and global issues—the way high school students would have you hear them. It includes a foreword by author Isabel Allende.

Talking Back: What Students Know about Teaching, 2004

Students from Leadership High School discuss the relationships they want to have with their teachers and the ways they view classroom life.

Each semester, 826 Valencia also publishes scores of chapbooks from workshops, field trips, and special projects with teachers and classrooms.

THE STAFF OF 826 VALENCIA

Executive Director, Leigh Lehman
Development Director, Lauren Hall
Design Director, María Inés Montes
Programs Director, Jory John
Programs Coordinator, Marisa Gedney
Programs & Events Coordinator, Eugenie Howard-Johnston
Programs Assistants, Emilie Coulson & Cherylle Taylor
Pirate Store Manager, Justin Carder

THE BOARD OF DIRECTORS OF 826 VALENCIA

Barb Bersche, Brian Gray, Abner Morales, Bita Nazarian,
Alexandra Quinn, Vendela Vida, Richard Wolfgram